ETHNIC IDENTITY AND
INEQUALITIES IN BRITAIN
The dynamics of diversity

Edited by Stephen Jivraj and Ludi Simpson

First published in Great Britain in 2015 by

Policy Press
University of Bristol
1-9 Old Park Hill
Bristol BS2 8BB
UK
t: +44 (0)117 954 5940
e: pp-info@bristol.ac.uk
www.policypress.co.uk

North American office:
Policy Press
c/o The University of Chicago Press
1427 East 60th Street
Chicago, IL 60637, USA
t: +1 773 702 7700
f: +1 773-702-9756
e:sales@press.uchicago.edu
www.press.uchicago.edu

© Policy Press 2015

British Library Cataloguing in Publication Data
A catalogue record for this book is available from the British Library.

Library of Congress Cataloging-in-Publication Data
A catalog record for this book has been requested.

ISBN 978-1-4473-2181-1 paperback
ISBN 978-1-4473-2182-8 ePub
ISBN 978-1-4473-2184-2 Kindle

Cover design by Hayes Design
Front cover: image kindly supplied by www.alamy.com
Printed and bound in Great Britain by CMP, Poole
Policy Press uses environmentally responsible print partners

Contents

List of figures and tables

Figures

Tables

Acknowledgements

The editors would like to thank the chapter authors without whom this book would have not been possible. Each chapter has built on briefings that have been published in two series by the Centre on Dynamics of Ethnicity (CoDE) at the University of Manchester and funded by the Joseph Rowntree Foundation (JRF) and CoDE. The contribution of the editorial team for the first series, comprising Laia Bécares, Mark Brown, Nissa Finney, Dharmi Kapadia and James Nazroo, and latterly the editors of the second series, Laurence Brown and Kitty Lymperopoulou, was essential to the development of the book. Each chapter has benefited from the critical and cooperative comments of other authors.

As editors we would also like to thank Aleks Collingwood and Emma Stone at JRF and Laura Vickers and Emily Watt at Policy Press for their support for the book. On behalf of the contributors we would like to thank Gareth Mulvey, Paul Norman, Albert Sabater and Satnam Virdee for their helpful comments.

Some of the chapters have benefited from other funding bodies, including Chapter Eight, which was conducted as part of Gemma Catney's Leverhulme Trust Early Career Fellowship (ECF-2011-065), and Chapter Nine, which was conducted as part of Laia Bécares' University of Manchester Hallsworth Research Fellowship, and benefited from an Economic and Social Research Council (ESRC) grant (ES/K001582/1).

This work contains statistical data that are Crown Copyright, from the Office for National Statistics (ONS) and National Records of Scotland (NRS). The use of the ONS and NRS statistical data in this work does not imply the endorsement of the ONS or NRS in relation to the interpretation or analysis of the statistical data. The images of census questions in Chapter One are reproduced by kind permission of the ONS, NRS and the Northern Ireland Research and Statistics Agency (NISRA). Without the work of these statistical agencies, social policy would flounder, and this book would not have been conceived.

Notes on contributors

Laia Bécares is a joint ESRC/Hallsworth Research Fellow at the Centre on Dynamics of Ethnicity (CoDE), University of Manchester. Her work examines the determinants of ethnic inequalities in health, with a focus on life course and neighbourhood effects. She is interested in understanding the pathways by which the racialisation of people and places lead to socioeconomic and health inequalities.

Bridget Byrne is Senior Lecturer in Sociology at the University of Manchester. She works in the areas of race, class, gender, national identity, feminist theory and citizenship. Her books include *White lives: 'Race', class and gender in contemporary London* (Routledge, 2006) and *Making citizens: Public rituals and personal journeys to citizenship* (Palgrave Macmillan, 2014). She is a member of the Centre on Dynamics of Ethnicity (CoDE) at the University of Manchester.

Gemma Catney is Lecturer in the Department of Geography and Planning at the University of Liverpool. She is a population geographer with interests in segregation, internal migration with an ethnic group dimension, and ethnic inequalities. She recently completed a Leverhulme Trust Early Career Fellowship, exploring how ethnic diversity and segregation have changed in England and Wales since the early 1990s. She is an affiliate member of the Centre on Dynamics of Ethnicity (CoDE) at the University of Manchester.

Ken Clark is Senior Lecturer in Economics at the University of Manchester and a Research Fellow at Institut zur Zukunft der Arbeit (IZA, Institute for the Study of Labor), Bonn. He researches in the area of applied labour economics with particular reference to the labour market outcomes of immigrants and minority ethnic groups.

Nissa Finney is Lecturer in Social Statistics at the University of Manchester and a member of the Cathie Marsh Institute for Social Research (CMIST) and the Centre on Dynamics of Ethnicity (CoDE). Her research is about where people live, why, and how this matters. She has a particular interest in ethnicity.

Bethan Harries is Research Associate in the Centre on Dynamics of Ethnicity (CoDE) and Sociology at the University of Manchester. Her research focuses on representations of geographical patterns of racism and inequalities, and the social, cultural and historical conditions in which these are produced.

Stephen Jivraj is Lecturer in Population Health at University College London. He is a Council Member of the British Society for Population Studies and a member of the Royal Statistical Society Statistics User Forum. His research interests include migration, social and spatial inequalities and neighbourhood effects. He is an affiliate member of the Centre on Dynamics of Ethnicity (CoDE) at the University of Manchester.

Dharmi Kapadia is a PhD student at the Cathie Marsh Institute for Social Research (CMIST) at the University of Manchester. Her research focuses on inequalities in mental health service use, with a particular interest on how social networks shape care pathways.

Omar Khan is Director of the Runnymede Trust. He is the chair of the advisory group to the Centre of Dynamics on Ethnicity (CoDE), chair of the Ethnicity Strand Advisory Committee to Understanding Society and a member of the Department for Work and Pensions' (DWP's) Ethnic Minority Employment Stakeholder Group. Omar is also chair of Olmec and a Clore Social Leadership Fellow.

Kitty Lymperopoulou is Research Associate at the Centre on Dynamics of Ethnicity (CoDE) at the University of Manchester. Her research interests include immigrant settlement, social integration and cohesion, ethnic inequalities and neighbourhood inequalities.

James Nazroo is Professor of Sociology at the University of Manchester and Director of the Centre on Dynamics of Ethnicity (CoDE) at the University of Manchester. His research focuses on questions of inequality in relation to both ethnicity and later life, with a particular interest in the social and economic processes that lead to inequalities in health outcomes.

Meenakshi Parameshwaran is an affiliate member of the Centre on Dynamics of Ethnicity (CoDE) at the University of Manchester. Her research interests include ethnic inequality, educational inequality and neighbourhood effects.

Ludi Simpson is honorary Professor of Population Studies at the University of Manchester. He has been President of the British Society for Population Studies and advises local and national governments on population analysis. His books include *'Sleepwalking to segregation'? Challenging myths about race and migration* (Policy Press, 2009, with Nissa Finney).

Andrew Smith is Reader in Sociology at the University of Glasgow. His research explores the politics of culture in colonial and post-colonial contexts. He has written most recently on the West Indian historian and radical C.L.R. James, and is author of *C.L.R. James and the study of culture* (Palgrave, 2010).

James Warren was previously Research Officer at the Office for National Statistics (ONS). He currently works at Acas. During his time at ONS he was part of the ONS Longitudinal Study Development Team.

ONE

Introduction: the dynamics of diversity

Stephen Jivraj and Ludi Simpson

Ethnicity is at the centre of major political debates in Britain. From diverse perspectives, politicians and campaigners have highlighted differences between ethnic groups in where they live, the skills and education they are provided with, the jobs they have and the healthcare they receive. The measurement of these ethnic group differences has become increasingly complex as identities evolve, and more people mix within families, neighbourhoods and workplaces. Comparisons made 50 years ago between immigrants from the British New Commonwealth as a whole and the average experience of UK residents are now made between family origins of many more world regions, between immigrants and their children and grandchildren born and educated in the UK. The context of social policies has moved from race relations to also encompass the management of immigration and the integration of immigrants, religious discrimination and the relationships between ethnic and religious claims and state services, as well as the state's response to terrorist threats.

In this book we show what the largest government statistical enquiry has to say about the dynamics of ethnic identity and inequality in contemporary Britain. The chapters draw on data from the decennial censuses of population in England, Wales and Scotland, which have asked a question on ethnic group since 1991. The first section shows how ethnic groups have grown, the places they are most diverse, how they perceive their national identity, and how ethnic identity changes over time. The second section looks at whether minority ethnic groups are residentially segregated and continue to face disadvantages in health, housing, employment, education and neighbourhoods.

This chapter introduces the concept of ethnicity, its measurement in the UK context, and the identities and inequalities that these data and other collected statistics have been able to identify. The chapter ends with a short description of the book and a section of reference material that is used throughout the book.

What is ethnicity?

Measuring ethnicity is fraught with difficulty because researchers try to reduce a subjective and dynamic concept to a categorisation that is meaningful to individuals and, at the same time, manageable in data analysis. Bulmer (2010) suggests an ethnic group is a collectivity within a large population with shared identity defined by kinship, religion, language, shared territory, nationality or physical appearance. The importance of these dimensions in what shapes ethnic identity will vary from person to person. Moreover, the differences become blurred in multicultural societies such as Britain, where living in diverse areas has meant minority groups have borrowed from one another and the majority culture to form new identities. This makes it more difficult than ever to distinguish meaningful categories (Neal et al, 2013). At the same time, the government uses ethnicity data to address inequalities that arise from prejudicial assumptions based not on subjective identity but skin colour or cultural stereotypes. The concept of ethnicity and the data that represent it are made to work very hard.

Ethnic group categorisation

The Office for National Statistics (ONS) has set the standard in measuring the concept of ethnic group in the England and Wales decennial censuses of population. The ONS recognises the subjective and dynamic aspect of ethnicity, which has led it to change questions and the answer categories over the last three censuses to reflect the evolving views of appropriate ethnic classifications and the changing family origins of the UK population itself. What has remained constant is that people have only ever been able to select one ethnic group category, unlike censuses in other countries, such as the US, where multiple responses are allowed. The National Records of Scotland (NRS) and the Northern Ireland Statistics and Research Agency (NISRA) are committed to harmonised approaches across the UK, but have made modifications to the answer categories used in the census in England and Wales.

The self-identification of ethnicity in the census is naturally affected by how people view their identity, but also by the list of predefined response categories that are presented to them (ONS, 2014). A challenge for the ONS has been to ensure that, while the categories remain meaningful, they can also be compared over time.

The 1991 Census question asked which ethnic group you 'descend from': White; Black Caribbean; Black African; Black Other; Indian; Pakistani; Bangladeshi; or Chinese. The question was the same in England, Wales and Scotland. The 2001 question asked about ethnic group in terms of 'cultural background'. There were additional response categories of 'Mixed' and 'White Irish' in 2001 as well as an 'Other' category for each broad group of 'White', 'Mixed', 'Asian' and 'Black' in the England and Wales census. Scotland added a 'White Scottish' category, and Northern Ireland asked the question for the first time.

The 2011 question mentioned neither descent nor culture; it simply asked about your 'ethnic group or background'. Categories were added for 'White Gypsy or Irish Traveller' and for 'Arab' in England and Wales, and also for 'White Polish' in Scotland. In England and Wales, the option for 'White British' was amended to read 'White English/Welsh/Scottish/Northern Irish/British'. (The census questions in each country of the UK in 1991, 2001 and 2011 are reproduced at the end of this chapter.)

The fact that some ethnic group answer categories in the census are tied to skin colour and region of origin (for example, White Irish, Black Caribbean and Black African) and others identify nationality or country of origin (for example, Pakistani and Bangladeshi) reflects the dual purposes of colour discrimination and recognition of cultural distinctions that motivated the inclusion of an ethnic group question in the census in 1991. It could be argued that the inclusion of the question and the way it has been designed has given unwarranted rigidity, or 'reified' ethnic groups, in British social policy because the census is the standard bearer for the measurement of socioeconomic variables with which other surveys and monitoring forms follow (Ahmad, 1999). Nonetheless, innovations in ONS surveys and research before each census have allowed alternative questions, response categories and methods of data collection to be tested, which have ultimately led to modification to the census ethnic group question.

For example, at the time of the 1991 Census a mixed ethnic group category was rejected because evidence suggested that people of mixed descent preferred to identify with the ethnic group of one of their parents (ONS, 2003). However, the category was deemed acceptable in 2001 based on tests of the question in fieldwork during the 1990s. User consultation was important in the creation of the original question in 1991 and has influenced the subsequent changes to the question and the response categories. The changes in the response categories, do add to the instability in individuals' responses over time (see Chapter Six, this volume).

Ethnic group inequalities

Prior to the inclusion of a question in the 1991 Census, a number of national and local studies examined experiences of people from minority ethnic groups. The Policy Studies Institute surveys examined a range of dimensions of the lives of minority ethnic people between the 1960s and 1990s. They showed how discrimination in housing and labour markets persisted throughout this period, as did structural disadvantage, such as low educational attainment (Modood et al, 1997). There was evidence of upward mobility in the experiences of some ethnic groups (Indian and Chinese), but disadvantage continued to prevail for others (Caribbean, Pakistani and Bangladeshi).

The justification for including an ethnic group question in the census was and remains to understand the social conditions between ethnic groups and to provide evidence to reduce inequalities (Bulmer, 2010). The ethnic group data from the census has confirmed a continuation of these trends in the 21st century, while also showing how disadvantage varies within ethnic groups (Platt, 2011), and is greater for people from minority ethnic groups born in the UK than those born overseas (Simpson et al, 2006). There is evidence from other national surveys that White men were advantaged in employment during 1972 to 2005 (Li and Heath, 2008). However, progress was evident in some groups, with Black African, Indian and Chinese men performing better than White men in gaining access to higher-status jobs. Pakistani and Bangladeshi men remained disadvantaged in both respects.

Aim of the book

The aim of this book is to update the evidence of differences between ethnic groups in the domains of housing, employment, health, education and residential location by presenting a contemporary picture based on the 2011 Census, and identifying changing patterns over time. Each census is a major landmark for our understanding of ethnic diversity, as there is no other source of evidence for ethnicity and social conditions for Britain and its localities.

Every chapter is centred on a question relevant to social policy. We have used standard data from the census offices available at the time of going to press, and some tables especially commissioned for this book. Based on Briefings intended to give a quick and authoritative response to the results as they emerged from the 2011 Census, each chapter has included new analyses, using innovative methods and providing new insights. Our aim has been to write accurately and transparently, with an eye to the needs of practical social policy, and in language that is accessible to all. We hope to be able to claim an authoritative review of these new data and their relevance for society.

The census in Northern Ireland uses different ethnic group categories from the rest of the UK – discussions of diversity intersect with the dynamics of religious identity in Northern Ireland, which we have not attempted in this book. We have included each country's census questions for comparison at the end of this chapter, and NISRA (2013) summarises ethnic diversity from the 2011 Census in Northern Ireland.

Outline

The majority of the book is presented in 12 chapters split across two sections. The first section (Chapters Two to Seven) explores the dynamics of ethnic diversity and identity in England, Wales and Scotland, and its changing spatial distribution at a sub-national level. The second section (Chapters Eight to Thirteen) describes socioeconomic inequalities between ethnic groups in health, housing, employment, education and residence.

Each chapter uses the same standard classification to compare differences between ethnic groups, whether focusing on data from 2011 or between 1991 and 2011. It is not possible to compare trends over time in every chapter because some of the data used were not available before 2011. Other chapters only use data from 2001 and 2011 because there is already substantial evidence documenting the change between 1991 and 2001, or because of the complexity of harmonising the changing census questions over time.

The only chapters that do not exclusively use data from the England and/or Wales census are Chapter Four, which profiles local diversity in English, Welsh and Scottish local authority districts, and Chapter Seven, which focuses specifically on Scotland's ethnic diversity. All of the chapters use aggregate data from the census, except Chapter Six, which is based on individual census records from the ONS Longitudinal Study (LS).

Chapter Two asks 'How has ethnic diversity grown?', and lays a platform for later analyses by outlining the change in comparable ethnic groups between 1991 and 2011. We look to see whether certain minority ethnic groups are becoming more or less concentrated in those local authority districts where they are over-represented. The chapter ends with a comparison of alternative measures of minority identity that can be used to measure social integration directly.

In Chapter Three, the components of population change are estimated to determine the contribution of international migration, births and deaths to the changing size of each ethnic group. We challenge the notion that the growth of minority ethnic populations are exclusively driven by immigration, and show how the importance of natural change varies by ethnic group.

'Does Britain have plural cities?' is the focus of Chapter Four. Ludi Simpson profiles the local authority districts where no one ethnic group is in the majority. He shows that places often labelled as segregated are, in fact, the most diverse, but that future growth in diversity will be limited. The chapter presents new population projections of ethnic diversity up to 2031.

Chapter Five presents data collected for the first time in the 2011 Census on national identity, and asks 'Who feels British?'. Stephen Jivraj and Bridget Byrne show how national identity varies by ethnic group, and how these patterns vary across local authority districts in England and by world region of birthplace and by religion.

In Chapter Six, anonymised individual data from the ONS LS are used to determine the proportion of people who changed their ethnic group between 2001 and 2011. Ludi Simpson, James Warren and Stephen Jivraj examine how this varies by ethnic group, country of birth and age, and make recommendations for stable comparison of ethnic groups over time.

Chapter Seven asks 'In what ways is Scotland's ethnic diversity distinctive?' Andrew Smith and Ludi Simpson describe Scotland's unique immigration history and the drivers of the growth in ethnic diversity, including the distinction between 'White: Scottish' and 'White: Other British'. The geographical pattern of diversity is shown for local authority districts and wards. The chapter ends with a profile of the ethnic diversity in Scotland's largest cities: Edinburgh and Glasgow.

'Has neighbourhood ethnic residential segregation decreased?' is the question posed by Gemma Catney in Chapter Eight. She challenges the popular discourse that ethnic segregation is rising using the Index of Dissimilarity between small areas, both within England and Wales, and within each local authority, showing patterns of increased residential diversity.

Chapter Nine, 'Which ethnic groups have the poorest health?', identifies variations in limiting long-term illness and self-rated general health between ethnic groups over the period 1991-2001-2011. It shows how health inequalities are persistent for some groups relative to the White British majority. Laia Bécares shows how ethnic group differences vary by age and in London compared with the rest of England and Wales.

The ethnic group divides between who lives in secure, spacious housing, and who lives in overcrowded housing and insecure tenure, are the focus of Chapter Ten. Nissa Finney and Bethan Harries chart the rise in private renting since 1991, and how it has disproportionately affected some ethnic groups more than others. They compare ethnic group patterns in housing tenure between local authority districts and between stages of the life course.

Chapter Eleven is concerned with inequalities in employment, and how they have persisted for some minority ethnic groups in each of the last three censuses, 1991, 2001 and 2011. Dharmi Kapadia, James Nazroo and Ken Clark explore the status of younger (aged 25-49) and older (aged 50-74) people in and out of the labour market, tracking progress and lack of it for each ethnic group, and separately for men and women.

Chapter Twelve asks 'Is there an ethnic group educational gap?'. Kitty Lymperopoulou and Meenaskshi Parameshwaran demonstrate differences in the average qualifications achieved by ethnic groups in 2001 and 2011. The authors highlight progress for most ethnic groups, although some remain disadvantaged in terms of educational attainment. They contrast the picture of recent immigrants with those who arrived in earlier periods, and those born outside the UK with those born in the UK.

'How likely are people from minority ethnic groups to live in deprived neighbourhoods?' is the focus in Chapter Thirteen. Stephen Jivraj and Omar Khan use the official government indices of multiple deprivation that measure area disadvantage for all neighbourhoods in England. The chapter ends with analysis of the unemployment and economic inactivity of ethnic groups in deprived neighbourhoods and all other neighbourhoods.

The book concludes with implications for policy and the cause for measuring ethnicity in Chapter Fourteen. We ask why, in spite of legislation and social policies geared towards minority ethnic groups, disadvantages persist, and summarise the nature of these disadvantages. The usefulness of ethnic data to measure diverse preferences and community relations is also discussed. We end by suggesting what should be measured to ensure effective policymaking and ask whether there is a future in ethnic group categories.

Reference material, sources and supporting online material

Throughout the book, shaded text refers to reference material that is relevant to the chapter: definitions, data sources and methods. The following pages present reference material that is used throughout this book, to avoid repeating it in each chapter. We reproduce the census questions from each country of the UK, in each of 1991, 2001 and 2011 Censuses, and include the numbers of people estimated in total in each ethnic group category. The reference material in this chapter also describes the comparisons that can be reliably made across time in spite of changes in the question, the labels we use to describe each group, how we have dealt with census undercount, the sub-national areas we have used, our sources for the census data, and the maps we have used throughout the book. Unless stated otherwise, the charts and tables presented throughout this book are based either on Crown Copyright data released from the censuses of 1991, 2001 and 2011, or on the estimates of full populations for 1991 and 2001 described later.

The book is supported by online material, where the detailed sources for each figure are provided along with the data themselves, and further analytical profiles for each local authority district are available. The online material is available from: http://www.ethnicity.ac.uk/dynamicsofdiversity/

Questions in the census

Against each category has been written the estimate of usual residents in that census, from standard census outputs. For England and Wales in 1991 and 2001, instead of the standard census outputs, full estimated populations are provided as described in a separate section later in this chapter.

England, Wales and Scotland, 1991

The same question was used in all three countries. An ethnic group question was not asked in Northern Ireland.

The responses written in under 'Any other ethnic group' which referred to any Asian origin, were reported as a separate category in the published output as in the population estimates below.

England, Wales and Scotland, 1991

Ethnic group	England and Wales	Scotland
White ☐ 0	47,429,019 (93.5%)	5,012,689 (98.6%)
Black-Caribbean ☐ 1	569,621 (1.1%)	1,130 (0.0%)
Black-African ☐ 2	255,336 (0.5%)	3,410 (0.1%)
Black-Other ☐ *please describe*	221,040 (0.4%)	3,132 (0.1%)
Indian ☐ 3	891,827 (1.8%)	11,198 (0.2%)
Pakistani ☐ 4	494,973 (1.0%)	24,142 (0.5%)
Bangladeshi ☐ 5	176,912 (0.3%)	1,283 (0.0%)
Chinese ☐ 6	173,184 (0.3%)	11,603 (0.2%)
Any other group ☐ *please describe*		
Other Asian	211,199 (0.4%)	5,066 (0.1%)
Other	324,922 (0.6%)	9,676 (0.2%)
Total	50,748,033 (100%)	5,083,330 (100%)

Please tick the appropriate box.

If the person is descended from more than one ethnic or racial group, please tick the group to which the person considers he/she belongs, or tick the 'Any other ethnic group' box and describe the person's ancestry in the space provided.

England and Wales, 2001 and 2011

On forms in Wales in 2011, the first box was titled 'Welsh/English/Scottish/Northern Irish/British'. In Wales, the form was also routinely available in Welsh.

England and Wales, 2001

8 What is your ethnic group?

Choose ONE section from A to E, then ✓ the appropriate box to indicate your cultural background

A White

☐ British	45,721,236 (87.3%)
☐ Irish	646,616 (1.2%)
☐ Any other White background, *please write in*	1,379,499 (2.6%)

B Mixed

☐ White and Black Caribbean	240,438 (0.5%)
☐ White and Black African	80,705 (0.2%)
☐ White and Asian	192,229 (0.4%)
☐ Any other Mixed background, *please write in*	158,582 (0.3%)

C Asian or Asian British

☐ Indian	1,053,302 (2.0%)
☐ Pakistani	727,727 (1.4%)
☐ Bangladeshi	286,693 (0.5%)
☐ Any other Asian background, *please write in*	247,157 (0.5%)

D Black or Black British

☐ Caribbean	572,212 (1.1%)
☐ African	494,669 (0.9%)
☐ Any other Black background, *please write in*	98,068 (0.2%)

E Chinese or other ethnic group

☐ Chinese	233,346 (0.4%)
☐ Any other, *please write in*	227,497 (0.4%)

Total 52,359,976 (100%)

England and Wales, 2011

16 What is your ethnic group?

Choose one section from A to E, then tick one box to best describe your ethnic group or background

A White

☐ English/Welsh/Scottish/Northern Irish/British	45,134,686 (80.5%)
☐ Irish	531,087 (0.9%)
☐ Gypsy or Irish Traveller	57,680 (0.1%)
☐ Any other White background, write in	2,485,942 (4.4%)

B Mixed / multiple ethnic groups

☐ White and Black Caribbean	426,715 (0.8%)
☐ White and Black African	165,974 (0.3%)
☐ White and Asian	341,727 (0.6%)
☐ Any other Mixed/multiple ethnic background, write in	289,984 (0.5%)

C Asian / Asian British

☐ Indian	1,412,958 (2.5%)
☐ Pakistani	1,124,511 (2.0%)
☐ Bangladeshi	447,201 (0.8%)
☐ Chinese	393,141 (0.7%)
☐ Any other Asian background, write in	835,720 (1.5%)

D Black/African /Caribbean /Black British

☐ African	989,628 (1.8%)
☐ Caribbean	594,825 (1.1%)
☐ Any other Black/African/Caribbean background, write in	280,437 (0.5%)

E Other ethnic group

☐ Arab	230,600 (0.4%)
☐ Any other ethnic group, write in	333,096 (0.6%)

Total 56,075,921 (100%)

Northern Ireland, 2001 and 2011

The responses written in under 'Any other ethnic group', which referred to any Asian origin, were reported as a separate category in the published output, as in the figures.

Northern Ireland, 2001

10 To which of these ethnic groups do you consider you belong?
✓ one box only.

White	1,670,988 (99.2%)
Chinese	4,145 (0.2%)
Irish Traveller	1,710 (0.1%)
Indian	1,567 (0.1%)
Pakistani	666 (0.0%)
Bangladeshi	252 (0.0%)
Black Caribbean	255 (0.0%)
Black African	494 (0.1%)
Black Other	387 (0.0%)
Mixed ethnic group, write in	3,319 (0.2%)

Any other ethnic group, write in

Other Asian 194 (0.0%)

Other ethnic group 1,290 (0.1%)

Total 1,685,260 (100%)

Northern Ireland, 2011

16 What is your ethnic group?
↪ Tick one box only.

White	1,778,449 (98.3%)
Chinese	6,303 (0.3%)
Irish Traveller	1,301 (0.1%)
Indian	6,198 (0.3%)
Pakistani	1,091 (0.1%)
Bangladeshi	540 (0.0%)
Black Caribbean	372 (0.0%)
Black African	2,345 (0.1%)
Black Other	899 (0.0%)
Mixed ethnic group, write in	6,014 (0.3%)

Any other ethnic group, write in

Other Asian 4,998 (0.3%)

Other ethnic group 2,353 (0.1%)

Total 1,810,863 (100%)

Scotland, 2001 and 2011

Scotland, 2001

15 What is your ethnic group?
Choose ONE section from A to E, then
✓ the appropriate box to indicate
your cultural background.

A White
- Scottish — 4,459,071 (88.1%)
- Other British — 373,685 (7.4%)
- Irish — 49,428 (1.0%)
- Any other White background, please write in — 78,150 (1.5%)

B Mixed
- Any Mixed background, please write in — 12,764 (0.3%)

C Asian, Asian Scottish or Asian British
- Indian — 15,037 (0.3%)
- Pakistani — 31,793 (0.6%)
- Bangladeshi — 1,981 (0.0%)
- Chinese — 16,310 (0.3%)
- Any other Asian background, please write in — 6,196 (0.1%)

D Black, Black Scottish or Black British
- Caribbean — 1,778 (0.0%)
- African — 5,118 (0.1%)
- Any other Black background, please write in — 1,129 (0.0%)

E Other ethnic background
- Any other background, please write in — 9,571 (0.2%)

Total 5,062,011 (100%)

Scotland, 2011

What is your ethnic group?
♦ Choose ONE section from A to F, then tick ONE box which best describes your ethnic group or background.

A White
- Scottish — 4,445,678 (84.0%)
- Other British — 417,109 (7.9%)
- Irish — 54,090 (1.0%)
- Gypsy / Traveller — 4,212 (0.1%)
- Polish — 61,201 (1.2%)
- Other white ethnic group, please write in — 102,117 (1.9%)

B Mixed or multiple ethnic groups
- Any mixed or multiple ethnic groups, please write in — 19,815 (0.4%)

C Asian, Asian Scottish or Asian British
- Pakistani, Pakistani Scottish or Pakistani British — 49,381 (0.9%)
- Indian, Indian Scottish or Indian British — 32,706 (0.6%)
- Bangladeshi, Bangladeshi Scottish or Bangladeshi British — 3,788 (0.1%)
- Chinese, Chinese Scottish or Chinese British — 33,706 (0.6%)
- Other, please write in — 21,097 (0.4%)

D African
- African, African Scottish or African British — 29,186 (0.6%)
- Other, please write in — 452 (0.0%)

E Caribbean or Black
- Caribbean, Caribbean Scottish or Caribbean British — 3,430 (0.1%)
- Black, Black Scottish or Black British — 2,380 (0.0%)
- Other, please write in — 730 (0.0%)

F Other ethnic group
- Arab, Arab Scottish or Arab British — 9,366 (0.2%)
- Other, please write in — 4,959 (0.1%)

Total 5,295,403 (100%)

Comparison through time of an ethnic group's population and characteristics

The census questions on ethnic group reproduced earlier have changed over time. Based on the research reported in Chapter Six, the following categories are most stable when people respond to each census, and are used in this book when making comparisons over time. For comparisons from 1991, the comparable categories are fewer because in 1991 'White' was a single category, and the 'Mixed' categories were only introduced in 2001.

2001-11 comparisons for England and Wales

1   White British (in 2011, labelled 'White English/Welsh/Scottish/Northern Irish/British')
2   White Irish
3   Other White (including 'White Gypsy or Irish Traveller' in 2011)
4   Mixed White & Caribbean
5   Mixed White & African
6   Mixed White & Asian
7   Indian
8   Pakistani
9   Bangladeshi
10 Chinese
11 Black Caribbean
12 Black African
13 All other categories (a residual category for completeness in tables, but not comparable over time)

Caution should be used when comparing Other Mixed, Other Asian and Other Black across the censuses because of the high instability of these responses between the two censuses, even though their labels and positioning in the census question was unchanged. A residual category 'Other' may be used in tables for completeness, but is not comparable across time. In 2001 it would include Other Mixed, Other Asian, Other Black and the final Other ethnic group. In 2011 it includes these and also Arab.

2001-11 comparisons for Scotland

1   White Scottish
2   White, Other British
3   White Irish
4   Other White (including 'White Gypsy/Traveller' and 'White Polish' in 2011)
5   Mixed
6   Indian
7   Pakistani
8   Bangladeshi
9   Chinese
10 Black Caribbean
11 Black African (including 'Other African' in 2011)
12 All other categories (a residual category for completeness in tables, but not comparable over time)

Research for Scotland equivalent to that reported in Chapter Six is not yet completed. The categories listed as comparable are based on those that have not changed their label between 2001 and 2011.

1991-2001-2011 comparisons for England, Wales and Scotland
1 White (including all categories under the 'White' heading in 2001 and in 2011)
2 Indian
3 Pakistani
4 Bangladeshi
5 Chinese
6 Black Caribbean
7 Black African (including 'Other African' in Scotland in 2011)
8 Other (a residual category for completeness in tables, but not comparable over time, including all other categories)
Those who in 1991 were recorded in the Other Black and Other Asian categories more often than not are found in different categories in later censuses.

Labels for each ethnic group
Good research practice would suggest that the labels used in the censuses should be reproduced wherever possible when describing our analyses. Deviation from the census labels themselves can be misleading, for example, where 'African' might be assumed to include White Africans unless the qualifying 'Black' is used, as in most census questions.

However, a precise reproduction of question labels is not possible because the census questions have headings and sub-headings and change over time. In England and Wales the label for 'White British' was expanded in 2011 to name 'English, Welsh, Scottish and Northern Irish'. In Scotland in 2011, 'Black' was dropped before the category 'African'.

In this book we have generally used the labels as listed in the section above on *Comparisons*. We have shortened them occasionally when the text or a figure is clearer by doing so.

Census undercount and its estimation: full population estimates
Non-response or 'census undercount' is generally regarded as having been estimated as accurately as possible within the 2011 Census output, partly because of a strategy to target follow-up in places where non-response was expected to be lower at the expense of places where it was expected to be higher. The 2011 Census output has not been subject to the challenge and revisions that were made after release of the 2001 and 1991 Censuses in England and Wales. Non-response is concentrated in young adult age groups, in urban areas, and among some minority ethnic groups. If this bias is not taken into account, comparisons of population over time can be misleadingly incorrect.

For this reason we have used, wherever relevant and possible, complete population estimates for 1991 and 2001 for each ethnic group, with details of age, sex and sub-national areas in England and Wales. These are consistent with the estimates of the total population in those years published by the ONS. The methods of estimation of complete population estimates for ethnic groups are described by Sabater and Simpson (2009). The estimates themselves are available from the Economic and Social Research Council (ESRC) UK Data Service (Study Numbers 6043 and 6044).

Sub-national areas

For sub-national analysis, many boundaries have changed. We have aggregated the data from the 1991 and 2001 Censuses to the 2011 local authority district boundaries to make a consistent time series. The word 'district' then refers to the 348 local authority county districts, unitary authorities, metropolitan districts and London boroughs of England and Wales, and Scotland's 32 council areas. A description in the relevant chapter describes smaller areas when these are analysed.

Access to data from the censuses

We have accessed data from the censuses using the public portal www.nomisweb.co.uk, from which most tabular data are released by the ONS, and the equivalent for Scotland at www.scotlandscensus.gov.uk. Occasionally we have used the academic portal INFUSE, or commissioned tables that are not standard, but are also available publicly.

All sources of figures and tables in this book, unless otherwise specified in the figure or table itself, are either the census or full population estimates for 1991 and 2001 described earlier. The specific census tables for all data used in the book and further details of analyses undertaken are provided in metadata companion notes available online at: http://www. ethnicity.ac.uk/dynamicsofdiversity/

Maps in this book

Population cartograms are used to display data across districts in England and Wales. The cartograms draw each area with boundaries so that it is proportional in size to its population. This makes it easier to discern patterns in cities that cover a small geographical area but have large populations. The cartograms maintain the shape and topology of area boundaries to make it as easy as possible to identify places on the map. Dorling and Thomas (2011) produced the cartograms using the open-source application ScapeToad that is available to download at scapetoad.choros.ch. A detailed key of each local authority district in England and Wales is available at: http://www.ethnicity.ac.uk/dynamicsofdiversity/

References

Ahmad, W. (1999) 'Ethnic statistics: better than nothing or worse than nothing?', in D. Dorling and S. Simpson (eds) *Statistics in society: The arithmetic of politics*, London: Arnold, pp 124–31.

Bulmer, M. (2010) 'Measuring race and ethnicity', in M. Bulmer, J. Gibbs and L. Hyman (eds) *Social measurement through social surveys. An applied approach*, Farnham: Ashgate, pp 109–25.

Dorling, D. and Thomas, B. (2011) *Bankrupt Britain: An atlas of social change companion website* (http://sasi.group.shef.ac.uk/bankruptbritain/index.html).

Li, Y. and Heath, A. (2008) 'Minority ethnic men in British labour market (1972-2005)', *International Journal of Sociology and Social Policy*, vol 28, no 5/6, pp 231–44.

Modood, T., Berthoud, R., Lakey, J., Nazroo, J., Smith, P., Virdee, S. and Beishon, S. (1997) *Ethnic minorities in Britain: Diversity and disadvantage*, London: Policy Studies Institute.

Neal, S., Bennett, K., Cochrane, A. and Mohan, G. (2013) 'Living multiculture: understanding the new spatial and social relations of ethnicity and multiculture in England', *Environment and Planning C: Government and Policy*, vol 31, no 2, pp 308–23.

NISRA (Northern Ireland Statistics and Research Agency) (2013) *Census 2011: Detailed characteristics for Northern Ireland on ethnicity, country of birth and language*, Statistics Bulletin, Belfast: NISRA.

ONS (Office for National Statistics) (2003) *Ethnic group statistics. A guide for the collection and classification of ethnicity data*, London: Office for National Statistics.

ONS (Office for National Statistics) (2014) *Guidance and methodology: Ethnic group* (www.ons.gov.uk/ons/guide-method/measuring-equality/equality/ethnic-nat-identity-religion/ethnic-group/index.html).

Platt, L. (2011) *Inequality within ethnic groups*, Programme paper: Poverty and ethnicity, 2607, York: Joseph Rowntree Foundation.

Sabater, A. and Simpson, L. (2009) 'Enhancing the population census: a time series for sub-national areas with age, sex, and ethnic group dimensions in England and Wales, 1991-2001', *Journal of Ethnic and Migration Studies*, vol 35, no 9, pp 1461–77.

Simpson, L., Purdam, K., Tajar, A., Fieldhouse, E., Gavalas, V., Tranmer, M., Pritchard, J. and Dorling, D. (2006) *Ethnic minority populations and the labour market: an analysis of the 1991 and 2001 Census*. DWP report No. 333, London: The Department of Work and Pensions.

Section 1
Ethnic diversity and identity

TWO

How has ethnic diversity grown?

Stephen Jivraj and Ludi Simpson

Key findings

- In 2011, one in five people in England and Wales (20 per cent) described their ethnic group as other than White British compared with 13 per cent in 2001.
- The population other than White British, White Irish and Other White has doubled in size since 1991, from 3 to 7 million, while remaining a small minority of the total population in 2011 (14 per cent).
- The Black African ethnic group has grown faster than any other minority group in the last two decades, doubling in 1991-2001 and 2001-11 to reach 990,000 in 2011.
- Ethnic diversity is increasing in all parts of England and Wales, and at a faster rate in those places where minority ethnic groups were fewest in 2001.
- Minority ethnic groups remained clustered in certain diverse urban areas, most notably London.
- There has been continued ethnic group mixing within families. The number of people identifying with a 'Mixed' ethnic category increased by 82 per cent between 2001 and 2011 to more than a million.
- The proportion of mixed households has grown in 346 out of 348 local authority districts in England and Wales. Excluding one-person households, one in eight households now have more than one ethnic group.
- New measures in the census show that the majority of people from minority ethnic groups describe themselves as British, do not have a minority religion, and speak English as their main language.

Context

British society is becoming increasingly ethnically diverse. This is a pattern that has been documented throughout the post-war period and more widely since the inclusion of an ethnic group question in the 1991 Census (Rees and Butt, 2004). Prior to the 1950s, the minority ethnic population was small and largely confined to a small number of dockland areas (Peach, 1996). The post-war immigration to Britain was initially dominated by people arriving from the Caribbean who quickly became outnumbered by those from South Asia, whose immigration was tied to events in the New Commonwealth countries (Coleman and Salt, 1996). By 1991, a youthful age structure meant many groups were growing rapidly through an excess of births over deaths.

This chapter and the next describe the growth of ethnic diversity between 1991 and 2011 in England and Wales. This chapter shows how it is occurring in all parts of the country, and not just in those places where minority groups are most clustered. It goes on to profile the Mixed ethnic group and multiple ethnic groups households. The chapter ends with a comparison of alternative indicators of minority identity that were included in the census for the first time in either 2001 or 2011. These show that the majority of people from minority ethnic groups see themselves as British, report no religion or being Christian, and speak English as their main language. Chapter Three then describes how minority ethnic groups have grown since 1991, and estimates the contribution of international migration, births and deaths.

Growth of ethnic diversity

In 2011, the White British ethnic group, including English, Welsh, Scottish and Northern Irish denominations, accounted for 80 per cent of the 56 million people living in England and Wales. Figure 2.1 shows that the group's population remained fairly stable in size during the 2000s, decreasing by only 1 per cent. The other 20 per cent of the population contained a diverse mix of minority ethnic groups that grew during the same decade by 4.2 million, a 64 per cent increase.

The largest minority group in 2011 was Other White, which describes the ethnicity of almost 2.5 million people. The Other White group grew by more than 80 per cent (or 1.1 million people) between 2001 and 2011, driven by immigration from Eastern Europe following European Union (EU) enlargement in 2004. The only minority ethnic group to decrease in size during the 2000s was White Irish, by almost 18 per cent. The source of these changes is described further in Chapter Three.

The White Irish and Other White groups were not separated from the White British group in 1991 when only a White group was measured. The White population, in total, remained relatively stable between 1991 and 2011, growing by only 2 per cent. The population other than White more than doubled in size

Figure 2.1: Minority ethnic population in England and Wales, 1991-2001-2011

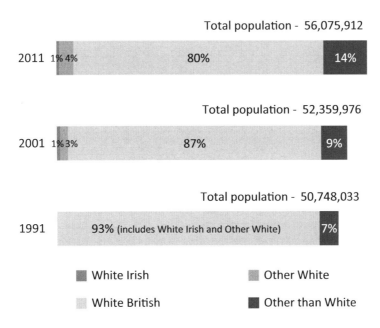

Figure 2.2: Ethnic groups other than White in England and Wales, 1991-2001-2011

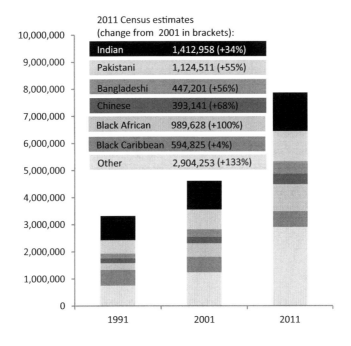

Note: the 'Other' groups are Mixed (see later) – 1,224,400 (+82%); Other Asian – 835,720 (+238%); Other Black – 280,437 (+186%); Arab – 230,600 (not measured before 2011); Other – 333,096 (+46%).

during the same period, from 3.3 million (or 7 per cent of the population) to 7.9 million (or 14 per cent of the population).

There has been growing diversity in the ethnic groups that make up the other than White population throughout the period 1991 to 2011 (see Figure 2.2). The faster rate of growth in some of the smaller ethnic groups meant that by 2011 the ethnic mix of the population was more varied than in 1991 or 2001. The ethnic group that has experienced the greatest increase in population between 1991 and 2011 is Black African, which grew almost three-fold to almost a million people by 2011. The Bangladeshi, Pakistani and Chinese groups doubled in size, and the Indian group grew by a little more than half. The Black Caribbean group grew by only 4 per cent between 1991 and 2001.

The Other category grew by 284 per cent between 1991 and 2011. This provides an indication of the increased diversity of the population in England and Wales. The Other group, however, should not be compared over time because it is not made up of the same ethnic groups between censuses (for example, Mixed), and because the stability of responses to the category by the same individuals was low between censuses (for example, Other Asian and Other Black). Chapter Six explores the high instability in the 'Other' ethnic group categories. The change in the Mixed ethnic groups between 2001 and 2011 is described later in this chapter.

Geographical spreading of ethnic diversity

The geographical distribution of minority ethnic groups continues to reflect the historic settlement patterns of immigrant groups in England and Wales. London remains the place of initial settlement of most new immigrants, and the location where minority ethnic groups remain most clustered. In 2011, people from minority ethnic groups accounted for more than half the population in the London region as a whole, and within 23 of the 33 local authority districts that make up the region (see Figure 2.3a). London includes the most ethnically diverse districts in the country, including Newham and Brent. Slough, Luton and Leicester became the first districts outside of London where no one ethnic group was in the majority in 2011. Chapter Four further discusses these 'plural' local authority districts.

Although the minority ethnic population remains clustered in and around selected towns and cities where they or their ancestors initially settled, clear indications of residential mixing between 2001 and 2011 are evident. Figure 2.3b shows the percentage change in the population other than White British between 2001 and 2011 in every district in England and Wales. The districts that have experienced the greatest percentage growth in the minority ethnic population are those places where they were fewest in 2001. This reflects dispersal of minority ethnic groups towards districts adjacent to immigrant settlement areas (for example, Bexley in London) as well as new immigration to parts of the country with very small minority ethnic populations (for example, Boston in the East Midlands).

Figure 2.3: Ethnic diversity and change in ethnic diversity, by local authority district in England and Wales, 2001-11

a) Percentage of population other than White British

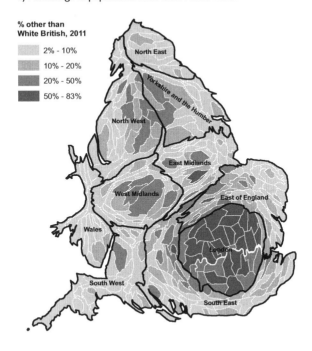

b) Percentage change in population other than White British

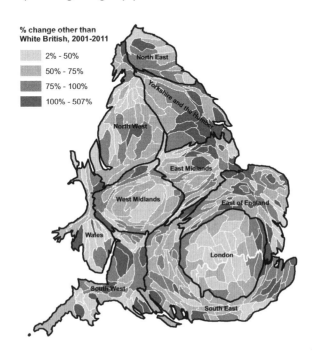

Figure 2.4: Growth in population by ethnic group in the districts where each group was most clustered, and everywhere else in England and Wales, 2001-11

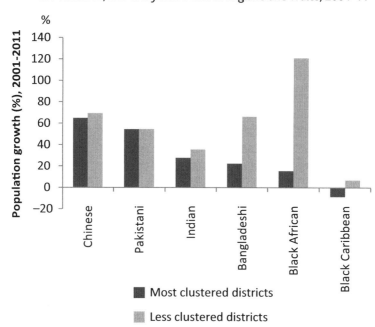

Figure 2.4 shows this pattern of residential spreading between 2001 and 2011 for selected ethnic groups. It shows the proportionate change in the population in districts where a group is most clustered (those containing a fifth of the population of each ethnic group in 2001), and the proportionate change of each ethnic group in all other districts. The pattern across each ethnic group is greater growth in those districts where they were less clustered compared with a smaller or negative change in the most clustered districts, except for the Pakistani group, where the difference is very small.

Ethnic mixing

Mixed ethnic groups

The Mixed ethnic group population, only measured in the 2001 and 2011 Censuses, almost doubled in size during the decade by adding more than half a million people to its population (see Figure 2.5). In 2011, more than 1.2 million people (2 per cent of the total population) described their ethnicity as Mixed. The largest Mixed ethnic group is the White & Black Caribbean (427,000), followed by Mixed White & Asian (341,000), Other Mixed (290,000) and Mixed White & Black African (166,000). All four groups grew by more than three-quarters between 2001 and 2011, with the smallest group, Mixed White & Black African, increasing at the fastest rate (106 per cent). This also signals the increased ethnic diversity in the England and Wales population.

Figure 2.5: Growth of Mixed ethnic groups in England and Wales, 2001-11

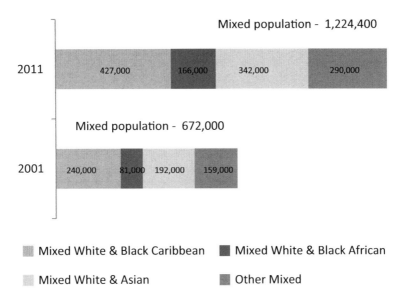

Figure 2.6a–d shows a commonality in the geographies of Mixed ethnic groups, with the greatest clusters of each Mixed group in London. The geographies of Mixed groups, however, are not as clustered in London as minority ethnic groups as a whole. For example, a lower proportion of those in the Mixed White & Black Caribbean and Mixed White & Asian groups live in London, especially inner London, compared with all minority ethnic groups. There are no districts where any Mixed group accounted for more than 4 per cent of the population.

The Mixed White & Black Caribbean group, which accounts for 0.8 per cent of the population nationally, is most clustered in Nottingham (East Midlands), Wolverhampton (West Midlands) and Lewisham (London), where at least 3 per cent of the population are in this group (Figure 2.6a). More than 2 per cent of the population in Lambeth, Croydon, Islington and Hackney in London, and Birmingham and Sandwell in the West Midlands, describe themselves as Mixed White & Black Caribbean.

Less than 2 per cent of the population describe themselves as Mixed White & Asian in any districts in England and Wales, and account for 0.6 per cent of the population nationally. The greatest clusters of the Mixed White & Asian group are in North and West London, including the districts of Kensington and Chelsea, Camden, Barnet, Westminster, Kingston upon Thames, Richmond upon Thames, and the City of London (Figure 2.6b).

Figure 2.6: Geography of Mixed ethnic groups in England and Wales, 2011

a) Percentage of Mixed White & Black Caribbean

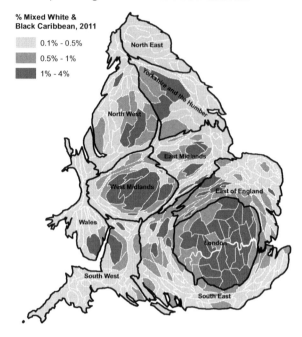

b) Percentage of Mixed White & Asian

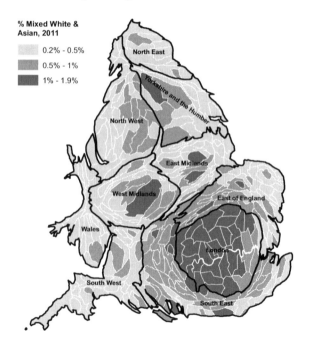

How has ethnic diversity grown?

c) Percentage of Mixed White & Black African

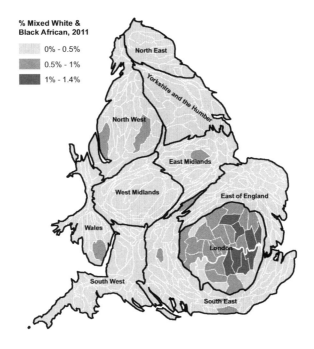

% Mixed White &
Black African, 2011

- 0% - 0.5%
- 0.5% - 1%
- 1% - 1.4%

d) Percentage of Other Mixed

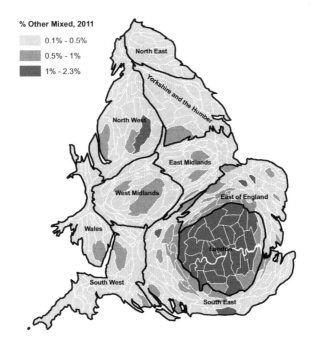

% Other Mixed, 2011

- 0.1% - 0.5%
- 0.5% - 1%
- 1% - 2.3%

There were only eight districts, all in London, where the Mixed White & Black African group accounted for more than 1 per cent of the population. The group accounts for 0.3 per cent of the population in England and Wales as a whole. The greatest clusters of Mixed White & Black African group are in South London, including Lambeth, Lewisham and Southwark (Figure 2.6c). The extremely diverse Other Mixed group accounted for more than 2 per cent of the population in Lambeth, Haringey, Islington and Hackney, and 0.5 per cent of the population nationally (Figure 2.6d). The only district outside London where more than 1 per cent of the population describe themselves as Other Mixed is Manchester (North West).

Households with more than one ethnic group

Multiple ethnic groups within a household became relatively common in 2011 – one in every eight households is formed of people from different ethnic groups living together. We count here only households of two or more people that can have multiple ethnic groups. In 2011, the number of households with multiple ethnic groups was 2 million, or 12 per cent. This figure has increased by half from 1.4 million in 2001.

Half of multiple ethnicity households have couples of different ethnic groups. About a quarter have different ethnicity only between generations, such as a White Irish parent with White British children. The rest, about a fifth, are different combinations – including different ethnicities between unrelated people, for example, lodgers or student households. The percentage of households with multiple ethnic groups varies between geographical areas, at its highest, 39 per cent, in inner London. Those areas with the most households of more than one ethnic group are also usually those with the greatest population from ethnic groups other than White British – in London and other major cities.

The number of multiple ethnicity households increased between 2001 and 2011 in every district, except for small decreases in Burnley and Hyndburn in East Lancashire.

Ethnicity and other minority identities

In the wake of rapid change in ethnic diversity, some interest groups have prompted fears about rights and responsibilities in British society, and about the status of those residents they do not consider to be part of Britain. The new measures included in the census in 2001 on religion and in 2011 on national identity, year of arrival in the UK, main language and English proficiency provide policymakers with direct measures of the process of integration. The process of integration of minority ethnic groups is better measured using these forms of identity, which say more about an individual than the colour of their skin or the place from where their descendants originated.

One of the greatest social integration concerns is the inability of some people from minority ethnic groups to speak English (O'Grady, 2013), which, although legitimate, should not be overblown. In 2011, less than 2 per cent of the population in England and Wales could not speak English (or Welsh in Wales) well or at all, which means the vast majority of people in minority ethnic groups can (see Figure 2.7). Only one in ten of those born abroad could not speak English well. However, the figure rises to more than a third among those who arrived in the UK after the age of 50. This suggests that English language support is required most by the elderly immigrant population in England and Wales.

Figure 2.7: Alternative measures of identity

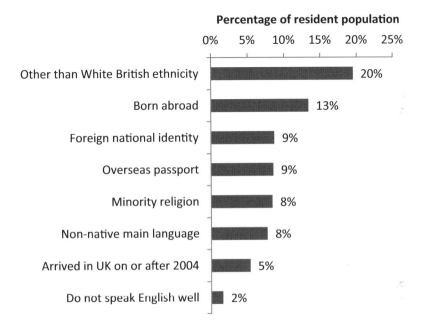

Note: Base resident population – 56,075,912, except for non-native main language and do not speak English well categories, which only include people aged three or over – 53,961,451.

More than 4 million people in England and Wales (8 per cent of the population) report that English (or Welsh in Wales) is not their main language. This has been misinterpreted as a sign of inability to speak English. In fact, 80 per cent of these 4 million people are able to speak English (or Welsh in Wales) well or very well, and therefore provide a bilingual resource that could be better utilised. The number of people not able to speak English (or Welsh in Wales) well or very well is 863,000.

Another fear that has had a profound affect on policymakers across the political spectrum is the increase in the population living in Britain who were born abroad. The rise in the population born abroad is common to all countries in Western Europe, and reflects an increasingly global economic system and labour force. The increase in the population born abroad was marked between 2001 and 2011 (up from 9 to 13 per cent) as a consequence of more migrants arriving during the 2000s than any other decade during the post-war period. It may surprise some people that a greater proportion of those who arrived since 2004 originated from Asia (33 per cent) compared with post-2004 EU Accession states (29 per cent).

The reactions to the disturbances in Northern English towns and cities with significant Muslim populations in 2001 and to Islamic terrorism at home and abroad during the 2000s has prompted fears that separation of people has been perpetuated by a support for minority cultures. These fears can be put into perspective by the fact that the majority of minority ethnic residents do not report a minority religion or a foreign national identity, and are less likely to do so the longer they have lived in Britain. The ethnic group differences by national identity are described in more detail in Chapter Five.

Policy implications

There is little policymakers can do to change the growth of ethnic diversity. Chapter Three will show that a benign and unavoidable demographic process of natural change largely explains this growth. Those concerned with geographical separation of the minority ethnic population can take an interest in the geographical spreading of diversity that is happening without direct intervention by government.

This might be welcomed as an opportunity to tackle prejudice in those parts of the country where anti-immigrant and minority ethnic views are fostered by a lack of experience of difference. Furthermore, the positive signals of tolerance and indifference to ethnic identity is no clearer than the growth in the Mixed ethnic group population and growth of people living within households of multiple ethnicities. While most people of Mixed ethnicity live in the same areas as other minorities, residential clustering of the Mixed groups is less and has decreased fastest, as discussed later in Chapter Eight.

The inclusion of questions in the census on religion in 2001 and national identity, time of arrival in the UK, main language and English proficiency in 2011 provide policymakers with evidence of clearer differences in how people view their own identity than ethnic group. These new measures can also indicate better whether people are able and willing to integrate in wider society. Much of the rest of this book identifies ethnic inequalities in housing, health, employment and education, which policymakers would do well to tackle if they wish to speed up the process of minority dispersal from settlement areas, and to foster even greater ethnic mixing in British society.

Note

Further information about data and sources are available from
http://www.ethnicity.ac.uk/dynamicsofdiversity/

References

Coleman, D. and Salt, J. (1996) 'The ethnic group question in the 1991 Census: a new landmark in British social statistics', in D. Coleman and J. Salt (eds) *Ethnicity in the 1991 Census: Volume One: Demographic characteristics of the ethnic ethnic minority populations*, London: HMSO, pp 1-32.

O'Grady, S. (2013) 'Migrants shun the English language', *Express*, 31 January (www.express.co.uk/news/uk/374550/Migrants-shun-the-English-language).

Peach, C. (1996) 'Introduction', in C. Peach (ed) *Ethnicity in the 1991 Census: Volume Two: The ethnic minority populations of Great Britain*, London: HMSO, pp 1-24.

Rees, P. and Butt, F. (2004) 'Ethnic change and diversity in England, 1981-2001', *Area*, vol 36, no 2, pp 174-86.

THREE

Why has ethnic diversity grown?

Ludi Simpson and Stephen Jivraj

Key findings

- Half of the population born abroad and living in England and Wales arrived in the UK aged 15–29. This is an age when they are economically productive and are unlikely to require or be eligible for state benefits.
- All ethnic groups in England and Wales have grown in size since 2001 through more births than deaths, apart from White British and White Irish groups. Most have also grown through net migration into England and Wales.
- The excess of births over deaths is because minority ethnic groups have a young age structure, not because of high fertility.
- The fertility of most groups has increased a little in the 2000s, but overall there is less difference in family size between ethnic groups than in past decades.
- For most ethnic groups whose first major immigration to the UK was over a generation ago, growth through further immigration is not as much as their 'natural' growth within England and Wales through an excess of births over deaths.
  - Pakistani and Bangladeshi groups have each grown by about 50 per cent during 2001-11, and mostly because more people have been born than have died.
  - For the Black Caribbean group, whose main immigration to the UK was now 60 years ago, growth has been less than 5 per cent; it was almost entirely due to the excess of births over deaths rather than further immigration.
  - The Indian group is an exception among established minority ethnic groups: it has grown through immigration during the period 2001-11 more than through an excess of births over deaths.
- During the 2000s, the Other White (including most Eastern Europeans), Black African and Chinese ethnic groups added rapidly to their population

from further immigration as well as from natural growth. Each grew between 70 and 100 per cent in total during the decade.

- The 'Mixed' groups have a very young age structure. Their growth was mainly due to children born in the decade. A smaller but significant growth of about 25 per cent was through immigration.
- The White Irish group in England and Wales reduced by 18 per cent over the decade, from an excess of deaths over births, from net emigration, and from a net movement out of the White Irish ethnic group largely to the White British group. The group is a relatively elderly population in England and Wales, although immigrants continue to arrive in their twenties.
- The census measure of immigration exaggerates the recent increase in immigration by excluding those people who have died or left the UK since they immigrated, and because it only counts the most recent arrival.
  - So, during the last 20 years, the census estimates that 53 per cent of all people born abroad arrived since 2004, while official measures of immigrant flows estimate that this figure is 44 per cent.

Context

The previous chapter has shown how Britain's minority population has grown, and changed its distribution in Britain. This chapter gives some explanations for why diversity has grown.

In national political debate it is common to interpret growth in ethnic diversity as solely the result of immigration. But a decreasing White British population and increasing minority population is not only the result of the emigration of the White British and immigration of minority groups. We shall see in this chapter that the age of immigrants also has a large impact. Those ethnic groups in Britain that have a relatively young age structure will have more children and suffer fewer deaths than others, and therefore grow more quickly in population irrespective of further immigration. From the age structure of each ethnic group in Britain we can learn about its past and its future.

Accounting for population change is a core task of demography, and the balance of births, deaths and migration takes centre stage in textbooks (Hinde, 1998; Siegel, 2002). Higher birth rates, lower death rates and an excess of in-migration over out-migration tend to increase a population. While births and deaths are quite well registered in the UK, migration is estimated from surveys and registration in the National Health Service.

However, none of these *components of population change* are separately measured in official statistics for each ethnic group. The census provides the most reliable and complete information about ethnic group populations, while between census years there are a variety of less reliable and incomplete sources of relevant data (Haskey, 2002; Wohland et al, 2010). The Office for National Statistics' (ONS) first attempt to estimate the ethnic composition of the population of each local authority in England and Wales between censuses in the 2000s grew more uncertain as years passed since the previous census, and was ended after the estimates for 2009 were found to be at odds with survey and other evidence (ONS, 2012a). New methods are being developed for the decade leading to the next census in 2021.

In this chapter we examine the age structure of each ethnic group from the two censuses of 2001 and 2011, to identify what led to increasing ethnic diversity. How much is due to age structure, to different birth rates, and to flows of migration? We also account for an additional component of change to ethnic group populations, changes to individuals' ethnic identity between one census and the next.

Many of the analyses could be repeated for areas within Britain, and we encourage readers to study their own areas in this way, using the methodology described later. The book's online interactive resources compare the age structures of each ethnic group, religion and national identity in the local authority districts of England, Wales and Scotland.

Immigration

A major source of increasing ethnic diversity in Britain is immigration. A little over half of the 3.7 million increase in England and Wales' population during 2001-11 was directly due to there being more immigration than emigration, and the net gain was entirely of minority ethnic groups. The 2011 Census asked people born abroad when they most recently arrived to live in the UK. Figure 3.1 shows the distribution of the foreign-born population by decade of arrival, highlighting key events associated with peaks and troughs of immigration. It also shows the official count of immigrant flows since 1975 of people born abroad (long-term international migration [LTIM], estimates from ONS, 2014).

Half of the population born abroad arrived in the previous 10 years. This reflects three trends: the sharp rise in immigration during the 2000s as a result of European Union (EU) enlargement in 2004, the arrival of increasing numbers of Asian and African nationals during the decade, and continued immigration flows from other countries including Ireland, Germany and the US (Blinder, 2012). This rise is shown in both the census and LTIM datasets. The difference between them widens during earlier decades. This is a result of the exclusion from the census of immigrants who have died or emigrated, and its counting of only the most recent arrival of each immigrant to the UK.

Half of the people born abroad and living in England and Wales arrived in the UK when they were between the ages of 15-29 (see Figure 3.2). Therefore, most came during the most economically productive stage of their life when they were less likely to be dependent on state provisions, including health and education. Less than 1 in 20 of the population born abroad arrived after the age of 45.

Figure 3.1: England and Wales residents born abroad, by year of arrival
The 2011 Census compared to ONS official immigration flows to the UK

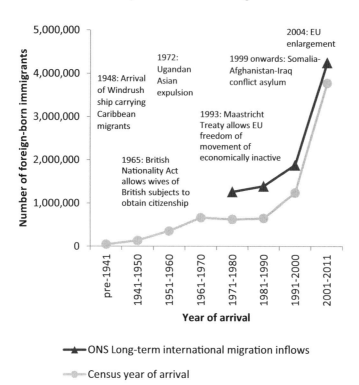

Year of arrival

━▲━ ONS Long-term international migration inflows

━●━ Census year of arrival

Figure 3.2: Foreign-born population in England and Wales, by age at arrival in the UK, 2011

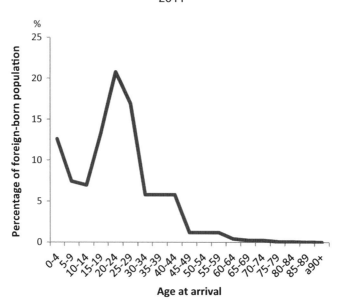

Age at arrival

Age structure

Census ethnic group categories are based on streams of migration to the UK in the past 60 years. Because of the youth of immigrants born outside the UK, half arriving when aged 15-29, it is not surprising to find that most groups other than White British are young in age structure (Figure 3.3). Not only are few immigrants old when they arrive in Britain, but most are ready to start or renew families within a few years of arrival.

The youngest ethnic group are those residents with a Mixed ethnic identity. Many of these will be children of parents of different ethnicities: for each of the four Mixed groups identified by the census, between 39 and 47 per cent are aged under 15, double the figure of 18 per cent for England and Wales as a whole. Less than 4 per cent of the Mixed group are aged 65 or older, compared to 16 per cent for England and Wales as a whole.

Only the ethnic groups with origins in large-scale immigration before 1970 have more than 5 per cent of their population aged 65 or older: Indian (8 per cent),

Figure 3.3: Broad age composition of ethnic groups, 2011

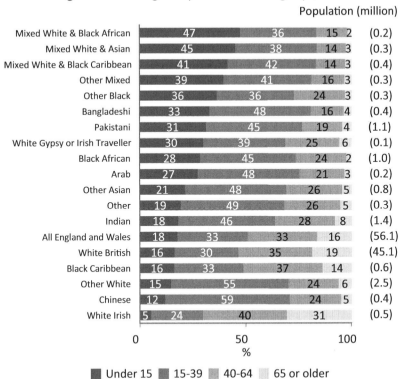

Note: Arranged by percentage of population aged under 15.

Black Caribbean (14 per cent) and White Irish (31 per cent). The immediate post–war European migration may account for the Other White group reaching 6 per cent elderly. In the future, it is likely that the percentage of elderly people will also grow for other groups that currently have a young age structure.

The Chinese and Other White groups have relatively low percentages of both young people and elderly people. Both groups had some immigration in the 1950s, and strong immigration in the 2000s with a period between of much lower immigration. Natural growth is not yet such a strong current feature as for other minority groups. This is confirmed by the low growth through natural change, shown in Figure 3.5.

Estimating fertility rates for ethnic groups

Since the numbers of births to mothers of each ethnic group are not collected as official statistics, fertility rates cannot be calculated as readily as is possible for the population as a whole. Estimates of some ethnic groups' fertility rates can be made from sample surveys (Coleman and Dubuc, 2010) or from the Office for National Statistics (ONS) Longitudinal Study (LS) (Storkey, 1999), but suffer from the small sample sizes for each ethnic group.

The aggregate census data of the whole population gives an opportunity for approximate estimates of fertility by comparing the number of children with the number of women of fertile ages. Groups with higher fertility will have a higher number of children per woman. The calculation is approximate for various reasons, but principally because the ethnic group of mother and child can be different. It is only reasonable to calculate a fertility rate in this way for groups where the mother and child are most likely to be of the same ethnic group. Matrices of mother's and child's ethnicity (for example, Wohland et al, 2010, Table 4.2, p 27) show that White British, Pakistani and Bangladeshi groups have least transfers in this way (the net change from mother to child's ethnic group was less than 5 per cent), Indian and Black African are moderately porous (a net loss from each of 10 per cent through ethnic group of children being different from the mother), Black Caribbean and Chinese more porous (a loss of a little over 20 per cent), while the Mixed groups gain many children from mothers of different ethnic groups.

The ratio (Children aged 0-4)/(Women aged 15-44) has been calculated for each ethnic group from each of the past three censuses, and for the total for all people in England and Wales. Since the children are born in the five years previous to the census, the women's fertility refers to that period. The Total Fertility Rate (TFR) for England and Wales (E&W) averaged for the five years previous to a census has been used to calibrate these Children-Women ratios (C-W ratios) in Figure 3.4 of this chapter. If the group's C-W ratio is higher than that of England and Wales as a whole, then its fertility is estimated as higher, and a lower C-W ratio leads to a lower estimate of fertility:

Estimated TFR (group) = TFR (E&W)*C-W ratio (group)/C-W ratio (E&W).

More accurate estimates of fertility by ethnic group for England and Wales for the period 1996-2004 give the same pattern of differences between groups as these Child-Women ratio estimates, but estimate a little higher fertility in each case (Coleman and Dubuc, 2010). This is because there is a net loss from other ethnic groups' mothers to Mixed ethnic groups' children.

The estimates of fertility given in the chapter are therefore a good guide to trends over time for ethnic groups, but more accurate estimates will be possible from other data.

Fertility rates

The growth of each ethnic group from births is the product of the group's proportion of women at fertile ages and their fertility rate. A comparison of the number of children with the number of women aged 15-44 provides estimates of fertility for each group for the period immediately before each of the past three censuses (see Figure 3.4).

Bangladeshi and Pakistani family size has reduced to an average of about three children per family, higher than other groups but considerably lower than in previous decades. Fertility of most other groups including White British has risen a little in the 2000s. The overall impact is a convergence of fertility rates. Chinese fertility is particularly low, partly because one-third of the Chinese population are students.

Figure 3.4: Estimated Total Fertility Rate (TFR)

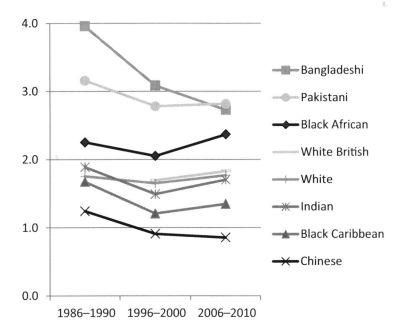

Births, deaths, net migration and changes in identity

During a decade, population change for an ethnic group is made up of *components* of three types, which are shown in Figure 3.5 and explained here. The calculations are provided in the online material supporting this book (see http://www.ethnicity.ac.uk/dynamicsofdiversity/).

a) Natural change: balance of births and deaths

Figure 3.5 uses the opportunity of the census, when population change over the decade is known quite accurately for each ethnic group, to estimate its components. The methods are developed from those used for the 1990s (Finney and Simpson, 2009). They could be applied to each sub-national area, when the net impact of migration would include movement within Britain as well as overseas migration.

Births are estimated as the number of children alive in 2011 aged under 10. Deaths during the decade are estimated by applying life table 10-year mortality rates from the mid-2000s to the age structure of each group's 2001 population. Births and deaths estimated in these ways for each ethnic group are scaled to be consistent with the known total number of births and deaths.

The estimate of births assumes a zero net impact of international child migration during the decade. Our birth estimates sum over all the ethnic groups to within 0.4 per cent of the registered births in the decade, which is reassuring. The assumption that mortality rates are the same for each ethnic group may also not be correct, although research suggests that any differences there are do not have a great impact (Haskey, 2002). The total estimated deaths were within 1.7 per cent of the registered total for the decade. To make the figures accurate for the England and Wales population as a whole, the estimates of births and deaths for each ethnic group have been scaled to be consistent with the registered totals for the decade.

b) Net migration: balance of immigration and emigration

Migration is not measured directly by ethnic group. It is calculated as a residual population change after births, deaths and changes in identity have been measured.

c) Net gain from changes of identity

Those who remained in the population during the decade but chose a different ethnic group.

The number of people who have changed their ethnic group is discussed in detail in Chapter Six. From the ONS LS, the number moving out of a group has been subtracted from the number moving to it, and expressed as a percentage of the 2001 population. This is the net impact on the population from changes in identity, and may increase or decrease the population. The estimate is a direct one, but from a 1 per cent sample, which for some groups is of less than 1,000 people.

Components of change

Immigration and births both add to Britain's population and make it more ethnically diverse. What is the contribution of each of these? Figure 3.5 summarises the answer, balancing immigration with emigration, and births with deaths. These balances are derived from analysis of the age structure of each group in the 2001 and 2011 Censuses. It also shows the extent to which populations change because some people change their ethnic group during a decade.

This chapter takes a more detailed look at individual ethnic groups, but Figure 3.5 makes clear that the rapid growth of minority ethnic groups has been due to both natural increase (births exceeding deaths) and net in-migration, and that overall these two sources contribute approximately the same amount of growth.

The growth of the Pakistani, Bangladeshi and Mixed groups in England and Wales is largely from children born in England and Wales. The growth of the Other White group that includes many of those with family origins in continental

Figure 3.5: Components of population change, 2001-11, England and Wales

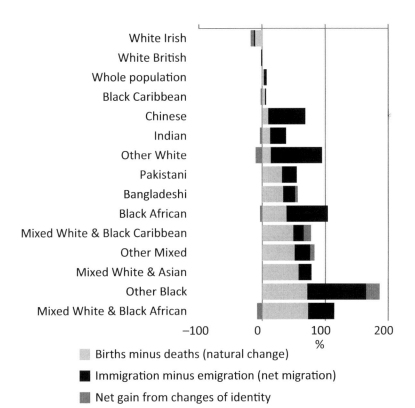

Note: Ethnic groups ordered by increasing net natural change.

Europe, and of the Indian, Black African and Chinese groups, is largely from migration to England and Wales.

The Black Caribbean group has grown a little, mainly from births exceeding deaths, while the White Irish group has lost, both from deaths exceeding births, and from net emigration during the decade.

These changes in the population size of each group tend to be much bigger than the net impact of people choosing a different ethnic group in 2011 from the group they chose in 2001. Most of this change has been towards the Mixed groups and the write-in 'Other' groups. However, White British gained from White Irish and Other White when its label changed to include White English/Welsh/Scottish/Northern Irish/British. These changes are discussed further in Chapter Six on the stability of ethnic group responses between the last two censuses.

Population pyramids reveal the sources of population change

In the population pyramids that follow, the 2011 age structure is outlined in bold. The shaded bars represent numbers of people in 2001, at the age they would have been in 2011. For example, the shaded 30- to 34-year-olds are the number of 20- to 24-year-olds in 2001. The changing size of a cohort in 2001 and 2011 shows whether it has grown from immigration, or reduced from a combination of emigration and mortality.

The labels on each pyramid are indicative of the drivers of change, showing that mortality is mainly at older ages and migration at young adult ages. The changing age structure tells the story of a group's migration. Explanation of the change in size of each age cohort is given beneath the pyramid. The smaller changes due to net changes of individuals' own ethnic identity are not known for each age group and so cannot be shown here. Pyramids for groups that are not shown are available in the book's online materials (see http://www.ethnicity.ac.uk/dynamicsofdiversity/).

Figure 3.6: England and Wales population at 2001 and 2011

Age at 2011
85+
80-84
75-79
70-74
65-69
60-64
55-59
50-54
45-49
40-44
35-39
30-34
25-29
20-24
15-19
10-14
5-9
0-4
Males
Females
Difference is mainly deaths
Mainly migration
Under 10s are new births
4,000,000 2,000,000 0 2,000,000 4,000,000
Males 2011
Females 2011
Males 2001
Females 2001

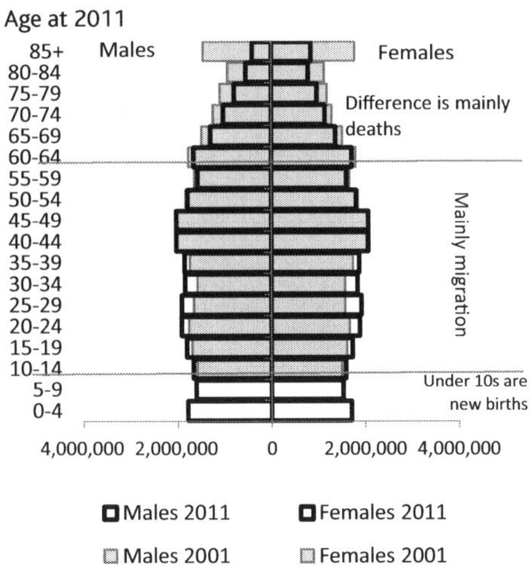

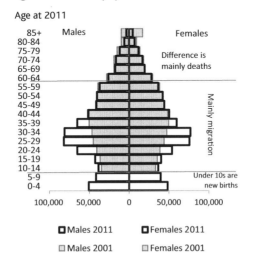

The pyramids show the England and Wales population in 2011, and in 2001 but aged 10 years. At older ages, the 2011 population is reduced mainly because of deaths during the decade. For ages under 10, the population has been born during the decade. Despite a growth in fertility rates during the 2000s, the number of children is not as large as the number now in their forties. For ages between 10 and about 60, changes in the size of a cohort are mainly due to migration. The pyramid shows the net in-migration of both men and women who, in 2011, were aged 20-34.

Figure 3.7: Indian population at 2001 and 2011

Age at 2011
85+
80-84
75-79
70-74
65-69
60-64
55-59
50-54
45-49
40-44
35-39
30-34
25-29
20-24
15-19
10-14
5-9
0-4
Males
Females
Difference is mainly deaths
Mainly migration
Under 10s are new births
100,000 50,000 0 50,000 100,000
Males 2011
Females 2011
Males 2001
Females 2001

The Indian population has been added to by migration, particularly of those now in their twenties and thirties. Migration accounts for two-thirds of the Indian group's growth from 2001–11 (see Figure 3.5). This reverses the estimates of change in the 1990s. The increase in immigrants from India is mainly students but also those joining family and for work (ONS, 2012b). The fertility rate of the Indian group in the UK is lower than the Pakistani group, resulting in a relatively smaller number of children.

Figure 3.8: White Irish population at 2001 and 2011

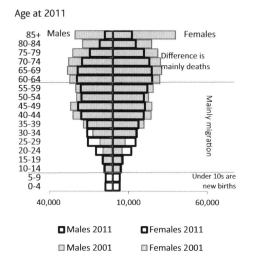

The White Irish population has an old age structure: many children and grandchildren of immigrants from Ireland are not recorded with the White Irish ethnic group in the census, by themselves or by their parents. Losses to those now aged 35 and older are due both to deaths and to emigration, perhaps back to Ireland during the early 2000s at the time of the booming 'Celtic tiger' economy. However, those now aged 20–34 have been added to by immigration, including students in higher education. Over all age groups, migration of the White Irish group is estimated to be a net loss of 2 per cent from England and Wales (see Figure 3.5).

Figure 3.9: Other White population at 2001 and 2011

Age at 2011

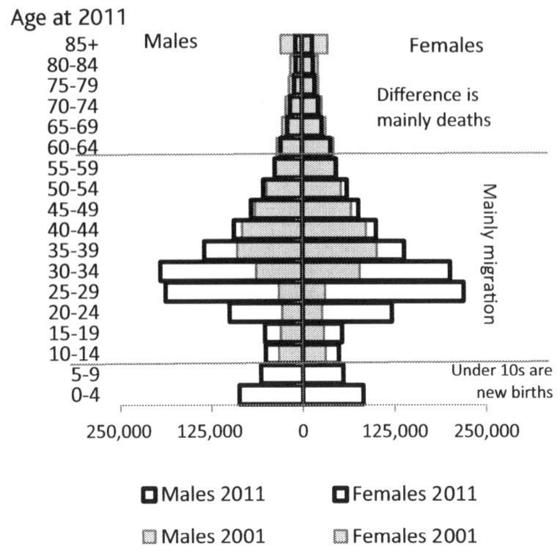

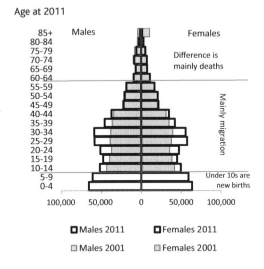

Immigration from Eastern Europe has in particular increased the size of the Other White population, among adults now aged in their twenties and thirties. The growing child population will have resulted from births in England and Wales, and child migrants during the decade.

Figure 3.10: Pakistani population at 2001 and 2011

Age at 2011

The Pakistani population has a younger age structure than the population of England and Wales as a whole. The number of children is larger than any other age group. Migration during 2001–11 has added to those now aged between 10 and 40.

Conclusions and implications

This chapter's demographic perspective has helped to show why ethnic diversity has increased, in four different ways. The first is recognition that most minority ethnic groups' age structure is influenced by the young age of migrants on their arrival in Britain; this has explained why most minority groups grow more through births outnumbering deaths. The second used the detailed age structure provided by the census to decompose population change into growth through the excess of births over deaths, and growth through the balance of immigration and emigration. The Pakistani and Bangladeshi groups' growth in the 2000s, for example, was less through migration and more through the excess of births over deaths.

The third demographic analysis used the ratio of young children to the women who could be their mothers to provide estimates of fertility for each ethnic group and its development over the past three decades. A reduction of differences between groups has shown that only the Black African, Pakistani and Bangladeshi groups have average fertility higher than two children, and all groups are now below three children per woman. Finally, a comparison of age cohorts between the 2001 and 2011 Censuses showed the impact of migration at different ages, revealing very different trajectories for each ethnic group.

The analyses paint a contrasting view of, for example, the White Irish and Indian groups in England and Wales. While the Indian group has had lower than average fertility rates for many years, its size has grown steadily from an excess of births over deaths because there are many more young adult Indian people than older adult Indian people. This is partly because the 2000s saw an increase in Indian immigration to Britain, coincident with India's economic growth and the attractiveness of British universities to an aspiring middle class. The White Irish population in England and Wales, on the other hand, is older and thus has a greater proportion of deaths, while many of its children take White British ethnicity rather than White Irish, a signal of assimilation that is not available to non-White children. The impact of migration has added to the young adult White Irish in England and Wales, but reduced the number of older adults as many emigrated to Ireland and elsewhere in the 2000s.

Knowledge of the age structure of a population is useful not only to understand its size and development, but also directly to shape appropriate services for children, and for young and older adults. The young profile of immigrants points to the role of immigration in filling a gap produced by an ageing population in England and Wales. Immigrants contribute to economic development, but they and their children often face discrimination long after they or their parents arrived as immigrants, evidenced by the inequalities examined later in this book. Knowledge of age structure is also necessary to make that examination of social change and inequalities, as Chapter Nine shows for health. Finally, it is a necessary starting point for projections of population size.

Note

Further information about data and sources are available from http://www.ethnicity.ac.uk/dynamicsofdiversity/

References

Blinder, B. (2012) *Settlement in the UK*, Oxford: The Migration Observatory (www.migrationobservatory.ox.ac.uk/briefings/settlement-uk).

Coleman, D.A. and Dubuc, S. (2010) 'The fertility of ethnic minorities in the UK, 1960s-2006', *Population Studies*, vol 64, no 1, pp 19-41.

Finney, N. and Simpson, L. (2009) 'Population dynamics: the roles of natural change and migration in producing the ethnic mosaic', *Journal of Ethnic and Migration Studies*, vol 35, no 9, pp 1479-96.

Haskey, J. (ed) (2002) *Population projections by ethnic group: A feasibility study*, Studies in Medical and Population Statistics 67, London: The Stationery Office.

Hinde, A. (1998) *Demographic methods*, London: Arnold.

ONS (Office for National Statistics) (2012a) *Population estimates by ethnic group: Quality and methodology information*, Newport: ONS (www.ons.gov.uk/ons/guide-method/method-quality/quality/quality-information/social-statistics/summary-quality-report-for-population-estmates-by-ethnic-group.pdf).

ONS (2012b) International Passenger Survey tables: *Countries of origin* (http://www.ons.gov.uk/ons/rel/migration1/long-term-international-migration/2013/table-3-20abc.xls), *Reasons for migration* (http://www.ons.gov.uk/ons/rel/migration1/long-term-international-migration/2013/table-3-09.xls) and for *India* (http://www.ons.gov.uk/ons/about-ons/business-transparency/freedom-of-information/what-can-i-request/published-ad-hoc-data/pop/june-2013/migration-to-and-from-india-2001-to-2011.xls).

ONS (2014) *Long term migrants*, Newport: ONS (www.ons.gov.uk/ons/taxonomy/index.html?nscl=Long-term+Migrants).

Siegel, J.S. (2002) *Applied demography*, San Diego, CA: Academic Press.

Storkey, M. (1999) 'Fertility of ethnic groups', *Longitudinal Study Update*, vol 23, pp 3-4.

Wohland, P., Rees, P., Norman, P., Boden, P. and Jasinska, M. (2010) *Ethnic population projections for the UK and local areas, 2001-2051*, Working Paper 10/2, Leeds: School of Geography, University of Leeds.

FOUR

Does Britain have plural cities?

Ludi Simpson

Key findings

- Britain's cities are more ethnically diverse than ever before. Slough, Luton and Leicester are the first local authorities outside London that are already plural, where no ethnic group is in the majority.
- The census itself has changed how Britain's diversity is measured, by dividing White into White British, Irish, Gypsy or Irish Traveller, and Other White.
- Cities labelled by politicians as 'segregated' are, in fact, the most diverse. For example, Bradford and Leicester both have more than 1,000 residents from each of 15 ethnic categories measured in the census, and over 30,000 residents from diverse groups that the census labels as 'Mixed' or 'Other White', 'Other Asian', 'Other Black' or simply 'Other'.
- Increased diversity over a decade is small but steady: every local authority district except Forest Heath has increased its diversity since 2001.
- A projection of ethnic diversity suggests that the future will include many local authorities where White British is not the largest group, but no other single ethnic group is likely to become the majority of any city's population.
- The future of Britain is a greater variety of diverse areas.

Introduction

Plural cities is a concept used in discussions about how local government policies might change when the population is so ethnically mixed that no one group is the majority.

   Local government deals with diverse areas on an everyday basis: not only ethnic and cultural diversity, but also the needs of young adults and older people, those in rural and urban neighbourhoods, those with powerful organisations to represent them, and those without. The changing ethnic composition of an area is a guide to changing needs inasmuch as it may indicate a variety of preferences for housing size, for types of school meals, for care of older people, for cultural and entertainment facilities, for funeral procedures or for other aspects of local services. Increasing ethnic diversity may also require and indicate resilience and an ability to cope with change, including the arrival of new migrants. Diverse areas offer a variety of resources and cultures to visitors and traders.

Managing ethnic diversity through appropriate services and by making connections between diverse cultures is an established area of study and practice in the UK and internationally (Wood et al, 2006; Reza, 2012). Needs are best measured directly by a variety of social indicators (see also Chapter Two, this volume).

In the 2000s many claims about which might be Britain's first plural city were clothed in the language of misfortune and fear. Finney and Simpson (2009, pp 141-59) trace how stories of Birmingham and Leicester becoming the first 'minority white city' were framed as 'a critical challenge' to democracy, requiring 'tough decisions' for city planning. More often than not, the claims of imminent plural cities were unsubstantiated by evidence, but repeated as news stories and in academic and government reports as a means to suggest a need for urgent action on immigration and integration, and a threatening loss of rights by the White population.

A decade later, the same association of immigration with ethnic diversity and with threats to the indigenous population are still common themes of political discourse. Peter Hitchens (2012) of the *Daily Mail* said that the census revealed an 'alien nation', and that Britain as we know it will soon disappear. However, the evidence on which to base our understanding has been boosted by the 2011 Census.

This chapter examines what the census says about the emergence of plural local authority districts, and presents pen portraits of the most diverse districts in Britain. Diversity does not stand still. The chapter also discusses how people make forecasts of ethnic diversity, and makes its own projections for the next two decades.

Plural towns and cities

Twenty-three of London's 33 boroughs were already 'plural' by 2011, as is London as a whole, whose White British population was 45 per cent of the capital's total. Leicester's total White population was more than half its residents, and so it was not yet a 'minority white city'. But restricting attention to White British shows that it was already plural, as the White Irish and Other White populations are substantial in Leicester. Thus the diversity in the census classification itself affects how we think of each city's composition. Slough and Luton are also already plural with White British less than half their population. It is possible that Birmingham will join them during this decade. However, in none of these districts will the

White British population be small; it is now the biggest in every district except two (Tower Hamlets and Brent, where it is the second biggest).

Newham

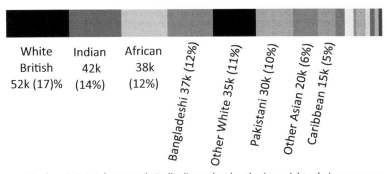

| White British 52k (17)% | Indian 42k (14%) | African 38k (12%) | Bangladeshi 37k (12%) | Other White 35k (11%) | Pakistani 30k (10%) | Other Asian 20k (6%) | Caribbean 15k (5%) |

Newham is Britain's most ethnically diverse local authority – eight ethnic groups are represented by 5 per cent or more of its residents. Of Newham's 308,000 residents, 143,000 were born in the UK; 52,000 have the ethnic group White British, while 203,000 have a British identity. Thirty-four per cent of households have more than one ethnicity, and 5 per cent of residents are of mixed ethnicity themselves. Of the 165,414 born abroad, 47 per cent arrived since 2004. Seventeen of the 18 ethnic groups counted in the 2011 Census have 1,000 or more residents.

Leicester

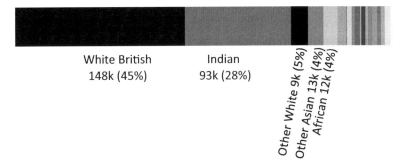

| White British 148k (45%) | Indian 93k (28%) | Other White 9k (5%) | Other Asian 13k (4%) | African 12k (4%) |

Leicester's Indian population is itself diverse, with Hindu, Muslim and Christian populations born in the UK, India and East Africa. Of Leicester's 330,000 residents, 219,000 were born in the UK; 149,000 have the ethnic group White British, while 273,000 have a British identity. Eighteen per cent of households have more than one ethnicity, and 4 per cent of residents are of mixed ethnicity themselves. Of the 110,843 born abroad, 36 per cent arrived since 2004. Seventeen of the 18 ethnic groups counted in the 2011 Census have 1,000 or more residents.

Slough

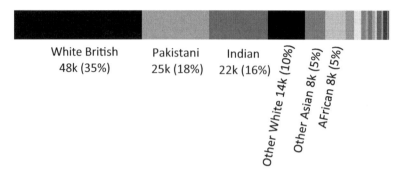

White British
48k (35%)

Pakistani
25k (18%)

Indian
22k (16%)

Other White 14k (10%)

Other Asian 8k (5%)

African 8k (5%)

Outside London, Slough is the most ethnically diverse local authority in Britain. Of Slough's 140,000 residents, 86,000 were born in the UK; 48,000 have the ethnic group White British, while 108,000 have a British identity. Twenty-one per cent of households have more than one ethnicity, and 3 per cent of residents are of mixed ethnicity themselves. Of the 54,652 born abroad, 41 per cent arrived since 2004. Thirteen of the 18 ethnic groups counted in the 2011 Census have 1,000 or more residents.

Luton

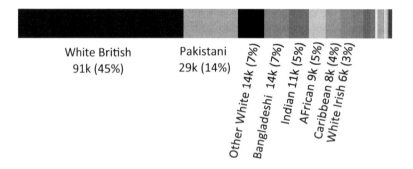

White British
91k (45%)

Pakistani
29k (14%)

Other White 14k (7%)

Bangladeshi 14k (7%)

Indian 11k (5%)

African 9k (5%)

Caribbean 8k (4%)

White Irish 6k (3%)

Luton is one of the three districts outside London where the number of White British is less than half of all residents, although still three times the next largest group, Pakistani. Of Luton's 203,000 residents, 140,000 were born in the UK; 91,000 have the ethnic group White British, while 165,000 have a British identity. Twenty-four per cent of households have more than one ethnicity, and 4 per cent of residents are of mixed ethnicity themselves. Of the 62,872 born abroad, 40 per cent arrived since 2004. Sixteen of the 18 ethnic groups counted in the 2011 Census have 1,000 or more residents.

Tower Hamlets

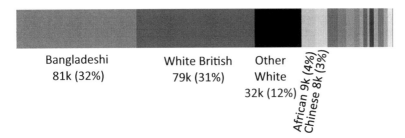

Bangladeshi
81k (32%)

White British
79k (31%)

Other
White
32k (12%)

African 9k (4%)

Chinese 8k (3%)

Tower Hamlets has Britain's largest Bangladeshi population. Of Tower Hamlets' 254,000 residents, 145,000 were born in the UK; 79,000 have the ethnic group White British, while 190,000 have a British identity. Thirty-three per cent of households have more than one ethnicity, and 4 per cent of residents are of mixed ethnicity themselves. Of the 109,434 born abroad, 44 per cent arrived since 2004. Seventeen of the 18 ethnic groups counted in the 2011 Census have 1,000 or more residents.

Brent

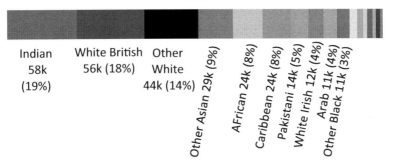

Indian
58k
(19%)

White British
56k (18%)

Other
White
44k (14%)

Other Asian 29k (9%)

AFrican 24k (8%)

Caribbean 24k (8%)

Pakistani 14k (5%)

White Irish 12k (4%)

Arab 11k (4%)

Other Black 11k (3%)

Brent is one of Britain and London's most ethnically diverse areas. Of Brent's 311,000 residents, 140,000 were born in the UK; 56,000 have the ethnic group White British, while 210,000 have a British identity. Thirty-four per cent of households have more than one ethnicity, and 5 per cent of residents are of mixed ethnicity. Of the 171,427 born abroad, 37 per cent arrived since 2004. Seventeen of the 18 ethnic groups counted in the 2011 Census have 1,000 or more residents.

Birmingham

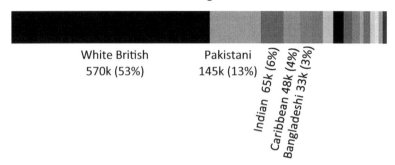

White British   Pakistani   Indian 65k (6%)
570k (53%)   145k (13%)   Caribbean 48k (4%)
                                           Bangladeshi 33k (3%)

Birmingham's large population means that its ethnic diversity includes 10 ethnic groups each with 20,000 people. Of Birmingham's 1.1 million residents, 835,000 were born in the UK; 570,000 have the ethnic group White British, while 952,000 have a British identity. Twenty-one per cent of households have more than one ethnicity, and 4 per cent of residents are of mixed ethnicity themselves. Of the 238,313 born abroad, 33 per cent arrived since 2004. Seventeen of the 18 ethnic groups counted in the 2011 Census have 1,000 or more residents.

Census data on cities

The information compiled about each local authority district is available with the online resources for this book (see http://www.ethnicity.ac.uk/dynamicsofdiversity/). It includes composition according to ethnic group and religion, UK-born, year of and age at arrival, numbers with a British passport, and with a British national identity, households with multiple ethnicities, and the diversity index. In this chapter we have included some of the most diverse districts. On their charts we have labelled each ethnic group that has 3 per cent or more of the district's residents.

The boundary of a local authority sometimes fits closely or even sits within an urban area. Such a close boundary emphasises ethnic diversity, as in Leicester. In contrast, the boundary of Bradford includes surrounding areas with less ethnic diversity, and does not reflect the diversity of the city alone.

Measuring diversity

Ecologists have a very useful notion of diversity that we have applied to calculate how closely each local authority district is to having an equal number of each ethnic group measured in the census. For better comparability with 2001, as in other chapters we have combined White Gypsy or Irish Traveller with Other White, and made a single 'Other' category from the 2011 Census categories of Arab, Other Mixed, Other Asian, Other Black and Other. To calculate the diversity index, the ecologists sum the 13 ethnic group proportions, first squaring them, and divide them into 1. Early analyses from the 2011 Census used 16 categories, before the research that informed this book (Simpson, 2013).

The index is greatest when there are equal numbers in each group, when it is equal to 13, and lowest when there is only one group in an area, when it is equal to 1. We have standardised the index by stretching it to be always within the range 0–100. The average across England and Wales as a whole has increased from 2.4 in 2001 to 4.3 in 2011.

Ethnic diversity on the increase

How diverse is each local authority district? How close is it to having an equal number of each ethnic group? The 2011 Census tells us that no local authority is very diverse in this sense. On a scale of 0–100 (see above), Newham is the most diverse district in England and Wales, at 56.

Diversity, averaged over the 348 local authority districts in England and Wales, has increased from 1.5 in 1991, to 2.4 in 2001 and to 4.3 in 2011. These seem small changes, but they are increases of more than 50 per cent in each decade. Every district except Forest Heath has increased its diversity since 2001 – Forest Heath hosts US air force bases, affecting its population composition from year to year.

There is a very strong relationship between diversity and the total percentage of minority ethnic groups in a district (the correlation coefficient is 0.96). The 10 local authorities with the greatest diversity are Newham, Brent, Ealing, Redbridge, Waltham Forest, Slough, Hackney, Haringey, Harrow and Lambeth, with Luton the next most diverse area outside London. In other words, areas with the fewest White British are also the most diverse. Those with little diversity are the areas where the population is almost entirely White British, although in the main, this is no longer a feature of modern Britain. Every district has at least 1 per cent of residents who described their ethnic group as other than White British in the 2011 Census.

Barking and Dagenham

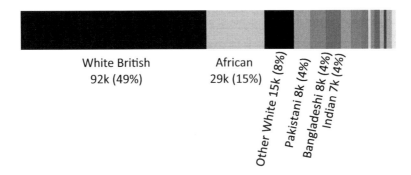

White British
92k (49%)

African
29k (15%)

Other White 15k (8%)

Pakistani 8k (4%)

Bangladeshi 8k (4%)

Indian 7k (4%)

Barking and Dagenham is home to many people who have moved away from inner London in the past decade, like many other outer London boroughs. Of Barking and Dagenham's 186,000 residents, 128,000 were born in the UK; 92,000 have the ethnic group White British, while 150,000 have a British identity. Twenty-three per cent of households have more than one ethnicity, and 4 per cent of residents are of mixed ethnicity themselves. Of the 57,447 born abroad, 40 per cent arrived since 2004. Sixteen of the 18 ethnic groups counted in the 2011 Census have 1,000 or more residents.

Lewisham

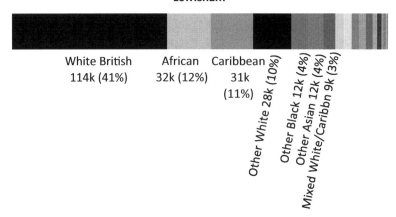

White British 114k (41%)

African 32k (12%)

Caribbean 31k (11%)

Other White 28k (10%)

Other Black 12k (4%)

Other Asian 12k (4%)

Mixed White/Caribbn 9k (3%)

Lewisham has the highest percentage of Caribbean population among Britain's local authorities, although larger districts including Birmingham have more Caribbean residents. Of Lewisham's 276,000 residents, 183,000 were born in the UK; 114,000 have the ethnic group White British, while 218,000 have a British identity. Thirty-nine per cent of households have more than one ethnicity, and 7 per cent of residents are of mixed ethnicity themselves. Of the 93,086 born abroad, 35 per cent arrived since 2004. Seventeen of the 18 ethnic groups counted in the 2011 Census have 1,000 or more residents.

Westminster

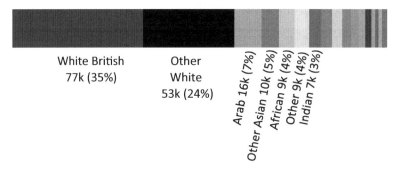

White British 77k (35%)

Other White 53k (24%)

Arab 16k (7%)

Other Asian 10k (5%)

African 9k (4%)

Other 9k (4%)

Indian 7k (3%)

Westminster is a gateway for many new residents of Britain from Europe and the Middle East. Of Westminster's 219,000 residents, 102,000 were born in the UK; 77,000 have the ethnic group White British, while 139,000 have a British identity. Forty-two per cent of households have more than one ethnicity, and 5 per cent of residents are of mixed ethnicity themselves. Of the 116,989 born abroad, 46 per cent arrived since 2004. Seventeen of the 18 ethnic groups counted in the 2011 Census have 1,000 or more residents.

Dynamics of change and population projections with an ethnic group dimension

Knowledge of the broad dynamics of population change after immigration makes it possible to project the population into the future, using a *cohort component* approach.

Immigration into the UK tends be of young adults, adding to the productive workforce. A growing child population results as most new migrants are of the age to start families. Not until many years later will those who immigrated become elderly and suffer significant numbers of deaths. Thus, for many decades, the population descended from immigrants will grow due to the number of births exceeding the number of deaths.

The UK government has investigated making population projections with an ethnic group dimension (Haskey, 2002), which would be useful for planning the nature of services in a changing society, as well as for implementing legislation against discrimination. However, there are three major difficulties, even though the dynamics of changing populations are known. First, the ethnic group dimension introduces complexity into a projection model because it must incorporate assumptions about moving between ethnic groups, both as individuals change their ethnicity during their lifetime, and because children may have different ethnicity from their parents. Second, the most unpredictable element of future population change is international migration, and this has a disproportionate impact on ethnic composition. And finally, the interpretation of population statistics referring to future years must acknowledge that by the time that future is reached, the politicians' focus on ethnic group will have changed, and will have probably introduced new categories, or a changed perspective on measurement of ethnicity, as has occurred at each of the past three censuses.

Finney and Simpson (2009, pp 151-5) reviewed population projections with an ethnic group dimension, a technique described by them as 'in its infancy'. The University of Leeds developed population projections with an ethnic group dimension for each local authority district of England, and the countries of Wales, Scotland and Northern Ireland (Rees et al, 2010; Wohland et al, 2010). Similar research will no doubt improve on these projections, updating the assumptions using results from the 2011 Census.

How much diversity will there be in the future?

It is clear that ethnic diversity will continue to increase in Britain, both nationally and in the vast majority of local areas. This is a safe prediction because the minority group populations are growing 'naturally' without the help of any further migration from overseas, due to their young age structures. Since global movement will continue to a lesser or greater extent, immigration will also add to the increasing diversity in Britain. The dynamics of change is explained in the box above. Each component of population change was measured in Chapter Three.

Within Britain, the spreading out of minority populations from cities to suburbs and to less urban areas is a consequence of existing integration in the labour and housing markets, as discussed and quantified from different perspectives in Chapters Two and Seven. This spreading of diversity within Britain will continue.

It is certain, then, that the number of plural cities in Britain will increase, as will the indices of diversity in most areas of Britain. A projection of diversity has been undertaken for this book that assumes a continued change at the pace of the decade 2001 to 2011, through to 2031. The projection aggregates the 'Other' categories that are not comparable across time (Chapter Six), to project the future share of 13 ethnic groups. The projection is not precise because immigration may be more or less than in the 2000s, and the labour and housing markets may encourage more or less internal movement. Ethnic groups may also become increasingly diverse in years to come with more categories, which will make this exercise almost impossible. Nonetheless, it serves to show the level of diversity to be expected in Britain based on current trends and ethnic groups, even if it happens sooner or later than suggested here.

Table 4.1: Indicators of ethnic diversity and the number of plural local authority districts, 2001-31

	Diversity index		Number of plural local authority districts		At least two groups have more than 5% of the population
	Average local authority	Maximum	No group has half the population, but White British is the largest group	White British is not the largest group	
2001	2.4	39.9	8	0	57
2011	4.3	55.8	24	2	101
2021	6.2	48.3	19	15	167
2031	7.6	46.2	22	26	214

Note: 348 local authority districts of England and Wales.

A projection of diversity for this book

For the purposes of this book, a projection of diversity in each local authority district in England and Wales up to 2021 and 2031 has been made by extrapolating each ethnic group's share of the local population, repeating the change that occurred between 2001 and 2011. Shares have been kept between 0 and 100 per cent, and in each year sum to 100 per cent in every area.

As with official projections of other types, the assumption is that the recent past will repeat itself. It must be stressed that this assumption is less reliable for projections of ethnic group shares of the population. These are more dependent on the volume and composition of future immigration that rarely repeats the pattern of previous decades.

A test of the projections was made, estimating diversity in 2011 by repeating the change during 1991-2001 in the next decade. This projection underestimated diversity because immigration was higher in 2001-11 than it had been during 1991-2001. Similarly, the projections reported in this chapter may overestimate diversity if immigration in 2011-31 is less than during 2001-11, and underestimate it if Mixed ethnic groups in 2011-31 grow faster than during 2001-11.

The projection shows that diversity will increase steadily, on average. However, the current most diverse local authority, Newham, is the most diverse that Britain's local authorities are likely to become. Six ethnic groups in Newham each have 10 per cent or more of its population, and no group has as much as 20 per cent. In future, other areas will approach similar levels of diversity but not exceed it (the maximum shown in Table 4.1 does not increase after 2011). It would simply be unlikely for any local authority to get closer to equal numbers of every minority. The future is likely to be a diversity of diverse areas, not a uniform sameness.

The number of plural local authorities will continue to increase. Whereas in 2001, the eight plural local authority districts were limited to London, in 2011 there are 26 that include Luton, Slough and Leicester outside London. In almost all cases the White British is the largest group, although no longer half of the population. However, it is this group of authorities where White British is not the largest group which will grow in number, according to our projection.

By 2031 we can expect 48 plural local authority districts, where no group has the majority of the population. Half of them will have a 'minority' ethnic group that is larger than White British. But the conclusion is even more telling than this. Those diverse and plural local authorities are expected to be made up of many smaller populations that currently do not have an ethnic group separately identified in the census, including many more Mixed ethnic groups. In 20 districts the largest group in 2031 is expected to be the write-in responses, for example, against the heading 'Other White' or simply 'Other ethnic group'. Of course, by then, the response categories may have changed. The census ethnic group question will either become very long to accommodate more world origins, or have acknowledged in some other way the multi-ethnic society that Britain will have become.

Even in the six areas where one group other than White British is projected to be the largest group, that group does not come to dominate the local ethnic composition. The projection does show that the largest group in Leicester is likely to be Indian, in Tower Hamlets it is likely to be Bangladeshi, in Luton and Slough, Pakistani, while in Barking and Dagenham and in Greenwich the Black African group is projected to be the largest. But these six areas would also remain diverse, because that largest group is not projected to have one-half of the district population. In most cases the largest group remains between one-quarter and one-third of the district population.

The evidence that began in Chapter Two to point to greater growth outside the main concentrations of any ethnic group is again emerging in these projections, where those main concentrations are limited in the future. So long as there is a continued degree of integration into the labour and housing markets, the areas of densest settlement by each ethnic group will not become ghettos of one ethnic group, but are likely to develop a diversity that will characterise most areas of Britain.

The final column of Table 4.1 suggests that most districts will have significant minority populations. More than 200 out of the 348 local authority districts of England and Wales will, in less than 20 years, have at least one ethnic group other than White British that makes up 5 per cent of its population.

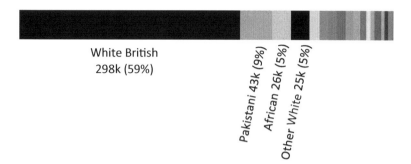

Bradford

White British
334k (64%)

Pakistani
107k
(20%)

Other White 16 (3%)

Bradford's Pakistani population is eight times the next largest minority ethnic group. A third of the local authority population lives outside the urban area of Bradford. Of Bradford's 522,000 residents, 433,000 were born in the UK; 334,000 have the ethnic group White British, while 481,000 have a British identity. Twelve per cent of households have more than one ethnicity, and 2 per cent of residents are of mixed ethnicity themselves. Of the 89,609 born abroad, 36 per cent arrived since 2004. Fifteen of the 18 ethnic groups counted in the 2011 Census have 1,000 or more residents.

Manchester

White British
298k (59%)

Pakistani 43k (9%)

African 26k (5%)

Other White 25k (5%)

Manchester's African population has more than trebled in the past decade. Of Manchester's 503,000 residents, 376,000 were born in the UK; 298,000 have the ethnic group White British, while 418,000 have a British identity. Twenty-five per cent of households have more than one ethnicity, and 5 per cent of residents are of mixed ethnicity themselves. Of the 127,061 born abroad, 51 per cent arrived since 2004. Seventeen of the 18 ethnic groups counted in the 2011 Census have 1,000 or more residents.

Edinburgh

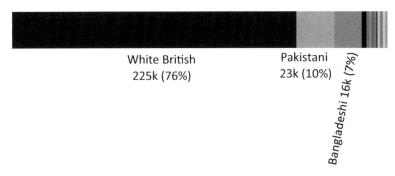

White British
225k (76%)

Pakistani
23k (10%)

Bangladeshi 16k (7%)

Edinburgh is the most ethnically diverse of Scotland's council areas. Of Edinburgh's
477,000 residents, 335,000 were born in the UK; 335,000 have the ethnic group
White Scottish, while 232,000 have a 'Scottish only' identity. Twenty-eight per cent of
households have more than one ethnicity, and 0.9 per cent of residents are of mixed
ethnicity themselves. Of the 75,698 born outside the UK, 63 per cent arrived since
2004. Fourteen of the 17 ethnic groups counted in the 2011 Census have 1,000 or more
residents. Scotland used different categories of ethnic group from England and Wales (see
Chapter Seven).

Glasgow

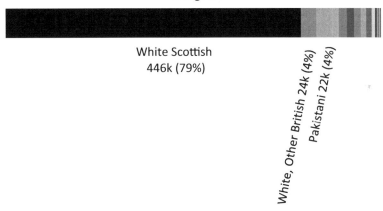

White Scottish
446k (79%)

White, Other British 24k (4%)

Pakistani 22k (4%)

Glasgow has the largest Pakistani population in Scotland. Of Glasgow's 593,000
residents, 486,000 were born in the UK; 466,000 have the ethnic group White Scottish,
while 367,000 have a 'Scottish only' identity. Sixteen per cent of households have more
than one ethnicity, and 0.5 per cent of residents are of mixed ethnicity themselves.
Of the 72,607 born outside the UK, 60 per cent arrived since 2004. Fourteen of the 17
ethnic groups counted in the 2011 Census have 1,000 or more residents. Scotland used
different categories of ethnic group from England and Wales (see Chapter Seven).

Conclusions and implications

The 2011 Census has confirmed that local authority districts have become more diverse to the extent that the whole of London, most London boroughs and three districts outside London have become 'plural', with no ethnic group making up half its population. But the key conclusion of this chapter is that the focus of attention should not be the fate of 'White British' relative to any other group, but on a future that is not about groups as such, but about diversity itself.

A projection of future local ethnic composition points away from islands of one ethnicity, towards a growing number of districts where no one group makes up more than a third of the population. Claims from different cultural groups will be important to balance with contact between groups, with permeability of group identities, and with encouragement of universal understandings and claims. Ethnicity is one among other dimensions of diversity. Ethnicity, age, gender, disability and income interact in the lived experience of a city, its services and its management.

Each city has its own particular development, illustrated by the pen portraits of diverse areas in this chapter. The most recent census and the data that supplement it during the decade are essential to developing plans that are truly local. Those plans will make the most of the resources of diversity including multilinguists and transnational networks.

As diversity develops, small minorities that are now not given a separate category in the official measurement of ethnicity will become the largest part of the population. The 'White' category used in the 1991 Census has now usefully been disaggregated to distinguish 'White British' from 'White Irish', and to allow those from Europe to choose 'White: Other'. The practice of distinguishing 'White Scottish' in Scotland might lead to 'White English' in England, and can be said to have already done so with the inclusion of English as an option in the new question on national identity (see Chapter Five). But the growing list of ethnicities has not diminished the number of residents who write in an ethnicity that has not been listed, which itself is an indicator that ethnicity is becoming increasingly diverse. Diversity begins to make the very categorisation of ethnicity less relevant to policy, and it will need to be rethought for future censuses.

Note
Further information about data and sources are available from
http://www.ethnicity.ac.uk/dynamicsofdiversity/

References
Finney, N. and Simpson, L. (2009) *'Sleepwalking to segregation'? Challenging myths about race and migration*, Bristol: Policy Press.
Haskey, J. (ed) (2002) *Population projections by ethnic group: A feasibility study*, Studies in Medical and Population Statistics 67, London: The Stationery Office.

Hitchens, P. (2012) 'Alien nation', *Daily Mail*, 15 December (www.dailymail.co.uk/news/article-2248707/Peter-Hitchens-The-new-census-reveals-Britain-unrecognisable-grandparents).

Rees, P., Wohland, P., Norman, P. and Boden, P. (2011) *What happens when international migrants settle? Ethnic group population trends and projections for UK local areas*, ESRC online summary (www.restore.ac.uk/UPTAP/wordpress/wp-content/uploads/2011/01/uptap-findings-rees-oct-10.pdf).

Reza, H. (ed) (2012) *Managing ethnic diversity: Meanings and practices from an international perspective*, Research in Migration and Ethnic Relations Series, Farnham: Ashgate Publishing.

Simpson, L. (2013) *Does Britain have plural cities?*, CoDE/JRF Briefing on the dynamics of diversity (www.ethnicity.ac.uk/medialibrary/briefings/dynamicsofdiversity/does-britain-have-plural-cities.pdf).

Wohland, P., Rees, P., Norman, P., Boden, P. and Jasinska, M. (2010) *Ethnic population projections for the UK and local areas, 2001-2051*, School of Geography Working Paper 10/2, Leeds: University of Leeds.

Wood, P., Landry, C., and Bloomfield, J. (2006) *Cultural diversity in Britain: A toolkit for cross-cultural co-operation*, York: Joseph Rowntree Foundation.

FIVE

Who feels British?

Stephen Jivraj and Bridget Byrne

Key Findings

- More than half of people in minority ethnic groups describe their national identity as British, English or a combination of the two.
- Bangladeshi, Pakistani, Indian and Black Caribbean ethnic groups are the most likely to consider themselves as exclusively British.
- An English-only national identity is favoured by more than seven tenths of the White British ethnic group.
- Those in the White British ethnic group are less likely to describe themselves as English if they live in London rather than other parts of the country.
- Immigrants from regions where there is a history of British colonialism are more likely to consider themselves as British than those born in other world regions.
- Fewer than a quarter of Muslims do not identify with a British national identity.
- Muslims living in communities where there is a greater cluster of other Muslims are more likely to describe themselves as British than Muslims living away from those clusters.

Introduction

This chapter presents national identity data from the 2011 Census. It starts with a brief review of the political context and theoretical debates in the field before describing how national identity varies by ethnic group, birthplace, religion and across local authority districts in England.

Policy context

In 2006 the Conservative Party leader, David Cameron, argued that "every child in our country, wherever they come from, must know and deeply understand what it means to be British" (British Political Speech, 2006). In this, he follows a long line of politicians (including John Major on the right and Gordon Brown on the left) who express concern about a perceived lack of affiliation to a notion of 'Britishness'. However, politicians struggle to define what it means to be British. Cameron himself could only offer: "the components of our identity – our institutions, our language and our history". Concerns about national identity have taken on particular force in the context of widespread critiques of state multiculturalism (Thomas, 2011). In part, these critiques are shaped by responses to civil disturbances in Oldham and Bradford in 2001 and in the declared War on Terror after the 9/11 bombings in New York and the 7/7 bombings in London. There have been debates as to how strong the multicultural policies are that have actually been introduced, particularly within the public sphere of law, government, employment, education and the market, as opposed to a rhetoric of multiculturalism (Grillo, 2007). However, critics of multiculturalism policy argue that multiculturalist rhetoric encourages a focus on difference and fosters segregation, and that it hampers confident assertions of national identity (Asari et al, 2008).

The Labour government (1997–2010) proposed various solutions to this 'crisis'. It introduced a raft of anti-terrorism measures laid squarely at young Muslims who are often perceived by politicians as being actively hostile to Britishness (Thomas, 2011). In addition, the government focused on concepts of citizenship with the introduction of citizenship studies in schools (2002) and reformed processes of naturalisation – including the introduction of citizenship ceremonies (2004) and the requirement to pass a citizenship test (initially, in 2005, this was required before naturalisation, and must now be passed before being granted permanent leave to remain in Britain). The coalition government (2010–15), led by the Conservative leader David Cameron, has continued to express concern about the dangers of multiculturalism and the need for a clear sense of shared national identity that is open to everyone. They have recommended to local authorities in England that they 'stop translating official documents into foreign languages' and 'do not give community grants to organisations that promote division in society' (DCLG, 2012a). The government continues to support the idea that there should be a strong attachment to 'British values', which include references to democracy, the rule of law and respect for others, but remain relatively vague on how this can be achieved.

Theoretical debates

The idea that nations are 'narrated' and made up of 'imagined communities' has long been a staple of academic argument (Anderson, 1991). At its heart, this is the suggestion that nationhood is the result of multiple acts of creation and 'inventions of tradition' rather than a question of objective or inevitable fact (Hobsbawm and Ranger, 1983). These narrations, using different communication technologies (print media, television, and so on) construct the idea of a national community – an 'us' that shares something profound in common which goes beyond the legal and administrative considerations of the state.

There are two models of national identity in the academic literature: ethnic and civic. The ethnic conception of national identity places emphasis on ancestry and is often considered to be fixed at birth. The civic model of national identity refers to a voluntary association of people who come together to share legal and political rights and duties, including speaking a national language. However, in practice, as the vast majority of citizens obtain citizenship by birth, the distinction between the two can become blurred. Civic models of national identity can also be overlain with exclusionary, and often racialised, ideas of who can belong.

Measuring national identity

National identity is made more complicated in the UK because of its multinational nature. For some, Englishness may be regarded as almost synonymous with Britishness. However, recent political developments, including Welsh and Scottish devolution, may have an impact on feelings of national identity in England.

Questions on national identity have become increasingly common in UK surveys since the turn of the last century. The government's 2010 Citizenship Survey revealed that the vast majority of the population in England and Wales feel a strong sense of belonging to Britain, with only minor variation across ethnic and religious groups (DCLG, 2012b). The question asked, 'What do you consider your national identity to be?' with respondents able to select multiple identities from 'English, Scottish, Welsh, Irish, British or Other'. Welsh replaced English as the first category in Wales. It is common to group together those who choose at least one from English, Scottish, Welsh and British and label this group as 'British', and categorise Irish and Other as 'Foreign'. The UK Labour Force Survey (LFS) asks the same question. Despite the multiple national identity options available in the LFS, very few people (less than 1 per cent in 2001-06) report dual identities. The British Social Attitudes (BSA) survey has asked a series of questions on national identity since the late 1990s that unpack the importance of multiple identities using the Moreno scale and what it means to be British (Curtice et al, 2013; Kiss and Park, 2014).

2011 Census question on national identity

A question on national identity was asked for the first time in the England and Wales census in 2011. The question was added in response to demand from census data users, especially regional and local government. During the planning for the 2011 Census, it was considered that a question on national identity would improve the acceptability of the ethnic group question by providing those who felt their identity of English, Welsh or Scottish was not recognised on the census form. The Office for National Statistics (ONS) piloted the LFS national identity question, and settled on a version which asked, 'How would you describe your national identity? Tick all that apply from English, Welsh, Scottish, Northern Irish, British and Other.' Those who ticked 'Other' were asked to write in their national identity. The national identity question precedes those on ethnic group, language, religion and passports held.

The option of reporting more than one national identity makes it difficult to aggregate responses to neat and meaningful categories. One could simply take together all those who say they are English, Welsh, Scottish, Northern Irish or British, including those who also report another identity as well, naming them all 'British'. However, this would not make full use of the data or allow one to determine the expected difference in English and British national identity between ethnic groups. Therefore, we have created four exclusive categories based on census output for people living in England:

- English only
- British only
- Other UK or UK combination: Welsh, Scottish, Northern Irish or a combination of more than one identity involving at least one UK country (for example, Scottish and British, English and British, Somali and British, and Irish and English)
- Foreign only, including Irish.

We have restricted the analysis to England because including Wales, Scotland and Northern Ireland would be better presented in separate analyses.

The aggregate 2011 Census tables on national identity provide a comparison, separately, between people of different ages and sex, ethnic group, religion and country of birth. More detailed comparisons by three or more census characteristics will be possible with the release of individual data from the 2011 Census in the form of the Sample of Anonymised Records (SARs). The published aggregate data are available at local authority district level, and therefore provide a unique spatial comparison not possible with existing sample surveys.

Ethnicity and national identity

Figure 5.1 shows the proportion of the population in each exclusive national identity category for each ethnic group, where each row totals 100 per cent. The ranking by ethnic group in the proportion of people who describe their national identity as some form of British or UK identity (that is, English only, British only, or Other UK or UK combination) is similar to that found by Manning and Roy (2010) using the LFS. In 2011, the White British ethnic group had the highest proportion, 100 per cent, followed by Mixed White & Black Caribbean, at 97 per cent. All minority ethnic groups had more than 50 per cent who described themselves as British in some form, except for the White Irish and Other White groups.

The minority ethnic groups with a longer history in Britain, for example, Black Caribbean, 88 per cent, Pakistani, 84 per cent, and Bangladeshi, 84 per cent, had a higher proportion who described themselves as British in some form compared with the ethnic groups whose population is largely made up of recent immigrants, for example, Other White, 22 per cent, Chinese, 52 per cent, Arab, 57 per cent, and Black African, 59 per cent. This suggests that assimilation to British national identity takes time and is more likely the longer a group has lived in the UK. This is supported by analyses of survey data that find people born in the UK and immigrants who have lived here for longer are more likely to consider themselves as British than those recent arrivals (Manning and Roy, 2010).

English versus British national identity

There is clear divergence between minority ethnic groups and the White British population in terms of whether they describe themselves as exclusively British or exclusively English. More than 70 per cent of the White British group describe themselves as English only, and 14 per cent describe themselves as British only. The majority of people in most other groups describe themselves as British only: Bangladeshi, 72 per cent, Pakistani, 63 per cent, Indian, 58 per cent, and Black Caribbean, 55 per cent. For all non–White ethnic groups, a higher proportion of people describe themselves as British only than English only, with the exception of the Mixed groups who were more likely to describe themselves as exclusively English rather than exclusively British. This may reflect the suggestion that Englishness is perceived by minority ethnic groups to be a 'white' identity. People with a mixed parentage, which consists of some form of white ethnic identity, might feel that they have claim to English national identity. Nonetheless, there is evidence to suggest that some people in those ethnic groups that have a longer history in Britain describe themselves as English. A quarter of the Black Caribbean ethnic group and a sixth of the Pakistani ethnic group describe themselves as exclusively English.

Geographical variation in 'Britishness' and 'Englishness'

Figure 5.2 shows that there is a geographical variation in the proportion of the White British population that describe themselves as (a) British only and (b) English only. Figure 5.2a shows that the White British population living in Central London are more likely to describe themselves as exclusively British compared with those living outside the capital. This may reflect an effect of living in the most diverse places in England, where the minority ethnic groups are most numerous and describe themselves as British. There might also be an effect of London, which, regardless of ethnicity, perhaps as the national capital, makes people more likely to feel British.

Figure 5.2b shows that fewer people describe themselves as English only in Central London. The areas where the White British ethnic group are most

Figure 5.1: National identity by ethnic group, 2011

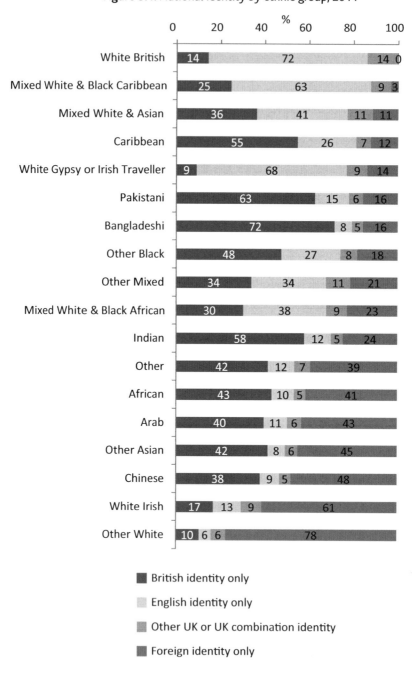

Note: Percentage of population in England; ethnic groups ordered by increasing foreign-only national identity.

likely to describe themselves as exclusively English are Sandwell and Walsall in the West Midlands, Barking and Dagenham and Havering in East London, and Castle Point and Thurrock in Essex. These areas tend to border ethnically diverse districts, and were targeted by radically right-wing political groups during the 2000s (Wilks-Heeg, 2008).

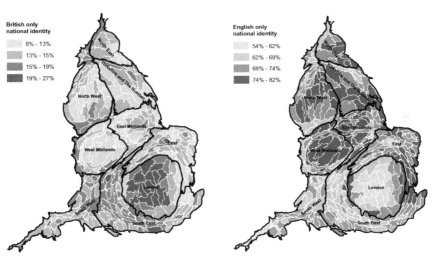

Figure 5.2a: Geographical distribution of British only national identity for White British ethnic group, 2011

Figure 5.2b: Geographical distribution of English only national identity for White British ethnic group, 2011

Figure 5.3 shows a very similar geographical pattern in British and English national identity of the Mixed ethnic groups. Figure 5.3a shows that the Mixed ethnic groups who describe themselves as British only are concentrated in outer London. Figure 5.3b shows an inverse geographical pattern where people in the Mixed ethnic groups are least likely to describe themselves as exclusively English in the capital and most likely to describe themselves as exclusively English in the Midlands and Northern England. The distribution of those who choose to describe themselves as either solely English or British suggests that place may have an effect on national identity assimilation in England.

Birthplace and national identity

Figure 5.4 shows the proportion of people in each exclusive national identity group by birthplace. A negligible number of those born in Britain do not consider themselves as being either British or English, which supports evidence from surveys (Manning and Roy, 2010). Those who were born in world regions where there is a history of British colonialism, for example, Africa and Asia, 60 per cent and 56 per cent respectively, describe themselves as having some form of UK national identity. In contrast, only 30 per cent of those born in European Union

Figure 5.3a: Geographical distribution of British only national identity for Mixed ethnic groups, 2011   **Figure 5.3b:** Geographical distribution of English only national identity for Mixed ethnic groups, 2011

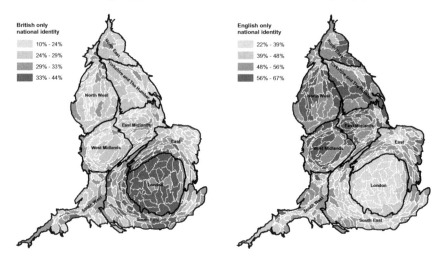

(EU) states describe themselves as having a UK national identity. EU citizens have unlimited rights to reside in the UK (and therefore have less incentive to naturalise). Migrants from EU Accession states, who have only begun to move to the UK in large numbers in last decade, are even less likely to describe themselves as British, English or some other UK combination, 14 per cent.

Religion and national identity

It has been suggested that Muslims, in particular, might find it difficult to identify with a British national identity because it conflicts with, or is secondary to, their religious identity. The existing empirical evidence from nationally representative surveys does not support this assumption, and rather, shows that religion is not an important determinant as to whether an individual considers themselves as British (Manning and Roy, 2010; Georgiadis and Manning, 2013).

The 2011 Census provides additional support to these findings. Figure 5.5 shows that more than half of Muslims describe themselves as British only. This sole affiliation to Britishness is higher than any other religious group, except Sikhs. Moreover, a quarter of Muslims (24 per cent) describe their national identity as foreign only, which is remarkable when considering that more than half of the Muslim population in England (53 per cent) were born abroad. Buddhists, 42 per cent, have the greatest proportion along with Hindus, 32 per cent, who describe their national identity as foreign. The minority religious group with the greatest proportion who describe themselves as British of some form, and more likely to describe themselves as exclusively English than British, is Jewish, which may reflect the time spent in the UK by the Jewish population, and the fact that most were born in the UK, 80 per cent.

Geographical variation in Muslim national identity

Figure 5.6 shows the geographical pattern of the Muslim population who describe themselves as (a) British only and (b) foreign only. The proportion of the Muslim population who describe themselves as exclusively British tends to be greater in areas where Muslims are most concentrated, for example, East London, Birmingham, East Lancashire and West Yorkshire. The proportion that describes themselves as foreign only is lowest in those areas with higher concentrations of Muslims. This is counterintuitive to the idea that Muslim areas are places where people live separate lives and choose not to assimilate to a British national identity. On the contrary, it appears that this is more likely in areas where Muslims are few and far between. This may suggest that areas with higher concentrations of religious minorities foster a more inclusive sense of Britishness.

Figure 5.4: National identity by birthplace, 2011

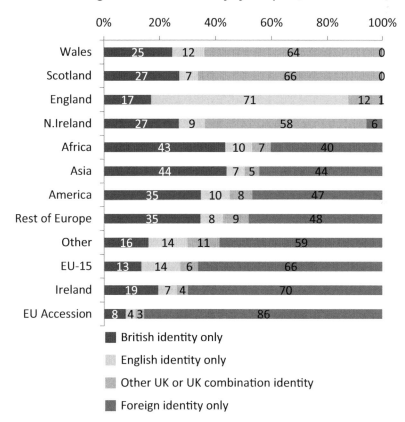

Note: Percentage of population in England; regions of birth ordered by increasing foreign-only national identity.

Figure 5.5: National identity by religion, 2011

	0%	20%	40%	60%	80%	100%

No religion: 17 | 65 | 13 | 5
Christian: 15 | 65 | 13 | 7
Religion not stated: 20 | 59 | 13 | 8
Jewish: 24 | 54 | 13 | 9
Other religion: 30 | 48 | 12 | 9
Sikh: 62 | 15 | 5 | 17
Muslim: 57 | 13 | 6 | 24
Hindu: 54 | 9 | 5 | 32
Buddhist: 27 | 23 | 8 | 42

■ British identity only

English identity only

Other UK or UK combination identity

■ Foreign identity only

Note: Percentage of population in England; religious groups ordered by increasing foreign-only national identity.

Figure 5.6a: Geographical distribution of British only national identity for Muslims, 2011

Figure 5.6b: Geographical distribution of foreign only national identity for Muslims, 2011

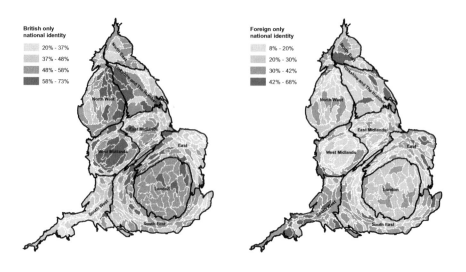

British only national identity
20% - 37%
37% - 48%
48% - 58%
58% - 73%

Foreign only national identity
8% - 20%
20% - 30%
30% - 42%
42% - 68%

Conclusions and implications

There has been an increased research and policy interest in national identity since the early 2000s. Considerable emphasis has been placed on the idea that the growing minority ethnic population has difficultly identifying with Britain, and that this has been compounded by multiculturalist policies that have fostered isolation. The empirical evidence from nationally representative surveys, however, does not support this suggestion. Rather, it suggests that affiliations are made to a British national identity, which takes time, but is not influenced by a particular ethnic or religious background.

This finding is supported by data on national identity collected for the first time in the 2011 Census. Ethnic groups with a long history in the UK, which are more likely to include people born in the UK, are more likely to identify with some form of British national identity. This is particularly the case for Mixed groups. Moreover, more than four-fifths of people in Black Caribbean, Pakistani and Bangladeshi groups describe themselves as British in one way or another.

The same is true for people affiliated to minority religions, including Islam, who, in the main, describe themselves as British, and exclusively British in most cases. Moreover, those Muslims living in areas with greater concentrations of fellow Muslims are also more likely to describe themselves as British. An implication for policymakers is to recognise that people born in the UK and those who have lived here for some time have already come to feel British without any strong intervention by the state.

The nationally representative surveys that ask about national identity can provide a richness in what is associated with national identity in a way that is not possible with the census. For example, Georgiadis and Manning (2012), using the Citizenship Survey, show that those minority ethnic groups who have not experienced discrimination from public organisations and feel they are treated with respect by others are more likely to consider themselves as British. This suggests that policies to strengthen national identity might be better focused on addressing socioeconomic inequalities faced by minority groups, for example, equal opportunities and anti-discrimination policies, which are often labelled as being part of the multicultural strategy.

Moreover, if policymakers are concerned about the growing immigrant and minority ethnic population not feeling British, they should target their efforts at those born in EU states, including Ireland. Another challenge for policymakers is to tackle the beliefs of a small but significant section of the population who believe it is not possible for non-White people to feel British. For example, Kiss and Park (2014) used the British Social Attitudes (BSA) survey to show that 50 per cent of people in England feel that ancestry and birthplace were both important to be truly British.

Surveys such as the BSA also show that there was a one-off rise from Scottish and Welsh devolution in the proportion of people who report an English exclusively identity, but that this was mainly of people who already prioritise their Englishness (Curtice et al, 2013). The census shows that most White British people report an English national identity, whereas minority ethnic groups are more likely to prioritise a British national identity than any other. Mixed groups are an exception in that they are more likely to describe themselves as exclusively English rather than exclusively British. This provides some support for the notion that Englishness is a white identity, but not that it is exclusively ethnic in its character because there are people in non-White, non-Mixed minority ethnic groups who feel exclusively English. This suggests both an acculturation to Englishness as well as Britishness in England, but that the former is slower for most minority ethnic groups.

There were suggestions in the testing of the national identity question for the 2011 Census that some people may have not understood that they could tick all that apply, and therefore the census may under-represent the proportion of the White British population who feel British as well as English (ONS, 2009). The priority given to British national identity by minority ethnic groups, however, suggests that they have sought out what was the fifth option on the census form, and this may reflect their interpretation of what is meant by national identity. Minority ethnic groups might prioritise citizenship over ethno-cultural references when describing their national identity, whereas White British people might be referring to cultural aspects of their identity, including sport (Manning and Roy, 2010). Whether the root of the divergence is interpretation or genuinely different feelings about national identity, it is important to recognise the importance of English identity to the majority population.

A unique feature of the census is that data on national identity can be disaggregated at small area geographies. This will not be possible again until the next census in 2021 because administration data do not contain subjective assessment such as national identity, and national surveys are rarely able to provide small area estimates. In this chapter we have been able to show that exclusive British national identity is stronger in London compared with other regions in England among the White British ethnic group. The same pattern is true for the Mixed ethnic groups. This suggests that there might be a London effect that makes people more likely to describe themselves as British. It could be the case that high levels of diversity in London mean that those who live there are more accepting of an inclusive British identity than many of the people around them, including greater numbers of minority ethnic groups than anywhere else in England, are claiming. There may also be an effect of London that is not related to ethnicity but the cultural references to Britain that are displayed more prominently in the capital compared with in other parts of the country.

As national identity is imagined and recreated through narrative, qualitative research that explores in-depth narrations of national identity are perhaps best placed for understanding how Englishness and Britishness are created. The question of national identity can be researched in a more open, conversational way, exploring associations, hesitations and contradictions in response to ideas of national identification, rather than requiring 'in-out' responses. Qualitative research can also reveal how understandings of national identity are classed, gendered and shaped by place as well as race (Byrne, 2007).

Note

Further information about data and sources are available from
http://www.ethnicity.ac.uk/dynamicsofdiversity/

References

Anderson, B. (1991) *Imagined communities: Reflections on the origin and spread of nationalism* (Revised edition), London: Verso.

Asari, E.-M., Halikiopoulou, D. and Mock, S. (2008) 'British national identity and the dilemmas of multiculturalism', *Nationalism and Ethnic Politics*, vol 14, no 1, pp 1-28.

British Political Speech (2006) 'Leader's speech, Bournemouth 2006b', David Cameron (Conservative) (www.britishpoliticalspeech.org/speech-archive.htm?speech=151).

Byrne, B. (2007) 'England – whose England? Narratives of nostalgia, emptiness and evasion in imaginations of national identity', *The Sociological Review*, vol 55, no 3, pp 509-30.

Curtice, J., Devine, P. and Ormston, R. (2013) 'Devolution: Identities and constitutional preferences across the UK', in A. Park, C. Bryson, E. Clery, J. Curtie and M. Phillips (eds) *British Social Attitudes: The 30th report*, London: NatCen Social Research, pp 139-72.

DCLG (Department for Communities and Local Government) (2012a) *50 ways to save: Examples of sensible savings in local government*, London: DCLG (www.gov.uk/government/uploads/system/uploads/attachment_data/file/39264/50_ways_2.pdf).

DCLG (2012b) *Creating the conditions for integration*, London: DCLG.

Georgiadis, A. and Manning, A. (2013) 'One nation under a groove? Understanding national identity', *Journal of Economic Behavior & Organization*, vol 93, pp 166-85.

Grillo, R. (2007) 'An excess of alterity? Debating difference in a multicultural society', *Ethnic and Racial Studies*, vol 30, no 6, pp 979-98.

Hobsbawm, E. and Ranger, T. (1983) *The invention of tradition*, Cambridge: Canto.

Kiss, Z. and Park, A. (2014) 'National identity: Exploring Britishness', in A. Park, C. Bryson and J. Curtice (eds) *British Social Attitudes: The 31st report*, London: NatCen Social Research, pp 61-77.

Manning, A. and Roy, S. (2010) 'Culture clash or culture club? National identity in Britain', *The Economic Journal*, vol 120, no 2, F72-F100.

ONS (Office for National Statistics) (2009) *Final recommended questions for the 2011 Census in England and Wales National identity*, Newport: ONS.

Thomas, P. (2011) 'All white? Englishness, "race" and ethnic identities', in A. Aughey and C. Berberich (eds) *These Englands: A conversation on national identity*, Manchester: Manchester University Press, pp 75–93.

Wilks-Heeg, S. (2008) 'The canary in a coalmine? Explaining the emergence of the British National Party in English local politics', *Parliamentary Affairs*, vol 62, no 3, pp 377–98.

SIX

Do people change their ethnicity over time?

Ludi Simpson, James Warren and Stephen Jivraj

Key findings

- Ethnic group is not a fixed characteristic during a person's life.
- Four per cent of all people chose a different ethnic group in 2011 than in 2001. This is twice the level of instability found for the decade 1991 to 2001.
- Among the main ethnic group categories, 1 per cent of White British in 2001 changed their ethnic group when asked again in 2011. Four per cent of Bangladeshi and 26 per cent of White Irish groups changed their ethnic group.
- A larger proportion of those in Mixed and 'Other' ethnic groups changed their recorded category (for example, 43 per cent of 'Mixed White & Black African' in 2001 identified with another census category a decade later).
- This should concern official statistical agencies responsible for setting ethnic group response categories in censuses and surveys, because 'Mixed' and 'Other' categories are the fastest growing groups as a result of natural change and international migration.
- A change of ethnic group category in the census is often due to a person's background fitting more than one category; it need not involve a conscious change of ethnic identity.
- The main categories of ethnic group can be compared from one census to another, but the residual 'Other' categories cannot. A recommended comparison of most stable groups identifies seven groups for comparison from 1991 to 2011, and 12 groups for comparison from 2001 to 2011.
- When a category names a region or a country, someone born there is more likely than others to stay with that category.

Introduction

Statistics of ethnicity are often treated rather like birthplace, sex or date of birth, as if there is little doubt about either the categories that have been used or their acceptance by respondents to the question. But while the measurement of ethnicity has become a norm in Britain and many other countries, the categories used are not at all fixed. And its reliability is limited: four in every 100 people asked their ethnic group in 2001 changed their answer when asked again in 2011. This chapter explores that reliability, asking why recorded ethnicity may change over time, and who is most likely to change their ethnic group.

Those who collect and review statistics of ethnicity are in no doubt about their fallibility. The Office for National Statistics (ONS) begins its guidance on ethnic group statistics by warning that:

> Collecting data on ethnic group is complex because of the subjective, multifaceted and changing nature of ethnic identification. There is no consensus on what constitutes an ethnic group and membership is something that is self-defined and subjectively meaningful to the person concerned. The terminology used to describe ethnic groups has changed markedly over time and however defined or measured, tends to evolve in the context of social and political attitudes or developments. (ONS, 2014)

The difficulty in pinning down ethnicity is not simply a matter of varied definitions between countries, but also that individuals in the same country can and do change their ethnicity. Responses to questions about ethnicity change over time as questions respond to new policy priorities, for example, towards existing minorities or to new origins of immigration; responses also change between cohorts as legislation or political movements have an impact in specific epochs, as, for example, when young adults in the Caribbean and in Australia have adopted Black and indigenous identities respectively; and responses change over a person's lifetime, particularly as an individual is able to adopt and record their own identity during childhood or early adulthood. Thus the major demographic dimensions of period, cohort and age all affect how an individual assesses their own ethnicity for official enquiries.

Comparison of responses to the 1991 and 2001 Censuses suggests that changes to the question, errors in recording and unreliability of responses when an individual finds more than one appropriate category, are all more important than conscious choices to move from one identity to another (Simpson and Akinwale, 2007). 'Why would a person's ethnic group change?' lists reasons for changing ethnicity between 2001 and 2011.

Knowing about instability in ethnic identity as it is measured in official enquiries helps in understanding the fluidity of the concept for individuals, and that official statistics of inequalities and demographic change are bound to be approximations.

The chapter suggests the level of approximation to expect, and in particular that some of the 'write-in' categories are very unstable in their composition. In some applications the change in identification that we know occurred during the decade 2001-11 can make analyses more accurate, as in the assessment of population change in Chapter Three.

In this chapter we discuss the stability of ethnic group identity from one census to the next. Acknowledging that movement between categories is in both directions, we identify the net transfers from a group. We then consider which categories are most stable over time and therefore can be reliably compared, and which should not be compared over time because their composition changes so much. We end by noting more instability in responses from those born in the UK, and a complex relationship with age and social characteristics.

Why would a person's ethnic group change?

More than one response is suitable for the same person. We cannot quantify this exactly, but it is likely to be the biggest reason for instability. For example, a person with Turkish family origins and British nationality might choose between 'White British', 'Other White' and 'Other' without changing their sense of identity. Someone with parents born in Ireland and Nigeria might also choose different ethnic categories on different occasions.

The census question has changed since it was introduced in 1991. Four Mixed categories were added in 2001, and the White category divided. The 2011 Census saw fewer changes; it added categories for 'Arab' and 'White Gypsy or Irish Traveller', and it moved 'Chinese' into the broad 'Asian' category, meaning, for example, that those of Far Eastern origins other than Chinese are likely to have moved from 'Other' (in 2001) to 'Other Asian' (in 2011). The new categories in 2011 account for 5 per cent of those who moved to a different category from their 2001 record.

When the question has not been answered, an answer is estimated by the census offices (it is 'imputed'). Records with estimated values in either 2001 or 2011 account for 20 per cent of those who moved to a different category from their 2001 record.

A different person may have filled in the form at each census. This is particularly likely when a child in 2001 had become an adult by 2011. We cannot quantify this effect, but it is likely to be small because we have found that stability in identification is not strongly related to age, except for White Irish.

A conscious change in identity. As we go through life, both our perception of official enquiries such as the census and our sense of ethnic identity may change, and for this reason we may decide to declare ourselves differently in the census.

Errors in the census collection. A person may unintentionally tick a box, or the process that scans answers from a form onto a computer may create an error. These are unlikely to be major reasons for instability in ethnic group, but will add a little 'noise' to the data.

Changes in the allocation of write-in responses. The census offices reviewed and changed some of the allocation of write-in answers. The major example is 'Kashmiri' which, in 2011, was added to the residual 'Other' categories, rather than to 'Pakistani' as in 2001.

About half the level of instability between two censuses a decade apart also occurred between the same question asked twice only six weeks apart in the Census Validation Survey (Simpson and Akinwale, 2007). This confirms that instability is to be expected due to the unreliability of responses rather than conscious changes in identity.

Stability of the ethnic group

The proportion of people staying in the same ethnic group from one census to the next is shown in Figure 6.1. Almost all of those who in 2001 ticked 'White British', 98.8 per cent, also ticked 'White English/Welsh/Northern Irish/Scottish/British' in 2011. The label had slightly changed between the censuses, but was adopted by almost all the same people. In 1991 there was only one 'White' option, and 99.2 per cent also ticked one of the 'White' options in 2001.

For the minority groups Bangladeshi, Pakistani, Chinese, Indian, Black African and Black Caribbean, the proportion staying in the same category was between 80 and 96 per cent. Significant proportions of people choosing a group in 2001 chose a different group in 2011. The proportions staying in or moving from a group changed a little from what was the case for 1991-2001, but not by much. Some people moved in opposite directions, which we examine later.

The Mixed categories were asked only from 2001, and so their stability in the census can only be measured for the period 2001-11. It is lower than the 'non-Mixed' groups, with over 40 per cent of those choosing 'Mixed White & Asian' or 'Mixed White & Black African' in 2001 moving to a different category in 2011.

The stability of the five residual 'Other' groups – the option under each broad heading to write in an answer – was generally low. Fifty-nine per cent of those ticking 'Other White' in 2001 stayed with that category in 2011, just under 50 per cent of 'Other Asian' stayed there, only 30 per cent of 'Other Mixed' and 'Other Black' stayed in those categories, and only 12 per cent stayed with the final category 'Other'. These low levels of stability were sometimes higher than those for the period 1991-2001.

This does not mean that a lot of people responded randomly or without thought to the question. It means that their family background does not fit easily into a single category, and so was entered differently at each census. For example, a Latin American person who had been in Britain for many years might enter themselves as 'White British' or 'Other White' or 'Other'. The child of parents with Chinese and Caribbean heritage might choose different categories on different occasions. This is a reason for research to consider national identity, country of birth, religion and language together with ethnic group.

The low stability of the residual categories apart from 'Other White' means that they not only include a diverse set of origins, but also that a comparison of the group from one census to another is comparing different sets of people, and should be made with great caution.

Although the White British group's stability is highest of all ethnic groups, it is so much bigger in population size that the number moving from it is more than from any other group.

Among all those who were enumerated in both censuses, 4 per cent changed their recorded ethnic group between 2001 and 2011. This is exactly double the instability between 1991 and 2001 (2 per cent), in spite of the greater changes to the question during the earlier period.

Figure 6.1: Stability of ethnic groups, 1991-2001 and 2001-11

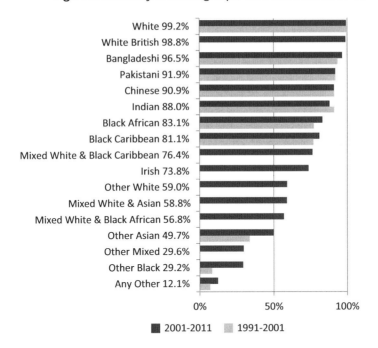

The percentage staying in the same ethnic group from one census to the next

Notes: After each group's name is the stability in 2001-11. The stability of the seven categories introduced in 2001 can be shown only for the period 2001-11. The groups are sorted in descending order of stability, 2001-11.

Source: ONS Longitudinal Study of England and Wales

Studying how an individual changes over time

The ONS Longitudinal Study (LS) links together census and other demographic data for about 1 per cent of the population in England and Wales. It does not retain name or address, and no identifiable information about individuals may be released. It offers a valuable perspective of how individuals change their circumstances that adds to the snapshot of the population that each census provides.

This chapter studies change over the decades 1991-2001 and 2001-11. It includes those who were enumerated in two censuses. About three-quarters of the 2011 resident population were enumerated in both the 2001 and 2011 Censuses and linked in the ONS LS. This proportion is 80 per cent for White British, and drops to about one-third for the Arab, Black African and Other White groups that had relatively large proportions of births and immigration during the decade.

For those who were enumerated in two censuses, for example, 2001 and 2011, our key measurement for each group is the number who were recorded with that group in both censuses, which is always less than the number recorded at the beginning and the end of the decade. Our main measurements for this chapter are:

- Proportion staying in a category (*stability*): Number staying in the group/Number in 2001.

- Proportion moving out of a category: (Number in 2001 – Number staying in the group)/ Number in 2001.

- Proportion moving into a category: (Number in 2011 – Number staying in the group)/ Number in 2001.

- Net proportion transferring: (Number in 2011 – number in 2001)/Number in 2001.

To define those who stay within a group, as elsewhere in this book, 'White: British' of 2001 has been considered the same category as 'White: English/Welsh/Scottish/Northern Irish/ British' of 2011.

For analyses with country of birth and with age, individuals whose ethnic group had been missing and therefore imputed during census processing have been omitted, while these have been included in the analyses of overall stability and net transfers between categories.

There are usually more changes of ethnic group than described in this chapter, when records for the same individual are compared from different data sources, because the method of asking a question also affects the responses (see, for example, Saunders et al, 2013). Lieberson and Waters (1993) investigate inconsistencies in the race and ancestry questions in the US.

The larger instability is due to the changed composition of the population, which now has more residents with ethnic identities that are not easily included within the existing census categories. It may also be that as people have grown used to the idea of defining their own ethnic group, more are choosing to define themselves differently. We can explore this by looking at the direction of change between groups.

Net transfers from other ethnic groups

While some people move away from each group, others move to it. Figure 6.2 shows the extent of moves to and from each group between 2001 and 2011, and the net impact on the size of the group.

For some groups, even the very unstable ones like 'Other', the moves to and from the group balance out, and the net transfer is very small.

For some groups like the 'White Irish' and 'Other White', the net transfer is negative – more people moved out than in – making a net loss of 8 and 17

Figure 6.2: Net transfer to each ethnic group from other categories, 2001-11

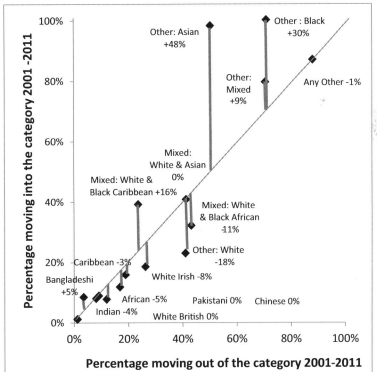

Note: The net transfer to a group between the censuses is the difference between those moving into it and those moving out of it.

Source: ONS LS of England and Wales

85

per cent respectively. The full matrix of moves shows that the net movement away from both these groups was mainly to 'White British', perhaps because that category was phrased more inclusively in 2011 as 'White English/Welsh/Scottish /Northern Irish /British' (Simpson et al, 2014).

Some groups gained substantially from net transfers from other groups, including Bangladeshi (+5 per cent), and 'Mixed White & Black Caribbean' (+16 per cent).

Three residual groups, 'Other Asian', 'Other Black' and 'Other Mixed', each gained substantially, which supports the suggestion that people were more willing in 2011 to write in what they felt to be their specific family origin when it was not named in the categories provided.

These net transfers, even when as large as causing an increase of 50 per cent in the 'Other Asian' group, should not be over-stated: they are still small relative to the change in population from births, deaths and migration. The 'Other Asian' population of England and Wales more than tripled in size between 2001 and 2011.

Amalgamated ethnic groups and broad categories

A little under half of the transfers between groups are within the broad headings of White, Asian, Black, Mixed and Other. However, the loss of meaning when using a broad category far outweighs the slight gain in stable responses. The three categories 'Black Caribbean', 'Mixed White & Black Caribbean' and 'Other Black' had significant exchanges between the two censuses, but similarly one could not amalgamate them without losing a great deal of value.

Comparable ethnic groups across censuses

Considering the instability of responses between censuses, it is recommended that when comparing 2001 and 2011 Census outputs, 12 comparisons may be made with reasonable confidence because of their relatively high stability: White British, White Irish, Other White, Mixed White & Black Caribbean, Mixed White & Black African, Mixed White & Asian, Indian, Pakistani, Bangladeshi, Chinese, Black Caribbean, and Black African.

Caution should be made when comparing 'Other Asian', 'Other Black' and 'Other Mixed' because of the high instability of these responses between the two censuses. They may be best amalgamated with the remaining categories as a single 'Other' category, or shown within each of the broad groups but only for completeness.

For comparisons between 1991, 2001 and 2011, it is recommended that seven categories be used: White, Black Caribbean, Black African, Indian, Pakistani, Bangladeshi, and Chinese. The remaining categories can be added into a single residual 'Other' category for completeness, but its composition has changed so much it that its characteristics should not be compared across time. For comparison between the three censuses, White cannot be easily divided because it was a single group in 1991.

Country of birth affects the stability of ethnicity

Within each broad group White, Asian, Mixed, Black, or Other, the labels used in the census for ethnic group are mostly national or regional indicators. Someone born in India is likely to relate quickly to the heading 'Indian', and someone born in Jamaica is likely to relate to 'Caribbean'. Those who were not born in the country or region associated with the ethnic group they chose in 2001 were more likely to move group when asked again in 2011 (see Figure 6.3).

For example, 13 per cent of those ticking 'White British' in 2001, but who were not born in the UK, moved to another category in 2011, compared to only 1 per cent of those who were born in the UK. The same is true for the other groups that have a label associated with a country or region – if you were born

Figure 6.3: Stability of ethnic group from 2001 to 2011, according to country of birth

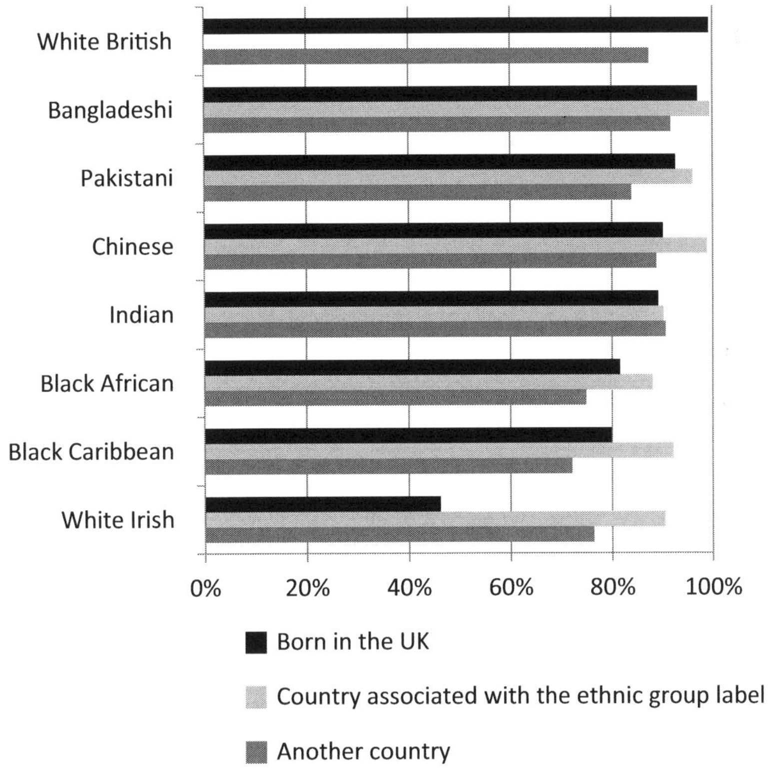

Percentage of ethnic group in 2001 who remained in the same group in 2011

Note: The sample size for each population shown is smallest for those born in 'Another country', which falls below 150 for the ethnic groups Black African (sample size 148), White Irish (74) and Bangladeshi (39).

Source: ONS LS of England and Wales

in that country you were more likely to stick with that label in both censuses than if you were born elsewhere.

More than half of the White Irish born in the UK chose a different category in 2011. The detailed matrix of moves (Simpson et al, 2014) shows that one-quarter of all the White Irish of 2001 moved to the 'White: English/Welsh/Scottish/ Northern Irish/British' of 2011. This may partly reflect assimilation and partly be a result of the inclusion of 'Northern Irish' in the label in 2011.

Since the proportion of minorities born in the UK is likely to increase, the lower stability of ethnicity for UK-born is important for our understanding of ethnicity. As one might expect, many second and later generations have a less clear 'affiliation' with the country of their ancestors than those who were born there. This is another reason why one might expect the concept of individuals' ethnicity to lose some of its value in social policy over time, and why markers of differences in preferences (for example, religion) might serve policymakers more effectively.

Does growing older create greater attachment to ethnicity?

Figure 6.4 shows differences in the proportion of young and elderly people staying with the ethnic group that they had been recorded with in 2001. The patterns are not the same for each ethnic group. For those aged 50 or older in 2001, who were 60 and over if they survived and were recorded in the 2011 Census, there is relatively high attachment to ethnic group for the White Irish and Black Caribbean compared to younger people in the same group. This may be a result of the higher stability for those born in Ireland and the Caribbean, as seen earlier. The pattern is reversed, with lower attachment among older people, for the Mixed groups, the Black African group, and the 'Other Black' group, although with smaller sample sizes for each of these. There are smaller differences between age groups for other ethnic groups.

One practical question arises for forecasters of Britain's future diversity: will these patterns of movement to and from different ethnic groups be repeated in the coming decades? The level of instability from one census to the next should sound a warning against putting too much faith in projections by ethnic group.

Figure 6.5 shows the net transfer at each age for four ethnic groups. The net transfer deducts moves out of each group from moves into it, and indicates the overall impact on population change that a projection is concerned with. The figure confirms that patterns of change are neither similar across ethnic groups, nor easily explained.

It shows, for example, that although the White Irish group lost 8 per cent through identity switching during the decade (Figure 6.2), and a loss was apparent for most age groups, those White Irish aged under 10 in 2001 were added to by nearly a fifth, by others of the same age who were counted as White Irish in 2011 but not before. These are net figures that hide a considerable movement in both directions (Figure 6.2), and so are the results of a variety of factors that

Figure 6.4: Stability of ethnic group by age group from 2001 to 2011

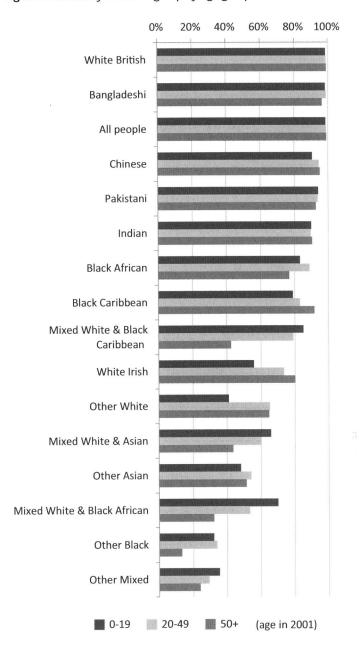

Note: Percentage staying in the same ethnic group from 2001 to 2011

Source: ONS LS of England and Wales. Categories sorted in descending order of stability for age 20-49

act differently for each age group. Perhaps there was an increasing awareness of Irishness that promoted the adoption of Irish identity among teenagers and their parent form-fillers, as shown in Figure 6.5 for those who were under 10 in 2001 but aged 10-19 in 2011. At the same time, the transfer of those White Irish who had been born in other parts of the UK to the White (English/Welsh/Scottish/Northern Irish/British) would work in the opposite direction, and was perhaps more relevant for older adults.

Figure 6.5: Net transfer of identity, selected ethnic groups, 2001-11, by age at 2001

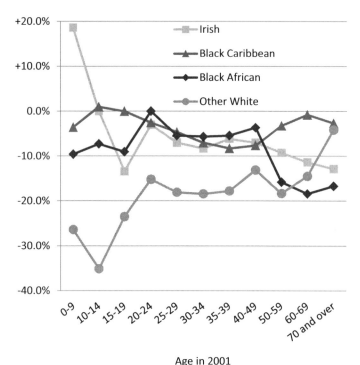

Age in 2001

Source: ONS LS of England and Wales

Conclusions and implications

Since the introduction of an ethnic group question in the 1991 Census, there have not been societal shifts in ethnic identification in Britain. While ethnic diversity and the lack of it play strongly in political rhetoric and general policy statements, the measurement of ethnicity has been used neither directly in legislation nor to define political identities in the UK. Thus there have not been the major shifts that have occurred in censuses in other parts of the world, for example, towards indigenous or Black identities.

Nonethless, there is significant instability in ethnic identity. Four in every 100 people recorded with an ethnic group in 2001 moved to a different category in 2011. Some of the categories made from write-in responses are very unstable in their composition, such that more than half of the people who were in such a category in 2001 moved to a different category in 2011. Minority categories were less stable than the White British category, even though that category had changed its label in 2011.

The instability that we have described in this chapter is mainly caused by measurement errors, by changes in the questions asked, and by the richness of many people's ethnic identity that allows different responses when they, or whoever fills a census form on their behalf, are asked their ethnicity on more than one occasion.

We have found that when an ethnic identity names a country or region, those who were born there are more likely than others to stay with that identity, as one might expect. However, stability is not strongly related to age in ways that can be easily explained. Other analyses show that stability is not strongly or clearly associated with social characteristics of individuals, which is, again, what one might expect if instability is mainly caused by changes to the question categories and the suitability of more than one category for many people.

This chapter's conclusions would be welcome to democrats who would hope that one's family background is not something that is fixed and defended when answering official enquiries such as the census.

There are, nonetheless, practical implications of the instability observed in individuals' ethnicity. Continued instability can be expected as changes in society and social policy lead to further change in the categories offered for our response. The instability is not sufficient to make statistics of ethnic diversity change worthless, but does clarify that all applications of statistics of ethnicity are approximate, whether they help to guide services, remedy inequalities, or understand demographic change. The residual categories of 'Other Mixed', 'Other Asian', 'Other Black' and 'Other' are so fluid that comparisons across time are of different sets of people.

This chapter has identified some ethnic group categories that can be most reliably compared over time. The quantified transfers between ethnic groups can be used to improve our understanding of population change, as in Chapter Three. An awareness of approximation in statistics of ethnicity, and its quantification, can be used to improve the recommendations that accompany social analysis.

Note

Further information about data and sources are available from
http://www.ethnicity.ac.uk/dynamicsofdiversity/

References

Lieberson, S. and Waters, M.C. (1993) 'Ethnic responses of White: what causes their instability, simplification and inconsistency?', *Social Forces*, vol 72, no 2, pp 421-50.

ONS (Office for National Statistics) (2014) *Guidance and methodology: Ethnic group* (www.ons.gov.uk/ons/guide-method/measuring-equality/equality/ethnic-nat-identity-religion/ethnic-group/index.html).

Saunders, C.L., Abel, G.A., El Turabi, A., Ahmed, F. and Lyratzopoulos, G. (2013) 'Accuracy of routinely recorded ethnic group information compared with self-reported ethnicity: evidence from the English Cancer Patient Experience survey', *BMJ Open*, vol 3, no 6.

Simpson, L. and Akinwale, B. (2007) 'Quantifying stability and change in ethnic group', *Journal of Official Statistics*, vol 23, no 2, pp 185-208.

Simpson, L., Jivraj, S. and Warren, J. (2014) *The stability of ethnic group and religion in the Censuses of England and Wales 2001-2011*, CCSR/CoDE Working Paper 2014, Manchester: University of Manchester.

SEVEN

In what ways is Scotland's ethnic diversity distinctive?

Andrew Smith and Ludi Simpson

Key findings

- Immigration and family-building have contributed to the rapid growth of Scotland's minority ethnic groups who, by 2011, numbered 850,000, or 16 per cent of Scotland's residents.
- The largest minority is 'White: Other British' numbering 417,000 in 2011, an increase of 10 per cent over the decade. About three-quarters of this group were born in England.
- Each minority group increased its population during the last decade.
- The African population grew rapidly, from 5,000 in 2001 to 30,000 in 2011. This growth was mainly from immigration, and was focused on areas beyond those where African people had mainly lived before.
- Other minority populations also dispersed across Scotland during the decade, growing faster outside of those areas in which they were most likely to be resident in 2001. The one exception is the Chinese population that has grown most in the student areas near universities where it was already concentrated.
- Change in the census question itself has added diversity, now identifying the Polish population, for example. At 61,000, they are the second largest minority in 2011.
- One in six of Scotland's households of two or more people have more than one ethnicity represented.
- Individuals with a 'Mixed or multiple' ethnic group number 20,000 people, or 0.4 per cent of the population.

- Over half of Scotland's residents in 2011 who were born outside the UK had arrived in 2004 or more recently. Immigration has increased more rapidly in Scotland in the past decade than in the rest of Britain.
- Scotland's diversity has increased both overall and in every local authority district. All of Edinburgh's population and two-thirds of Glasgow's population live in wards that are more diverse than Scotland as a whole. Both have become more diverse, and their diversity has spread more evenly through their cities, as it has through Scotland as a whole.

Introduction

It has been recognised for some time that there are distinctive aspects to ethnic diversity in Scotland. The reasons for this are, in no small part, historical: significant Irish immigration to Scotland in the 19th century, especially to the west of Scotland, created a large migrant labour force, as did the migration southwards of displaced Highlanders who were seen as being culturally, if not 'racially', distinct by lowland Scots. This, allied to the effects of deindustrialisation, limited the opportunities for incoming workers in the 20th century, and therefore discouraged immigration from Commonwealth countries on the scale experienced in England and Wales. Immigration to Scotland in this period thus had a particular character; there was relatively little labour migration from the Caribbean, for example, and the migrant population which arrived from Asia or via East Africa in this period tended to be somewhat better off and more entrepreneurial than that which settled in England, and was therefore less likely to be associated with labour competition (see, for example, Hopkins, 2008).

The presence of a significant Irish Catholic population, and the extent of sectarian discrimination against that population, suggests that there are good reasons to be wary of a public discourse which associates Scotland with tolerance, and which attributes that 'tolerance' to the supposed absence of minority groups (Wells and Williams, 2003). It is important to be clear, in this regard, that racism has been a long-standing experience for many of Scotland's minority ethnic communities, and that those communities continue to face significant forms of prejudice and exclusion (Haria, 2014), as well as socioeconomic disadvantage (Netto et al, 2011). Nevertheless, public discourse north of the border has tended not to invoke a 'racialised' version of 'Scottish' identity in the way that some forms of English nationalism have; indeed, post-war Scottish nationalism has often presented itself self-consciously as 'in opposition' to an Englishness portrayed as 'extreme, right-wing and authoritarian' (Kyriakides et al, 2009, p 295; see also Kiely et al, 2005). Since 1999, then, governments in Edinburgh have supported public campaigns intended to sustain a civic, rather than ethnic, conception of Scottish-ness (Williams and de Lima, 2006).

Wider demographic and economic issues are a factor in all of this: an ageing population means that the devolved Scottish government has set explicit targets for population growth in the decade between 2007-17, and has been relatively open about Scotland's economic reliance on current and future immigration (McCollum et al, 2014). Indeed, for more than a decade now the country has gained population through net immigration, both internally from the rest of the UK, but also internationally. In contrast to the situation in England, this has not led to political interest groups, at least at the national level, seeking to change the Scottish government's position in respect to migration, and there is some evidence that public attitudes to migration in Scotland may be somewhat different from those reported in the rest of the UK (McCollum et al, 2013). Racism against minority populations remains considerable, however, and is particularly prevalent against the Pakistani population (CRER, 2013). Anti-English sentiment, especially in rural areas, is the subject of periodic press interest, and some research has suggested that this has taken an increasingly 'racialised' form (McIntosh et al, 2004), although questions of class, nation and ethnicity are entangled in complicated ways in this context.

It is against this background, then, that this chapter seeks to describe some of the significant changes in ethnic diversity in Scotland over the last decade through a comparison of data from the 2001 and 2011 Censuses. The chapter does not explore questions of 'identity' as such, nor does it focus on the inequalities that might be associated with perceptions of ethnic difference. The concern here is to identify key patterns in changing ethnic diversity in Scotland in this period. We address, in particular: the scope, nature and development of that diversity over the period between the two censuses; the spreading of that diversity across the country; the profile of that diversity at the level of local areas; and finally, specific changes in the ethnic diversity of Scotland's largest and most cosmopolitan cities, Edinburgh and Glasgow.

Ethnic group categories

This chapter compares data on ethnicity from the 2001 and 2011 Scottish Censuses. Scotland has developed its ethnic group question independently from other parts of the UK. Thus the Scottish question distinguished 'White Scottish' from 'White: Other British' in 2001 and in 2011. In 2011 it also identified 'White: Polish', 'White: Gypsy/Traveller' and 'Arab' for the first time, and it made African a separate category from 'Caribbean or Black'. There is one 'Mixed' category rather than the four used in England and Wales. Chapter One reproduces the census questions.

Most answers that were 'written in' rather than ticked are collected under 'Other' categories and cannot be reliably compared from one census to the next. The categories that we considered as equivalent across the censuses are described in Chapter One. In the Scottish context, specifically, we have combined 'White: Gypsy/Traveller' and 'White: Polish' with 'Other White', as well as 'Arab' with 'Other', in order to ensure better comparability with 2001.

Areas within Scotland

Where we come to compare areas of Scotland, we have used the 32 council areas, referred to as districts, and the 353 multi-member wards with boundaries established in 2007. Census output approximates these wards from both the 2001 and 2011 Censuses by adding together census output areas (OAs). The approximation means that small changes between censuses for individual wards may not be reliable, and consequently, we have focused on major results rather than marginal changes for single areas.

Measuring diversity

The measure of diversity that we use is called the Reciprocal Diversity Index and is the same as that used for England and Wales in Chapter Four.

Measuring changes in composition

Where we discuss geographical dispersal, we have done so by measuring changes in the concentration of each group. More specifically, for each group, we identified the wards that included a fifth of the group's population in 2001 and had the highest percentage of the group. We then measured the growth of the group between 2001 and 2011 in those most clustered areas, and the growth outside of those areas. Higher growth outside of the previously 'most clustered' areas suggests movement away from them, creating a more even spread of population in 2011. This is the same approach as used in Chapter Two.

All but 'White Scottish' are minorities

In this chapter we have taken 'minority ethnic' to refer to all those who described themselves as other than 'White Scottish'. This includes, therefore, those living in Scotland who were born in England or other parts of the UK and who chose not to identify themselves as Scottish when they responded to the census question on ethnic group. Other analyses of the 2011 Census, including the Scottish government's own, have chosen to define minority ethnic rather differently, taking it to refer to 'to all those who ticked a box outside of the "White" section' (Scottish Government, 2014, p 4). While it is true that this latter definition may well reflect common usage of the term 'ethnicity' in some everyday situations in contemporary Scotland, we believe there are justifications for the approach we have taken.

Discounting all 'White' minority groups from the definition would have the effect of making 'minority ethnic' a category that is only applicable to those who are seen to be visibly different from the majority Scottish population; it risks leaving us with a 'colour-coded' understanding of ethnicity. This is problematic not least because it conceals from view significant diversity within the 'White' group and within areas that might otherwise appear to be homogenously 'white'. It makes it harder to reckon with the history and potentially enduring consequences of discrimination against some of those who are of Irish descent, for example, as well as the distinctive trajectories of more recent 'white' migrant communities: Polish, for example, or English migrants to the Highlands and Western Isles. Therefore, and with a concern to bear in mind the particular ways in which ethnicity may 'work' in Scotland, we have treated as 'minority ethnic' all groups other than that described as 'White Scottish'.

Scotland's growing ethnic diversity

The overall picture in Scotland between 2001 and 2011 is one of growing ethnic diversity. Four-and-a-half million of Scotland's population describe their ethnic group as 'White Scottish'. There was no significant change, in this respect, between the censuses of 2001 and 2011. The remaining one-sixth of Scotland's population total – 850,000 – is a diverse mix of minorities that has increased in size by 29 per cent across the course of this decade. Just under half of Scotland's minority ethnic population (417,000) described themselves as 'White: Other British' in 2011. White Polish, White Irish, Pakistani, Chinese, Indian and African ethnic groups each numbered between 30,000 and 61,000.

As Figure 7.1 shows, each minority ethnic population grew between 2001 and 2011. Several groups more than doubled their population in this period. This growth has occurred as a result of immigration and from an excess of births over deaths among these populations, as might be expected in groups mainly comprising young adults. A number of these populations – including the African, Black Caribbean, Chinese, Indian and Bangladeshi groups – grew much more rapidly in Scotland than they did in England in the same period, albeit from a

Figure 7.1: Ethnic group populations of Scotland, 2001 and 2011

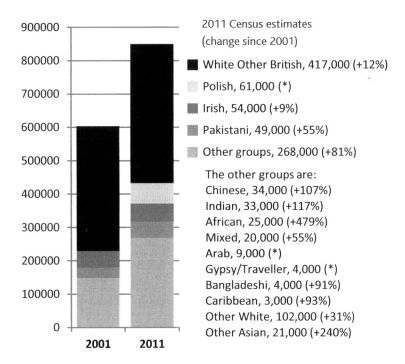

Note: * Arab, Gypsy/Traveller and Polish are new categories in 2011.

much lower starting point (more details about the situation in England and Wales can be found in Chapter Two).

In the 2011 Scottish Census 130,000 people did not find a single ethnic group category that they felt to be applicable to their sense of themselves, and so chose one of the 'Other' categories. The number of people choosing these 'Other' responses grew since 2001, despite the addition of three new census categories: White Polish, White Gypsy/Traveller and Arab. This suggests that the census ethnic group categories cannot capture the complexity of everyone's ethnic self-identification.

The census also asks questions that explore the diversity of family and cultural origins through religion, language and country of birth. (Note that, in Scotland, the language question asks about the language used at home, where the England and Wales census asks about 'main language': see Chapter Two.) National Records of Scotland (NRS) provides a more detailed breakdown of responses to these questions (2014); it is worth noting, however, that while more than 300,000 of Scotland's residents speak a language other than English at home, most of these respondents are bilingual or multilingual, since only 75,000 do not speak English well or very well. The 2011 Census also reveals that 85,000 understand the Gaelic language, and 58,000 of these can speak Gaelic. The numbers, in this respect, have not changed greatly since 2001. Respondents who identified themselves as Gaelic-speakers may not speak it at home, and so this figure may be additional to the 300,000 above.

This growth in ethnic diversity in Scotland is also reflected at the level of individuals and households. Figure 7.2(a), for example, shows the proportion and distribution of people who described themselves as being of mixed ethnicity, which we might take as one indication of the most intimate form of the mixing of ethnic groups in Scotland. There were 20,000 people recorded as 'Mixed or multiple ethnic groups' in the 2011 Census, up from 13,000 in 2001, although still less than 0.5 per cent of the population. As can be seen, the proportion of those claiming mixed ethnicity is highest in the urban areas where ethnic diversity is also high. Another striking indication of mixing is that among households with two or more people in Scotland, one in six are home to people of different ethnic groups.

Figure 7.2(b) shows the percentage change between 2001 and 2011 in the proportion of people with mixed ethnicity in the population for each local authority district in Scotland. It is notable that these proportions have increased rapidly outside the areas where mixed ethnicity is most common, although from a low level. This, again, suggests the spreading of diversity across Scotland.

Figure 7.2: Distribution of the Mixed ethnic group in Scotland, 2011

a) Percentage in the Mixed ethnic group, 2011

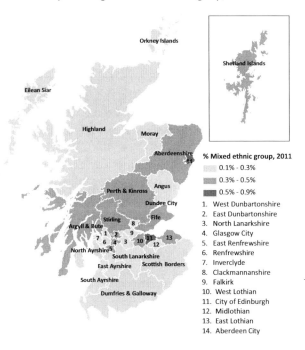

% Mixed ethnic group, 2011

- 0.1% - 0.3%
- 0.3% - 0.5%
- 0.5% - 0.9%

1. West Dunbartonshire
2. East Dunbartonshire
3. North Lanarkshire
4. Glasgow City
5. East Renfrewshire
6. Renfrewshire
7. Inverclyde
8. Clackmannanshire
9. Falkirk
10. West Lothian
11. City of Edinburgh
12. Midlothian
13. East Lothian
14. Aberdeen City

b) Percentage change in the Mixed ethnic group, 2001-11

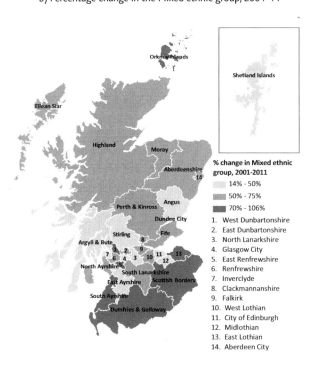

% change in Mixed ethnic group, 2001-2011

- 14% - 50%
- 50% - 75%
- 70% - 106%

1. West Dunbartonshire
2. East Dunbartonshire
3. North Lanarkshire
4. Glasgow City
5. East Renfrewshire
6. Renfrewshire
7. Inverclyde
8. Clackmannanshire
9. Falkirk
10. West Lothian
11. City of Edinburgh
12. Midlothian
13. East Lothian
14. Aberdeen City

Many recent arrivals in Scotland from overseas

The 2011 Census allows us to explore the rate of immigration in recent history, and shows a major difference between Scotland and the rest of Britain. The census asked all those who were born outside the UK to state the year of their most recent arrival, not counting short visits away from the UK. As explained in Chapter Three, this tends to emphasise more recent immigration, because it counts only the most recent arrivals, and because those who have emigrated or died since they came to the UK will not have been included in the 2011 Census. But there is no reason to believe that this will affect Scotland more than England or Wales.

Figure 7.3 shows the increase in immigration in the last two decades. In Scotland, the rise was slower than in England and Wales up until 2003, but since then it has been faster. Seven per cent of all Scotland's residents who had been born outside the UK arrived in each of the three years 2007, 2008 and 2009. Twelve per cent arrived each year in 2010 and 2011, nearly twice the rate for England and Wales.

Figure 7.3: Residents born outside the UK, year of arrival

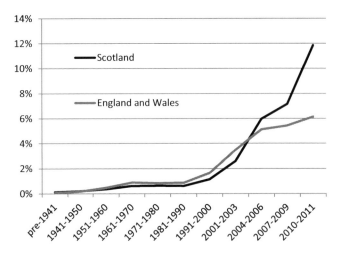

Notes: Arrivals per year during each period, percentage of all born outside the UK. For Scotland, 16% arrived in 2010-11. The figure per year of 12% per year for 2010-11 allows that there were only four months of 2011 up to the census on 29 April.

Over half of Scotland's residents born outside the UK arrived in 2004 or more recently (55 per cent, compared to England and Wales' 40 per cent). This emphasises one of the aspects of Scotland's distinct history of immigration and diversity. The lower demand for labour in the second half of the 20th century, described at the start of the chapter, may well have been reversed in the 21st century, but other factors, including growth in migration for purposes of education, are also clearly significant.

Spreading of ethnic diversity across Scotland

Not only does a comparison between 2001 and 2011 show a growth in the ethnic diversity of Scotland; it suggests the geographical spreading of that diversity. In other words, it shows the extent to which minority groups are moving into new parts of the country. Figure 7.4 demonstrates that the growth in minority ethnic populations has been at least as great outside those wards in which given groups were most 'clustered' in 2001 as it has been within those wards.

For example, the Indian population grew by about a quarter in those areas where it was most clustered in 2001, including wards in Glasgow and East Dunbartonshire. But it grew much faster elsewhere, more than doubling in other areas. We can safely conclude that those of Indian ethnicity were moving in substantial numbers to areas where they were not previously established. The same is true of other minorities, including the White Other British and the White Irish groups: on balance, their populations grew faster in wards outside those in which they had been most concentrated in 2001.

The Chinese population is the exception. It grew fastest in the areas in which it was already established, including in Anderston and Hillhead in Glasgow and Southside in Edinburgh. The extent of student immigration to university areas is likely to explain why the Chinese population grew faster in these wards than elsewhere. This is indicative of a more general point. The number of European Union (EU) and international students in Scottish universities has increased considerably over the last decade, nearly doubling in the case of both groups, and they now make up a greater proportion of the overall student population than is the case even in other parts of the UK (22 per cent as opposed to 18 per cent of the student body comes from overseas, with an additional 13 per cent coming from other parts of the UK; see UKCISA, 2014). Educational migration is clearly a key factor in growing diversity within Scotland. This population is nonetheless small relative to the total 250,000 growth of minority ethnic group populations in Scotland between 2001 and 2011 (Figure 7.1).

Scotland's African population is another special case, and has grown nearly five-fold between 2001 and 2011. This growth has created new areas of settlement larger than the ones in which the African population were mostly clustered in 2001. Springburn in Glasgow had 322 African residents in 2001, and the highest proportion of the African population in Scotland, followed by two wards in Edinburgh. In 2011 Springburn's African population had increased rapidly to 2,360, but was now followed by other wards in Glasgow and in Aberdeen, all of which had fewer than 100 African residents in 2001, but between 690 and 1,100 residents in 2011. Since 2000, policies to disperse asylum-seekers from the South of England have increased the African population in Scotland, and Springburn has been the site at which much of this population has been relocated (by the

Figure 7.4: Population growth of ethnic groups in the wards where each group is clustered, and population growth everywhere else, 2001-11

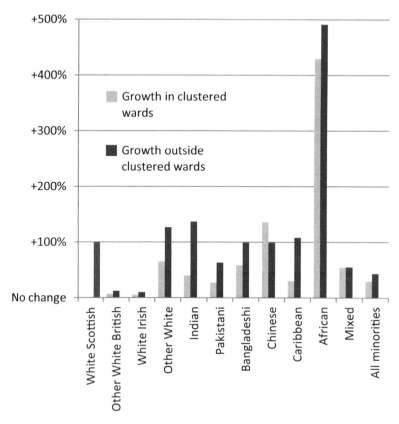

Notes: The 'clustered wards' for each ethnic group include a fifth of the group's population in 2001 with the highest percentage of the group. The other wards include the remaining four-fifths. The most clustered wards include:

Other White British: Lomond North (Argyll & Bute), Forres (Moray), North Isles (Orkney), Annandale East (Dumfries & Galloway)

White Irish: Southside Central, Langside, Anderston and Linn (Glasgow), West End (Dundee)

Pakistani: Pollokshields and Southside Central (Glasgow)

Indian: Pollokshields (Glasgow), Bearsden South and North and Bishopbriggs South (East Dunbartonshire)

Chinese: Anderston and Hillhead (Glasgow), Southside and Liberton (Edinburgh), George St (Aberdeen)

African: Springburn (Glasgow), Tillydrone and George St (Aberdeen), West End (Dundee)

end of 2004, Glasgow had just under 6,000 resident asylum-seekers, the highest number of any UK local authority; see Sim and Bowes, 2007, p 730). The data suggest, however, a growing diversity of trajectories within African migration to (and around) Scotland, which is likely to include migration for purposes of education to university cities in the North East and elsewhere.

Ethnic diversity in different areas of Scotland

The data suggest, then, that ethnic diversity is on the increase, but how diverse is each area in Scotland? The 2011 Census tells us that no district is very diverse. On a scale of 0–100 (see earlier), Edinburgh is the most diverse local authority district in Scotland, at 7.2, and the average for the whole of Scotland is just over 3. Scotland's diversity measured in this way has increased from 2.1 in 2001 to 3.1 in 2011. This may seem a small change, but it is an increase of 50 per cent in a decade. Moreover, every district has increased its diversity since 2001. All but nine of the 353 wards in Scotland have increased diversity. Six of these decreased by a very small amount. The only wards in which there has been a significant decrease in diversity are in Argyll & Bute and Moray; in these cases the closure or restructuring of military bases is likely to account for this decrease.

Eight of the ten wards with the greatest diversity are close to universities: City Centre, Southside and Meadows in Edinburgh, St Andrews in Fife, Anderston and Hillhead in Glasgow, and George St/Harbour and Tillydrone/Seaton in Aberdeen City. In each of these areas a third or more of the adult residents are students. The five most diverse wards that are not also student areas are Pollokshields and Southside Central in Glasgow, Leith and Leith Walk in Edinburgh, and North Isles in Orkney. In North Isles it is the large proportion that chose 'White: Other British' which makes its ethnic diversity; 34 per cent of North Isles residents were born in England.

There is a very strong relationship between diversity and the total population of minority ethnic groups in a ward (the correlation coefficient is 0.97). The areas with the fewest people describing themselves as White Scottish are also the most diverse. Conversely, the areas with little diversity are the areas where the population is almost entirely White Scottish, although in the main this is no longer a common feature of modern Scotland. Wards with a population which is more than 90 per cent White Scottish are located mostly in the west of Scotland, on the edges of the Glasgow conurbation, and also in the Shetland Isles. On the other hand, White Scottish remains the largest ethnic group in every ward in Scotland, and only in the City Centre ward of Edinburgh did it constitute less than half of a ward's population. In short, we can say that Scotland's growing diversity is not creating polarised islands of specific groups, but rather a mosaic of differently mixed areas.

Ethnic diversity in Edinburgh and Glasgow

Edinburgh and Glasgow are the largest Scottish districts, and are home to one-fifth of Scotland's population overall, and 32 per cent of Scotland's minority ethnic population, or 44 per cent of the minority population, if 'White: Other British' is excluded. This is comparable to the situation in London, which is home to 41 per cent of all of England and Wales' minorities other than 'White English/ Welsh/Scottish/Northern Irish/British'. At the same time, there were notably different patterns of diversity within these two cities in 2001, with the minority ethnic population much more widely dispersed in Edinburgh than Glasgow.

Is this still the case? Using the same measure of diversity as earlier, we find that in 2011 all of Edinburgh's wards had higher diversity than Scotland's overall value of 3.1, while in Glasgow, 68 per cent of its population lived in wards with higher diversity than Scotland. All of Edinburgh's wards already had higher values of diversity than the national level in 2001. For Glasgow, however, there has been a significant increase in diversity in the same period: only 44 per cent of its wards were above the national level of diversity a decade ago.

In both cities the geographers' measure of separation, the Index of Dissimilarity (see Chapter Eight) for White Scottish versus all minorities, decreased in the decade. It started from a higher point and declined more rapidly in Glasgow (30 down to 25 per cent) than in Edinburgh (25 down to 22 per cent). As city boundaries are changing and housing stock in the two cities is very different, it is not reasonable to draw strong conclusions from differences in these measures of diversity, but what is clear is that both cities are becoming more ethnically diverse, and that their diversity has become more widely spread across their wards. Beyond Edinburgh and Glasgow, where the majority of Scotland's population live, and where the majority of its minorities live too, diversity is growing even faster, as is described earlier. This growth is perhaps less noticeable because it is spread across a wider area.

Conclusions and implications

Direct comparisons between the findings regarding ethnicity in England and Wales and those in Scotland are not easily made. The respective ethnic group response categories differ, as does the size of relevant local areas. Nevertheless, it is clear that in important ways there are distinctive aspects to the shape of ethnic diversity in Scotland. To a certain extent this distinctiveness is a consequence of the different ways in which ethnicity was measured in the Scottish census. Here, in contrast to England and Wales, for example, 'White: Scottish', 'White: Other British' and 'White: Polish' were included as separate categories.

A 'White: Other British group', three-quarters born in England, remains the largest minority community in Scotland, and continues to grow in size. This is an important reminder of the considerable diversity that exists within so-called 'white' populations, which are too often treated as homogeneous or monolithic. In a more general sense, it is often the case that the ethnicity of majority groups goes unremarked; one advantage of a comparative approach to ethnic diversity is that shifts in perspective – in this case, a shift which allows us to consider 'Englishness' outside of the English context – can help bring that 'invisible' ethnicity back into view. Thus this aspect of Scotland's particular diversity offers us an important reminder about how ethnicity works more generally.

There are other specific features of ethnic diversity in Scotland, including the relatively rapid growth of most minority communities, albeit from a much lower starting point than in England and Wales. While it is not possible, on this analysis, to explain absolutely what may have caused these trends, it seems likely that they are at least partly attributable to the particular demographic situation north of the border which, as was explained in the introduction of this chapter, makes Scotland particularly reliant on the economic contribution of immigrant communities, and which has meant that the Scottish government – despite its limited ability to shape migration policy directly – has adopted a rather different rhetoric with regard to immigration from that which has tended to predominate in English politics. The specificity of patterns of migration for purposes of education may also be a factor here: Scottish universities have a higher proportion of international students than their counterpart institutions in the rest of the UK. It is unsurprising, in this regard, that a significant component of diversity in Scotland is found in wards closest to universities.

This combination of a differently inflected political discourse around immigration, economic opportunity and educational migration may help explain, then, why immigration has grown more rapidly in recent years in Scotland than in England and Wales. However, we should be cautious about attributing growing diversity only to the presence of greater opportunities or to a supposedly more welcoming public conversation in Scotland. Part of the notable growth of the African population in Scotland, for example, is the consequence of the presence of a population of 'dispersed' asylum-seekers, a reminder of how often migration is a matter of neither choice nor opportunity.

The data considered here also allow us to recognise some broad similarities in the overall pattern of diversity across the UK. In particular, there is evidence in Scotland, as in England and Wales, of both a growth in ethnic diversity and of the broadening out of that diversity. We can see evidence of this growth in diversity at all levels in Scotland: regionally, in the movement of minorities beyond those areas in which they were most established in 2001; locally, in the rise of the number of households which include residents of more than one ethnicity; personally, in the growth of those who describe themselves as being, in some sense, of 'mixed ethnicity'. Diversity does not have a single shape or form: a comparison of the dynamics of ethnicity between different parts of the UK reveals the diversity *of* diversity, as well the inescapably contextual nature of ethnicity as a concept. Yet there is a shared lesson here as well: while diversity is growing in Scotland, as it is in England and Wales, in neither context does the evidence suggest that growing diversity, in and of itself, creates division. What we see, rather, is the growth of new forms of inter-mixture and new patterns of living together, which take time and are not dependent on integration programmes motivated by a fear of difference.

Note

Further information about data and sources are available from
http://www.ethnicity.ac.uk/dynamicsofdiversity/

References

CRER (Coalition for Racial Equality Rights) (2013) *The state of the nation: Race and racism in Scotland; Criminal justice*, Glasgow: CRER.

Haria, J. (2014) 'Near the start of our journey', *Scottish Left Review*, vol 80, pp 4–5.

Hopkins, P. (2008) 'Politics, race and nation: The difference that Scotland makes', in C. Dwyer and C. Bressey (eds) *New geographies of race and racism*, Aldershot: Ashgate, pp 113-24.

Kiely, R., McCrone, D. and Bechofer, F. (2005) 'Whither Britishness? English and Scottish people in Scotland', *Nations and Nationalism*, vol 11, no 1, pp 65-82.

Kyriakides, C. Virdee, S. and Modood, T. (2009) 'Racism, Muslims and the national imagination', *Journal of Ethnic and Migration Studies*, vol 35, no 2, pp 289-308.

McCollum, D., Nowok, B. and Tindal, S. (2014) 'Public attitudes towards migration in Scotland: exceptionality and possible policy implications', *Scottish Affairs*, vol 23, no 1, pp 79-102.

McCollum, D., Findlay, A., Bell, D. and Bijak, J. (2013) *Patterns and perceptions of migration: Is Scotland distinct from the rest of the UK?*, ESRC Centre for Population Change Briefing Paper 10 (www.esrc.ac.uk/_images/cpcbriefing-10_tcm8-26550.pdf).

McIntosh, I., Sim, D. and Robertson, D. (2004) 'It's as if you're some alien...': exploring anti-English attitudes in Scotland', *Sociological Research Online*, vol 9, no 2.

Netto, G., Sosenko, F. and Bramley, G. (2011) *Poverty and ethnicity in Scotland*, York: Joseph Rowntree Foundation.

National Records of Scotland (2014) *2011 Census: Ethnicity, identity, language, and religion* (www.scotlandscensus.gov.uk/ethnicity-identity-language-and-religion).

Scottish Government (2014) *Overview of the equality results from the 2011 Census release 2*, Edinburgh: Scottish Government.

Sim, D. and Bowes, A. (2007) 'Asylum seekers in Scotland: the accommodation of diversity', *Social Policy and Administration*, vol 41, no 7, pp 729-46.

UKCISA (UK Council for International Student Affairs) (2014) *International student statistics: UK higher education* (www.ukcisa.org.uk).

Wells, P. and Williams, R. (2003) 'Sectarianism at work: accounts of employment discrimination against Irish Catholics in Scotland', *Ethnic and Racial Studies*, vol 26, no 4, pp 632-62.

Williams, C. and de Lima, P. (2006) 'Devolution, multicultural citizenship and race equality: from laissez-faire to nationally responsible politics', *Critical Social Policy*, vol 26, no 3, pp 498–522.

Section 2
Ethnic inequalities

EIGHT

Has neighbourhood ethnic residential segregation decreased?

Gemma Catney

Key findings

- Residential segregation, the extent to which an ethnic group is unevenly spread across neighbourhoods, has been decreasing steadily over the last two decades.
- Neighbourhood residential mixing is increasing – segregation has decreased within most local authority districts of England and Wales, for all minority ethnic groups.
- In over two-thirds of districts, segregation decreased for the Black Caribbean, Indian, Mixed and Black African ethnic groups, between 2001 and 2011.
- There is increased residential mixing between the White British and minority ethnic groups and, while White British segregation has increased slightly in many districts, segregation remains low for this group.
- There has been increased ethnic diversity in previously less diverse neighbourhoods, and those identifying with the White British group are more likely than ever to live next door to someone of a different ethnic group to their own.
- There are few districts that have seen a large increase in segregation; this has occurred in areas where there are small numbers of people in a particular ethnic group, and not in the areas where minority ethnic groups are most populous.
- There has been increased residential mixing in inner and outer London. In outer London, for example, segregation decreased by 12 percentage points for the Bangladeshi ethnic group and 11 percentage points for the Chinese ethnic group.
- Large cities such as Leicester, Birmingham, Manchester and Bradford have seen a decrease in segregation for most ethnic groups.

- The processes associated with changing residential segregation are multifaceted, but an important mechanism for decreasing segregation is movement away from existing clusters of an ethnic group or groups.

Introduction: 'segregation' in debate

This chapter considers how far the increased ethnic diversity in England and Wales discussed in Chapters Two and Three has been accompanied by the growth or decline of ethnic group concentrations in neighbourhoods. Are people mixing more in their residential environments, or have neighbourhoods become more ethnically segregated? The chapter explores how ethnic group residential segregation is changing nationally and at the neighbourhood level. It uses the widely applied Index of Dissimilarity to show how segregation has changed for all ethnic groups between 1991-2001-2011. The chapter begins by discussing in brief the contemporary policy context and academic literature surrounding British ethnic segregation. The next section is an analysis of how segregation has changed for each ethnic group, for England and Wales, before exploring smaller geographical areas, and considering the geography of these changes.

'Segregation' is a difficult term to conceptualise, and despite decades of research on its measurement, there is no consensus as to how best to quantify the level of segregation in a given place or for a given population group (such as an ethnic group). In day-to-day discourse, what is understood as segregation is no more straightforward, and it means different things to different people. Mixing with members of another ethnic group can take place in many spheres of life; living next door to a person of a different ethnic group is not the only (or indeed necessarily best) measure of positive social interactions – people may mix in the workplace, in schools, in religious establishments, and in various social settings. While there have been some British-based studies of ethnic group mixing in schools and in employment, most research to date has focused on *residential* segregation. Likewise, contemporary policy on inter-ethnic group relations has tended to focus on mixing in neighbourhood residential environments, as has political and popular debate.

So why is ethnic mixing in neighbourhoods of such interest? Debates about inter-ethnic and religious group neighbourhood dynamics were thrown into the spotlight in the aftermath of a series of disturbances (which became known colloquially as the 'race riots') in several urban towns in the North of England in the early 2000s. This was accompanied by a very direct policy response, concerned with improving community interactions at a local level, and a shift in focus from multiculturalism (celebrating differences) to community cohesion (emphasising a shared culture, identity and belonging). A series of local (in Bradford, Oldham and Burnley) and national reports into community dynamics placed emphasis on the negative role of segregation in promoting 'parallel lives' with 'no meaningful interchanges' between communities (Home Office, 2001, p 9). The policy response was to actively promote community cohesion, and a community cohesion unit was established to achieve this aim at the national and local level, through a variety of schemes from housing plans to community events. An overview and critical appraisal of these reports and ensuing local and national level policies can be found in Robinson (2005).

These programmes sound very positive, and certainly the promotion of more inclusive and tolerant neighbourhoods, more quality social engagement, stronger relationships and lower levels of anti-social behaviour are nothing but desirable. However, the policy developments that ensued were not without controversy, raising questions about the strength of the evidence on which new policies were based, the relevance of policy aims, and their usefulness at tackling structural inequalities between ethnic groups.

A particularly difficult tension between the *choice* to live in a particular neighbourhood and the *constraints* faced by people to realise their housing or locality preferences has at least been recognised in policy. Official reports from 2001 and later the Commission on Integration and Cohesion (2007) report, *Our Shared Future*, recognise these complexities, the latter explicitly acknowledging that the focus on segregation might have been over-emphasised in policy. The positive reasons for living in a neighbourhood with higher levels of one's own ethnic group are well known – strong familial and social networks, protection from intolerance, and well established services and institutions catering for specific ethno-cultural, religious and/or language requirements are obvious attractions, particularly for newly-arrived migrants. Areas of initial migrant settlement also typically have more employment opportunities and cheaper housing. Hence, ethnic group 'concentrations' might be a result of choice and preference, particularly at a certain stage in the life course (Peach, 1996a). While policy has recognised residential preferences, it has been fairly hard-hitting about the potential of co-ethnic clustering to lead to social isolation, particularly when combined with other forms of 'culturally-specific' activities, such as attending non-mixed faith schools, or a lack of inter-ethnic mixing in the workplace.

However, there is a considerable evidence base demonstrating the constraints that minority ethnic groups face in the housing market. The existence, and indeed persistence over time, of ethnic inequalities in the labour market may render certain residential locales and even housing types financially impossible for those who suffer from marginalisation and discrimination (see Chapters Ten, Eleven and Twelve). Catney and Simpson (2010) demonstrated that migration away from immigrant settlement areas is by the most financially able, across minority groups. While housing and locational aspirations may be shared between ethnic groups, racial steering by housing institutions and estate agents can restrict mobility, as well as fear or experience of racial intolerance (Phillips et al, 2007). There is strong evidence that the 'self-segregation' by minorities purported in policy is not a dominant process (Finney and Simpson, 2009).

While policy agendas have changed since the initial push for community cohesion in the early 2000s, this aim lives on in policy and political discourse, most recently with a focus on 'creating the conditions for integration', with a strong emphasis on the local level and community-led strategies (see, for example, DCLG, 2012). Ideas such as the maintenance of a 'mainstream British' culture, the failure of multiculturalism and the existence of 'parallel lives' and self-segregation are still strong in political debate, particularly in the context of wider events which took place throughout the last decade – the threat from international terrorism fuelled by tragedies like the London bombings of July 2005, a growing right-wing politics and a sensationalised debate about immigration levels.

What do we already know about ethnic residential segregation? Peach (1996b) tested the existence of 'ghettos' in the British social landscape, concluding that segregation was lower than in the US; the lack of evidence of intense concentrations of minority populations was again demonstrated a decade on by Finney and Simpson (2009). Rees and Butt (2004) showed decreasing segregation and deconcentration from urban clusters, and the role of internal migration in dispersing minority populations from concentrations was evidenced in several studies including by Stillwell and Hussain (2010). Each of these studies makes use of data from the census, and each has made a considerable impact on our knowledge of the patterns and processes of ethnic geographies. Catney (2015) has explored how residential segregation has been changing more recently. There exists in the international literature a long-standing debate about how best to measure segregation (dubbed the 'index wars'; see 'How is segregation measured?' below), and the British case has been no different (for some insight, see Peach, 2009). This chapter adopts a straightforward approach to the measurement of segregation, favouring measures that are fairly intuitive to interpret, and commonly applied in the segregation literature.

The last two decades have been a time of increased ethnic diversity in terms of absolute population growth, but also *geographically*; there has been a spreading out of ethnic diversity into new locales previously less diverse, and beyond the metropolitan centres we most traditionally associate with high diversity (see Chapter Two). How have levels of segregation responded in the context of these higher levels and new geographies of diversity?

Ethnic group data and 'neighbourhoods'

Neighbourhoods are difficult to define, but in this chapter small geographical areas form the main zones for comparison. The analysis of segregation for 1991-2011 is for wards within England and Wales (see Figure 8.1). The same areas for all three time points, aligned to the 2001 ward boundaries, are used here (8,850 wards; with a mean population of approximately 5,700 in 1991, 5,900 in 2001 and 6,300 in 2011), using the procedure outlined in Norman et al (2003).

The geographically refined study of segregation for more detailed ethnic groupings between 2001 and 2011 (see Figure 8.2) is for output areas (OAs) within local authority districts. OAs are the smallest geographical areas at which ethnic group data are released, with an average of around 300 people. There were 348 local authority districts in England and Wales in 2011, which are variable in size and with an average of approximately 161,000 people; examples of districts include Birmingham, Newham, Leicester and Cardiff.

The results for 1991 and 2001 make use of population estimates by ethnic group that take account of undercount in the census outputs (see Chapter One).

How is segregation measured?

Segregation is traditionally measured using numerical indices that capture the different ways ('dimensions') in which people might mix or live apart (Massey and Denton, 1988). The most frequently used measure of segregation, or separation, is the Index of Dissimilarity, which indicates to what extent a group's population is evenly spread across an area. The proportion of an ethnic group's total population in England and Wales that lives in a neighbourhood is subtracted from the proportion of the rest of the population that lives in that same neighbourhood. The absolute difference in proportions is added up across all neighbourhoods in England and Wales, and multiplied by fifty. The index can have a value between 0 and 100 per cent, with 0 per cent indicating a completely even spread of the ethnic group's population, and 100 per cent meaning complete separation. Thus, the greater the decrease in the index, the more the population has spread out, and hence experienced a decline in segregation.

National change in residential segregation, 1991-2001-2011

Figure 8.1 shows segregation between 1991 and 2011, for the whole of England and Wales. As 'Other' groups are difficult to compare over time (see Chapter One), they have not been included on this graph. Figure 8.1 shows how each ethnic group has become more dispersed over time; for example, between 1991 and 2011, by 10 percentage points for the African group, and 8, 6 and 5 percentage points for the Indian, Bangladeshi and Pakistani groups respectively. Mixed groups are combined together for the years where data for these groups are available, and show a small decrease between 2001 and 2011. Analysed individually (not shown), the Mixed White & Black Caribbean, Mixed White & Black African and Mixed White & Asian groups each experienced a decrease of 3 percentage points or less, while the Other Mixed group saw a small (less than 1 per cent) increase in segregation. The Chinese group had consistently low levels of segregation, and the slight increase by the Chinese group between 2001 and 2011 might be explained by migration from overseas of young people for education in university towns and cities, into fairly localised student clusters. Ethnic group populations in areas may grow or decline through natural change (births and deaths), immigration/emigration, and through migration into or out of the area from and to other parts of the country. The processes associated with these changes will be multifaceted, but an important mechanism for decreasing segregation is movement away from existing clusters of an ethnic group or groups.

Figure 8.1: Ethnic group segregation in England and Wales, 1991-2011

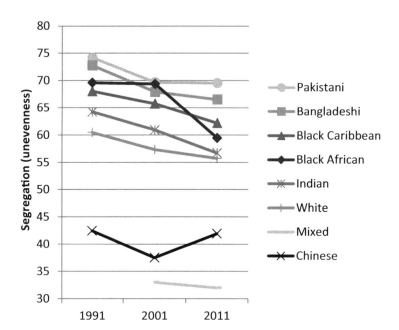

Local change in residential segregation, 2001-11

Figure 8.2 shows change in the Index of Dissimilarity, this time calculated for OAs within each local authority district in England and Wales, between 2001 and 2011. The histograms are shaded in dark grey where segregation decreased during 2001-11. In the majority of districts, segregation has decreased for all minority ethnic groups. The Black Caribbean, Indian, Mixed, and Black African ethnic groups have seen a decrease in neighbourhood segregation in more than two-thirds of districts. The groups labelled 'Other', apart from Other White, are not included as it is not possible to compare them over time (see Chapter One). The Black African and Mixed groups experienced the largest median change in segregation (−7 and −6 percentage points respectively). The four Mixed groups are combined here given space constraints; separate analyses of individual mixed groups reveals a decrease in segregation by each group in more than 80 per cent of districts where their population meets the threshold (see notes to Figure 8.2).

Why might neighbourhood segregation decrease for minority ethnic groups? The two mechanisms behind decreasing segregation are the spreading out of diversity (migration away from co-ethnic clusters) and natural change (the balance of births and deaths). Initially high segregation levels may be expected given chain immigration and the attractiveness of diverse areas to new immigrants, and in some cases subsequent UK-born people, particularly young people who might prefer or require cheap housing and centrality. Higher fertility among

Figure 8.2: Percentage point change in neighbourhood segregation, 2001-11

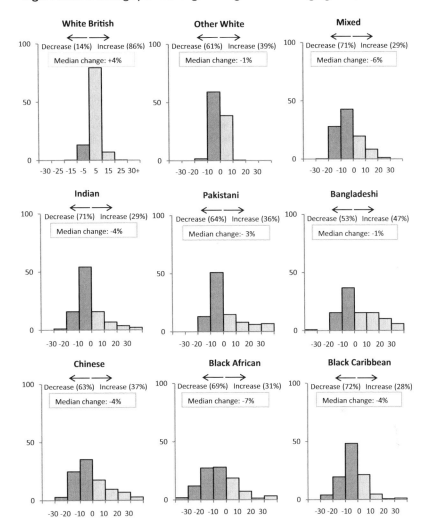

Notes: (i) Other White includes White Irish and Other White in 2001, plus White Gypsy or Irish Traveller in 2011. Mixed includes all four Mixed categories.

(ii) Dark grey bars show the proportion of districts with decreased segregation, and light grey bars the proportion with increased segregation. The percentage of districts that have increased or decreased is shown in brackets. The x-axis classes are expressed as a decrease or increase of 30 percentage points or more, and categories of 10 percentage points between –30% and +30%. The median change value is provided for each ethnic group.

(iii) Districts with an ethnic group population of less than 200, in either 2001 or 2011, are not included here as the populations are too small to reliably monitor change in segregation. This mainly affects rural areas and results in a different number of districts being analysed for each ethnic group, out of a possible 348: White British = 348; Other White = 347; Mixed = 337; Indian = 264; Pakistani =161; Bangladeshi = 117; Chinese = 239; Black African = 150; Black Caribbean = 149.

new immigrants who are typically younger might increase these concentration ('segregation') values. Over time, as knowledge of local housing markets increases or the protection of co-ethnic clusters becomes less important, a spreading out away from specific locales to other parts of the city, or indeed migration out of the city completely, might be expected. Movement away from urban clusters has been shown regardless of ethnic group but differentiated by socioeconomic position (Simpson and Finney, 2009; Catney and Simpson, 2010), and research has shown common housing aspirations favouring locales outside the inner city, although this should not, of course, be essentialised or over-simplified (Phillips et al, 2007). Housing pressure, improved financial status, or simply a transition along the life course in search of a bigger house, more green space, or a quieter lifestyle, will inspire this movement out of (often urban) clusters and lead to increased ethnic mixing in suburban and rural areas.

Very few districts experienced a large increase in segregation for any ethnic group (Figure 8.2), and where this occurred it was in areas where there were small numbers of people in that ethnic group (for example, rural areas), not in the areas where minority groups were most populous. For example, every district that experienced an increase in segregation by 10 per cent or more for the Pakistani population had in 2011 a Pakistani population of less than 1 per cent of the district's total. Segregation for an ethnic group may 'increase' where that group is found only in a small number of areas within a district and there is growth within those areas, or there is movement into a small number of areas from a relatively low population base. Thus, a small population and the geographical distribution of an ethnic group in combination may lead to an increased segregation value, despite more residential mixing. These processes may be the result of deconcentration from cities over time, discussed later.

Increases in segregation in some locales should also be understood in the context of minority ethnic disadvantage. *Spatial* inequalities in ethnic group distributions within certain residential neighbourhoods may be the outcome of *socioeconomic* inequalities in the housing and/or labour markets (see Chapters Ten, Eleven and Twelve) and a result of marginalised populations seeking protection from racism in areas with greater support networks.

The White British group saw a slight increase in segregation for the majority of districts (an increase of less than 5 percentage points in most districts which saw an increase in the period; for wards within England and Wales as a whole this group saw an increase of less than 1 percentage point). Segregation remained low for the White British group; this group is very populous and evenly spread throughout most districts. This increase in segregation for the White British group is largely a function of the decreasing segregation of minority ethnic groups, which have considerably smaller populations in most districts in England and Wales. A large percentage of many areas of England and Wales are predominantly White British. Where these areas become more ethnically mixed (due to members of one or more minority group moving in), unevenness of the White British group in relation to everyone else will increase. 'On the ground', there is increased residential mixing between the White British population and other ethnic groups. The segregation value for the White British group (and thus the population other than White British as a whole, given that this measure of segregation is symmetrical) may increase, while each individual minority group's value decreases. This apparently contradictory scenario is explained by the co-residence of minority ethnic groups in the same neighbourhoods. With more than one minority ethnic group that is spatially distributed equally but differently from the majority ethnic group, the segregation value for the majority is more than the value for any minority group individually. This is because the minority ethnic groups individually are compared with 'the rest' of the population, which includes the other minority group(s) with which they have a common spatial pattern.

This increased residential mixing between the ethnic majority and minority groups is explored further in Figure 8.3, which is a concentration profile for the White British group. It shows the percentage of individuals identifying with the White British group (left, vertical axis) who lived in neighbourhoods (OAs) with a percentage of the White British population greater than the percentage indicated on the bottom axis (horizontal axis). For example, in 2001, 96 per cent of the White British population (shown on the vertical axis) lived in neighbourhoods that were more than 60 per cent White British (shown on the horizontal axis). By 2011, residential mixing between the White British and minority groups had increased, meaning that this value had decreased by 3 per cent (to 93 per cent). In other words, in 2011 a person identifying as White British is more likely to have a neighbour from a different ethnic group than they were in 2001. Figure 8.3 shows how there has been increased ethnic diversity in previously less diverse neighbourhoods, and that people affiliating with the White British group are not becoming increasingly concentrated.

Figure 8.3: White British residential mixing with other ethnic groups, 2001-11

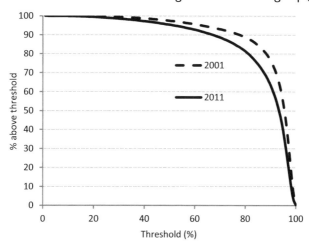

Notes: This figure is the percentage of the White British population in England and Wales living in neighbourhoods (OAs) with a White British population of more than the threshold shown.

Where has this decrease in segregation taken place?

This section explores the geography of the changing patterns of segregation outlined so far. Figure 8.4 shows cartograms (see Chapter One) of the classes of segregation change in Figure 8.2, refined into four categories of increase and decrease in separation levels, for the two largest 'non-White' ethnic groups – Indian and Pakistani. The approximately two-thirds of districts which have experienced a decrease in segregation by both ethnic groups can be seen in the maps. Increases in segregation of these populations are mainly in rural areas where their population tends to be very small. The Indian group shows decreasing segregation in urban centres such as Liverpool and Manchester, and some marginal increase in rural areas, suggesting a deconcentration from cities over time. Districts with the largest decreases for the Pakistani group (that is, where the Pakistani group is more evenly spread than it was a decade earlier, shown by the darkly shaded areas) include the London Boroughs of Barking and Dagenham, Lewisham and Tower Hamlets.

Figure 8.4: The geography of change in segregation, 2001-11

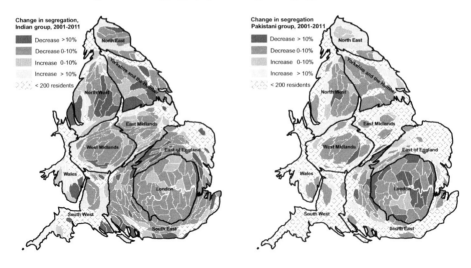

For many of the ethnic groups shown in Figure 8.2, segregation has decreased by over 5 percentage points in large cities such as Leicester and Birmingham. These cities saw a decrease in segregation for the White British and all minority ethnic groups except Other White, which had a very small increase. Manchester experienced a decrease in segregation for all ethnic groups, including by 13 percentage points for the Indian ethnic group. Segregation has decreased in Bradford for all ethnic groups, except a marginal (under 2 percentage points) increase for the White British and Other White groups. Reduced segregation here included 16 percentage points for the Black African and 13 percentage points for the Chinese ethnic groups.

As discussed earlier, cities are attractive to young people, recent immigrants and students. New arrivals to the UK may only stay a short time in one locale, their 'settlement area', before leaving the UK or moving away from these areas. Other research has shown dispersal away from ethnically diverse urban areas – a process common across ethnic groups (Simpson and Finney, 2009). So what is happening to neighbourhood segregation in large cities? Figure 8.5 shows percentage point change in levels of segregation for neighbourhoods within districts for each ethnic group, by category of large urban district (see 'Area classifications' below). Inner London saw a decrease in segregation for most ethnic groups, and a small increase of 3 percentage points or less for the White British, Black Caribbean and Black African groups. Outer London's decreasing segregation was particularly notable for the Bangladeshi (–12 percentage points), Chinese (–11 percentage points) and Mixed (–8 percentage points) groups. Segregation has decreased in metropolitan districts for all ethnic groups except White British, which experienced a slight (less than 2 percentage points) increase. The White British group saw a marginal increase in segregation in other large cities. For all other ethnic groups, segregation decreased in these urban districts, in particular for the Black African group, with a decrease of 20 percentage points. The picture is one of increased residential mixing in urban areas. An important mechanism for this change will be dispersal from major cities to suburban and rural areas, in particular by families.

Area classifications

The *types* of area that have experienced a change in ethnic group segregation can be explored using a categorisation of areas, using the characteristics that they share to group them together. The area classification scheme used in this chapter is based on common socioeconomic and demographic characteristics and administrative status (see Champion, 2005, applied here to 2011). Major urban districts have been categorised as inner London, outer London, metropolitan areas, and other large cities (Figure 8.5). Examples of metropolitan areas include Birmingham, Bradford, Leeds and Manchester. Other large cities include Cardiff and Nottingham.

Conclusions and implications

During the last 15 years sensationalised claims have been made about minority ethnic groups living parallel lives from the White British majority via a process of self-segregation, despite academic research which suggested greater mixing and dispersal from concentrations. The early 2000s saw a major policy shift towards community cohesion, and a concern with segregation in local communities. The 2011 Census revealed a growth of ethnic diversity in England and Wales (see Chapter Two). This chapter challenges the public and policy discourses of rising ethnic residential segregation, showing how this increased ethnic diversity has not been accompanied by greater segregation in neighbourhoods; the extent to which members of different ethnic groups live in separate residential locales has

Figure 8.5: Urban segregation, 2001-11

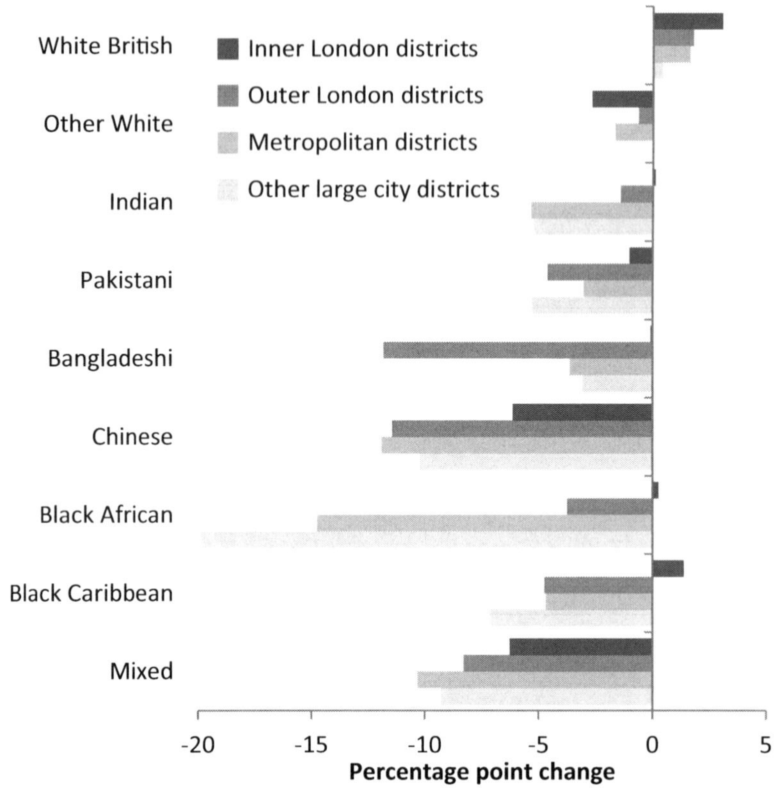

Notes: This figure is the change in the Index of Dissimilarity for OAs within local authority district types: districts in inner London, outer London, metropolitan, and other large city districts.

decreased over the last 20 years, and the 2011 Census has provided compelling evidence of increased residential mixing. Previous research has demonstrated common housing aspirations and shared migration processes within the country, from urban concentrations towards greater mixing, regardless of ethnic group. This has been supported by the results presented here. However, the more limited opportunities and persistent discrimination in housing and employment (shown in Chapters Ten and Eleven) which disproportionately affect some minority groups in achieving upward residential mobility will result in *spatial* inequalities. In addition to providing services and support to increasingly diverse neighbourhoods, pertinent issues for future policy would be in ensuring the conditions for realising housing needs and neighbourhood preferences, by reducing discrimination and inequalities in housing, the labour market, and in education.

Note

Further information about data and sources are available from
http://www.ethnicity.ac.uk/dynamicsofdiversity/

References

Catney, G. (2015) 'Small area ethnic (de-)segregation in England and Wales', *Urban Studies*, in press.

Catney, G. and Simpson, L. (2010) 'Settlement area migration in England and Wales: assessing evidence for a social gradient', *Transactions of the Institute of British Geographers*, vol 35, no 4, pp 571-84.

Champion, T. (2005) 'Population movement within the UK', in R. Chappell (ed) *Focus on people and migration*, Houndmills: Palgrave Macmillan, pp 91-114.

Commission on Integration and Cohesion (2007) *Our Shared Future*, London: Department for Communities and Local Government.

DCLG (Department for Communities and Local Government) (2012) *Creating the conditions for integration*, London: DCLG.

Finney, N. and Simpson, L. (2009) *'Sleepwalking to segregation'? Challenging myths about race and migration*, Bristol: Policy Press.

Home Office (2001) *Community cohesion: A report of the Independent Review Team (Chaired by Ted Cantle)*, London: HMSO.

Massey, D.S. and Denton, N.A. (1988) 'The dimensions of residential segregation', *Social Forces*, vol 67, no 2, pp 281-315.

Norman, P., Rees, P. and Boyle, P. (2003) 'Achieving data compatibility over space and time: creating consistent geographical zones', *International Journal of Population Geography*, vol 9, no 5, pp 365-86.

Peach, C. (1996a) 'Does Britain have ghettoes?', *Transactions of the Institute of British Geographers*, New Series, vol 21, no 1, pp 216-35.

Peach, C. (1996b) 'Good segregation, bad segregation', *Planning Perspectives*, vol 11, no 4, pp 379-98.

Peach, C. (2009) 'Slippery segregation: discovering or manufacturing ghettos?', *Journal of Ethnic and Migration Studies*, vol 35, no 9, pp 1381-95.

Phillips, D., Davis, C. and Ratcliffe, P. (2007) 'British Asian narratives of urban space', *Transactions of the Institute of British Geographers*, New Series, vol 32, no 2, pp 217-34.

Rees, P. and Butt, F. (2004) 'Ethnic change and diversity in England, 1981–2001', *Area*, vol 36, no 2, pp 174-86.

Robinson, D. (2005) 'The search for community cohesion: key themes and dominant concepts of the public policy agenda', *Urban Studies*, vol 42, no 8, pp 1411-27.

Simpson, L. and Finney, N. (2009) 'Spatial patterns of internal migration: evidence for ethnic groups in Britain', *Population, Space and Place*, vol 15, no 1, pp 37-56.

Stillwell, J. and Hussain, S. (2010) 'Exploring the ethnic dimension of internal migration in Great Britain using migration effectiveness and spatial connectivity', *Journal of Ethnic and Migration Studies*, vol 36, no 9, pp 1381-403.

NINE

Which ethnic groups have the poorest health?

Laia Bécares

Key findings

- Persistent inequalities in limiting long-term illness are seen in the health of Pakistani and Bangladeshi women. Their illness rates have both been 10 per cent higher than White women in 1991, 2001 and 2011.
- The White Gypsy or Irish Traveller group, identified for the first time in the 2011 Census, have particularly poor health. Both men and women had twice the White British rates of long-term limiting illness and poor self-rated health, and throughout the life course they are the group most likely to report a limiting long-term illness.
- Ethnic inequalities in health are most pronounced at older ages:
  - 56 per cent of all women aged 65 or older reported a limiting long-term illness, but over 70 per cent of Pakistani, Bangladeshi and White Gypsy or Irish Traveller women at this age reported a limiting long-term illness;
  - Arab and Indian women aged 65 or over also reported high percentages of limiting long-term illness (66 and 68 per cent respectively);
  - 48 per cent of White British men aged 65 or older reported poor self-rated health, but 75 per cent of White Gypsy or Irish Traveller, 74 per cent of Bangladeshi and 66 per cent of Pakistani men of the same age reported poor self-rated health.
- The Chinese group reported persistently better health in 1991, 2001 and 2011, half or under half the White illness rates for both men and women.
- Gender differences exist in ethnic inequalities in health across census years and health measures. For example, in 2011 White Irish men had higher rates of limiting long-term illness than White British men, whereas the opposite

was true for White Irish women, who had lower rates of limiting long-term illness than White British women. Conversely, Indian men reported in most cases better health than White British men, whereas Indian women reported worse health than White British women.

• Health inequalities for ethnic groups with poorer health were more pronounced in London in 2011 than elsewhere in England and Wales.

• Health advantages among minority ethnic groups that have lower rates of limiting long-term illness than the White British group, including Chinese and Black African groups, were larger in regions outside of London.

Ethnic health inequalities and the social determinants of health

Poor health is caused by a wide range of factors, including biological determinants (age, sex, hereditary factors), and wider social determinants such as education, social position, income, place of residence, social support and experiences of discrimination (Dahlgren and Whitehead, 1991). The greater significance of the social over the biological determinants in patterning health across different groups in society is well documented (Acheson, 1998; Commission on Social Determinants of Health, 2008), and it is now clear that addressing the social determinants of health is key to improving the health of the population of England and Wales, and to reducing wider health inequalities.

The social determinants of health are unequally distributed across ethnic groups, leading to unjust and preventable ethnic inequalities in health. For example, Bangladeshi people in England and Wales are over–represented in the lowest socioeconomic positions, and live in the most deprived areas of the country (see Chapters Eleven and Thirteen). They also report the highest percentage of bad and very bad self-rated health among all ethnic groups (Nazroo, 2003). The poorer health profile of some ethnic groups has been shown for children and adults across a wide range of markers of morbidity and mortality (Davey Smith et al, 2000). Although explanations relating to genetic differences and lifestyle choices have been put forward to explain ethnic inequalities in health, these arguments have failed to demonstrate genetic underpinnings, and disregard the contextualisation of biological and lifestyle factors within wider social determinants (Dahlgren and Whitehead, 1991). Framing ethnic inequalities in health as a result of underlying social and economic determinants provides a clear understanding for the consistent patterns of health inequality, across and within ethnic groups, experienced by the most disadvantaged minority ethnic groups.

This chapter illustrates these inequalities using census data from 1991, 2001 and 2011. It compares inequalities across census years to describe persistent inequalities in health among some minority ethnic groups since 1991, and provides new information for ethnic groups that had not been previously captured in the census, including the White Gypsy or Irish Traveller group, for whom health statistics are not as widely available.

Measuring health

The 2011 Census included two measures of health: limiting long-term illness, and general self-rated health. Limiting long-term illness was measured by asking, 'Are your day-to-day activities limited because of a health problem or disability which has lasted, or is expected to last, at least 12 months? Include problems related to old age.' Responses could be 'Yes, limited a lot', 'Yes, limited a little' and 'No.'

General self-rated health was measured by asking, 'How is your health in general?' with the following options as responses: 'Very good', 'Good', 'Fair', 'Bad' or 'Very bad'.

These two measures are commonly used in health studies as they are a predictor of mortality and health service use (Cohen et al, 1995; Idler and Benyamini, 1997).

The measurements of limiting long-term illness and general self-rated health have been asked using slightly different questions in previous censuses. In 2001, general health was measured by asking, 'Over the last 12 months would you say your health has on the whole been: Good? Fairly good? Or Not good?' And limiting long-term illness was asked with the following question: 'Do you have any long-term illness, health problem or disability that limits your daily activities or the work you can do? Include problems related to old age. Yes or No.'

Limiting long-term illness is the only health measure that was asked in 1991, and it was captured by asking respondents: 'Do you have any long-term illness, health problem or handicap which limits your daily activities or the work you can do? Include problems which are due to old age.' Possible responses were 'Yes, I have a health problem which limits activities' or 'I have no such health problem.'

These changes in wording have important implications for how people interpret the question, and so comparisons across years have to be interpreted with caution. For this reason we have compared *inequalities* in each year, showing illness relative to the White British group in 2011 and 2001, and relative to the White group in 1991.

Throughout the chapter, 'poor health' is referred to as either having a limiting long-term illness, or reporting 'fair', 'bad' or 'very bad' self-rated health in the 2011 Census, and 'not good' health in the 2001 Census.

Why age-standardised ratios?

Older age is strongly associated with a decrease in health, and since most minority ethnic groups are younger than the White British group, the overall proportion of a group that is ill can be low even when their illness rates are high at each age. Figures presented here are produced with the indirect standardisation method, which calculates how much higher or lower the group's poor health is compared to the average for England and Wales. For men and women separately, the calculation applies the England and Wales age-specific illness rates to the group's population to compute an 'expected' number ill. The age-standardised ratio is the observed number ill divided by the expected number ill. In order to compare the illness rates of minority ethnic groups to that of the White British group, we have divided the age-standardised rate of limiting long-term illness, or poor health, of each ethnic group by the rate of the White British. A figure greater than 1 means more illness, and a figure lower than 1 means less illness than the White British population.

Ethnic inequalities in limiting long-term illness

This chapter uses census data on limiting long-term illness and self-rated health to examine inequalities in health between ethnic groups in England and Wales. Across census years and health measures, results show an advantaged health profile for some ethnic groups, including White British and Chinese groups, and poorer health status among other ethnic groups, such as Pakistani and Bangladeshi groups. Health status varies by gender, so in this chapter rates of poor health are presented separately for men and women.

In 2011, men from the White Gypsy or Irish Traveller, Mixed White & Black Caribbean, White Irish, and Black Caribbean groups had higher rates of limiting long-term illness than White British men (see Figure 9.1). Men in the White Gypsy or Irish Traveller group, identified for the first time in the 2011 Census, reported the highest rates of limiting long-term illness, almost twice the rate of White British men.

Twelve of the 17 minority ethnic groups had lower limiting long-term illness among men than the White British group, with Chinese and Black African men reporting the least illness. Men from Bangladeshi, Arab and Pakistani ethnic groups also reported slightly lower rates of limiting long-term illness compared to White British men.

This health advantage is not observed among Bangladeshi, Arab and Pakistani women, or in analyses of self-rated health, the other health outcome measured in the census, where men from these ethnic groups reported poorer health than White British men. Findings on self-rated health are discussed later in this chapter.

White British women had similar rates of illness as White British men, but had considerably better health than women of several minority ethnic groups (see Figure 9.1). White Gypsy or Irish Traveller women had the highest rates of limiting long-term illness, almost twice the White British rate. Pakistani and Bangladeshi women also had considerably higher rates of limiting long-term illness than White British women (a ratio of 1.27 and 1.20 respectively, relative to the White British illness rate). Women from some ethnic groups had better health than White British women; Chinese, Other White, Black African, and Other Asian groups had the lowest rates of limiting long-term illness.

Figure 9.1 shows further gender differences in ethnic health inequalities. Whereas Indian men in 2011 had 25 per cent less limiting long-term illness than White British men, this health advantage was only 3 per cent for Indian women. In contrast, White Irish men had 8 per cent higher rates of limiting long-term illness than White British men, whereas White Irish women had slightly lower illness than White British women.

Figure 9.1: Ethnic inequalities in limiting long-term illness for men and women, 2011

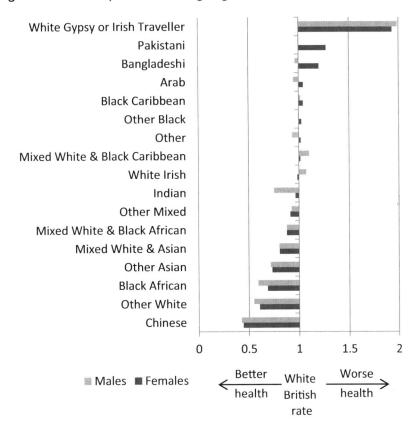

Note: Age-standardised illness ratio, each group relative to the White British group. A value of 0.5 indicates half the White British illness, and 2 indicates twice the White British illness. See information on age standardisation on page 125. Groups have been sorted in the chart from highest to lowest illness for women.

Figure 9.2 shows greater ethnic inequalities in limiting long-term illness at older ages. Fifty per cent of all men aged 65 or over living in England and Wales reported a limiting long-term illness in 2011, but this figure is much higher for some minority ethnic groups; 69 per cent of White Gypsy or Irish Traveller, 69 per cent of Bangladeshi and 64 per cent of Pakistani men aged 65 or over reported a limiting long-term illness. Fifty per cent of White British men aged 65 or over reported a limiting long-term illness, the same as the national average.

Older men from Mixed White & Asian, Black African, and Chinese ethnic groups were least likely to report a limiting long-term illness, 5 to 10 per cent less likely than White British men of that same age.

Among younger age groups, the percentage of people from minority ethnic groups who had a limiting long-term illness in 2011 is not very different compared to the England and Wales average (5 per cent among men aged 0-15, and 12 per cent among men aged 16-64). But the White Gypsy or Irish Traveller group stands out, with much higher limiting long-term illness for all age groups (8 per cent among men aged 0-15, and 30 per cent among men aged 16-64).

Figure 9.2: Percentage of men reporting limiting long-term illness, by age and ethnic group, 2011

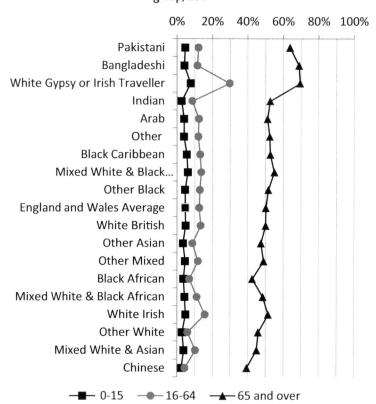

Ethnic inequalities in limiting long-term illness across age groups are also seen for women (see Figure 9.3). Fifty-six per cent of White British women aged 65 or older reported a limiting long-term illness in 2011 – the same as the national average, and slightly more than men. Pakistani, Bangladeshi and White Gypsy or Irish Traveller groups had a much higher percentage of elderly women with a limiting long-term illness (77, 76 and 73 per cent respectively). Women aged 65 or older from Arab and Indian ethnic groups also reported high percentages of limiting long-term illness (66 and 68 per cent respectively), whereas women of the same age from Chinese and Mixed White & Asian ethnic groups reported the lowest limiting long-term illness (47 and 51 per cent respectively).

Similar to men, health inequalities are less extreme among women under 65. But as with men, young White Gypsy or Irish Traveller women stand out with high illness rates. Figure 9.3 shows that whereas 13 per cent of all women in England and Wales aged 16-64 reported a limiting long-term illness, this percentage is more than twice as high for White Gypsy or Irish Traveller women of the same age.

Figure 9.3: Percentage of women reporting limiting long-term illness, by age and ethnic group, 2011

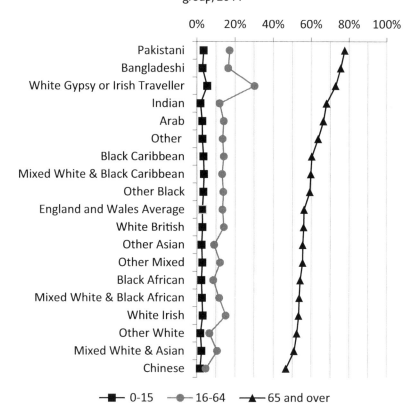

Prior to 2011 there were no categories of White Gypsy or Irish Traveller and Arab, so we do not know from census data whether the stark inequalities in limiting long-term illness have persisted over time. We can, however, observe a persistent inequality in the illness rates of other ethnic groups that are comparable in the 1991, 2001 and 2011 Censuses. Figures 9.4 and 9.5 show the rates of limiting long-term illness among men and women from minority ethnic groups, relative to the White British rate in 2001, and relative to the rate of the White group in 1991.

Figure 9.4 shows that in 2001 the Pakistani, Bangladeshi, Black Caribbean, White Irish, and the Mixed White & Black Caribbean ethnic groups all had worse health than the White British, for both men and women.

Yet this is not the case across all groups. Other minority ethnic groups had lower rates of illness than the White British, both for men and women. Rates of limiting long-term illness are particularly low for both men and women in the Chinese group, who had more than 40 per cent improvement on the rates of illness of White British.

Gender differences can be observed in the health of Indian men and women. Indian men had lower rates of limiting long-term illness than White British men, but the opposite is true for Indian women, who had higher rates of illness than White British women.

The rate of illness for Indian women is nonetheless lower than that of women from more disadvantaged ethnic groups, including Pakistani, Bangladeshi and Black Caribbean women.

Figure 9.4: Ethnic inequalities in limiting long-term illness for men and women, 2001

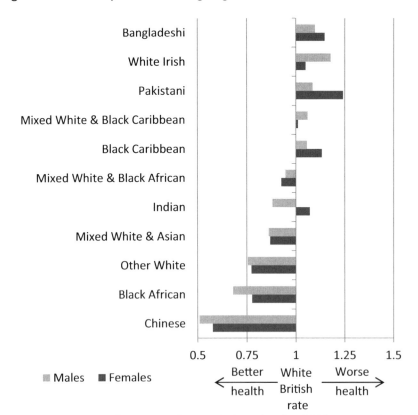

Note: Age-standardised illness ratio, each group relative to the White British group. A value of 0.5 indicates half the White British illness, and 2 indicates twice the White British illness. See information on age standardisation on page 125. Groups have been sorted in the chart from highest to lowest illness for women

Fewer minority ethnic groups were identified in the 1991 Census (see Chapter One), but, as Figure 9.5 shows, we can still observe more illness among men and women in the Pakistani, Black Caribbean, and Bangladeshi ethnic groups when compared to the illness rates of the White ethnic group. The health disadvantage of Bangladeshi men was much larger than that for Bangladeshi women – an illness rate of 1.53 among Bangladeshi men, relative to White men, compared to the illness rate of 1.20 for Bangladeshi women, relative to White women.

Women from the Indian and Black African ethnic groups had slightly higher rates of limiting long-term illness than White women in 1991, unlike men of these minority ethnic groups who had lower rates of illness than White men (see Figure 9.5). As in other years, Chinese men and women reported much less limiting long-term illness than the White British.

Figure 9.5: Ethnic inequalities in limiting long-term illness for men and women, 1991

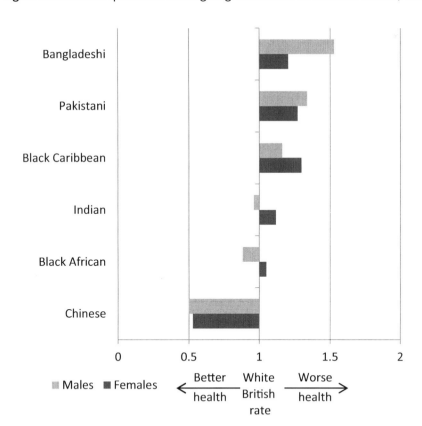

Note: Age-standardised illness ratio, each group relative to the White British group. A value of 0.5 indicates half the White British illness, and 2 indicates twice the White British illness. See information on age standardisation on page 125. Groups have been sorted in the chart from highest to lowest illness for women.

Ethnic inequalities in self-rated health

The other measure of health available in the England and Wales census, self-rated health, has been asked since 2001 (see 'Measuring health' earlier). Analyses using this health outcome show a similar pattern of inequality across ethnic groups, although inequalities in self-rated health are larger than inequalities in limiting long-term illness.

Figure 9.6 shows the rates of reporting poor self-rated health across minority ethnic men and women, compared to the White British group. In 2011, White Gypsy or Irish Traveller men and women had by far the highest rates of poor self-rated health – over twice the rate of White British men and women, and higher than all other minority ethnic groups.

Men who had higher rates of limiting long-term illness than White British men, such as White Irish, Black Caribbean, and Mixed White & Black Caribbean men, also had higher rates of poor self-rated health. Self-rated health captures inequalities in health not observed with analyses of limiting long-term illness. Studies show that minority ethnic groups tend to under-report long-term illnesses due to different notions, as compared to the White population, of what constitutes an illness grave enough to be considered a long-term illness (Nazroo, 1997). For example, in the data presented in this chapter, men from Bangladeshi, Pakistani, Other Black, and Arab ethnic groups reported poorer self-rated health than White British men, but had better rates of limiting long-term illness.

The same patterns of ethnic health inequalities observed with self-rated health are also documented with doctor-diagnosed outcomes, including cardiovascular disease and diabetes (Sproston and Mindell, 2006).

Among women, Pakistani, Bangladeshi, Arab, Black Caribbean and Other Black women also had much higher rates of poor health than White British women. White Irish women, who had similar rates of limiting long-term illness than White British women (see Figure 9.1), had poorer self-rated health (see Figure 9.6).

Gender differences appear again among the Indian group, as women had higher rates of poor self-rated health than White British women, but Indian men had lower rates of poor self-rated health than White British men. As with limiting long-term illness, despite having poorer health than Indian men, Indian women had better rates than women from most other minority ethnic groups.

As with limiting long-term illness, inequalities in self-rated health are largest among older people. Whereas 48 per cent of White British men aged 65 or older reported poor self-rated health in 2011, 75 per cent of White Gypsy or Irish Traveller, 74 per cent of Bangladeshi, and 66 per cent of Pakistani men of the same age reported poor self-rated health. Among women aged 65 or older, 76 per cent of White Gypsy or Irish Traveller, 81 per cent of Pakistani and 83 per cent of Bangladeshi women reported poor self-rated health, as compared to 52 per cent of White British women of that same age (data not shown).

Younger age groups have lower rates of poor self-rated health, but inequalities in health are also evident. For example, whereas 16 per cent of White British men aged 16–64 reported having poor self-rated health, 36 per cent of White Gypsy or Irish Traveller men of that same age group reported poor self-rated health.

Figure 9.6: Ethnic inequalities in self-rated health for men and women, 2011

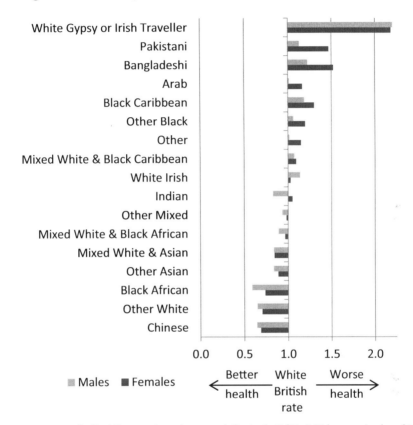

Note: Age-standardised illness ratio, each group relative to the White British group. A value of 0.5 indicates half the White British illness, and 2 indicates twice the White British illness. See information on age standardisation on page 125. Groups have been sorted in the chart from highest to lowest illness for women.

We can contrast inequalities in self-rated health in 2011 with 2001. Although the question wording and response choices differed in the two censuses, the pattern of ethnic inequalities is the same. As Figure 9.7 shows, inequalities in poor self-rated health among Pakistani, Black Caribbean, Bangladeshi, White Irish, and Mixed White & Black Caribbean ethnic groups, as compared to the White British group, were already present in 2001. Among women, the health disadvantage of Indian women, as compared to White British women, is also seen in 2001 (see Figure 9.7).

Figure 9.7: Ethnic inequalities in self-rated health for men and women, 2001

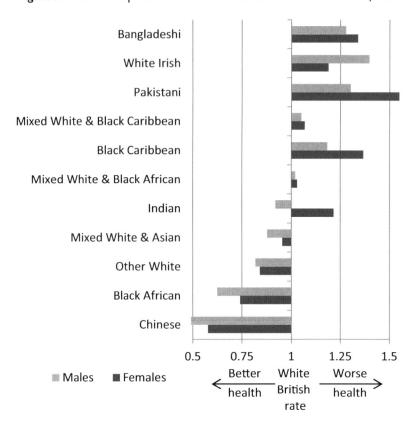

Note: Age-standardised illness ratio, each group relative to the White British group. A value of 0.5 indicates half the White British illness, and 2 indicates twice the White British illness. See information on age standardisation on page 125. Groups have been sorted in the chart from highest to lowest illness for women.

Regional differences in ethnic health inequalities

Using limiting long-term illness as an example to examine regional differences in ethnic health inequalities, Figures 9.8 and 9.9 show variations in the patterns of inequality between the London region and everywhere else in England and Wales, for men and women, respectively. In summary, groups with poorer health have greater disadvantage in London, while groups with better health have less advantage in London.

Health disadvantages are more pronounced in the London region. For example, Black Caribbean men living in London were 11 per cent more likely than White British men to report a limiting long-term illness in 2011, but Caribbean men living in other regions of England and Wales were only 3 per cent more likely than White British men to report a limiting long-term illness. Among women, Black Caribbean women living in London were 11 per cent more likely that

White British women to have a limiting long-term illness, but only 6 per cent more likely among Black Caribbean women living outside of London.

Health advantages among some of the minority ethnic groups that have lower rates of limiting long-term illness than the White British group are larger in regions outside of London. This is the case for the Black African, Other Asian, Chinese, Mixed White & Asian, Mixed White & Black African, and Other White ethnic groups.

For some groups, ethnic health inequalities that exist in London are not present in other regions. Women from the Other ethnic groups, and men from the Bangladeshi, Other Black, and Other minority ethnic groups who in 2011 lived in regions outside London had lower rates of limiting long-term illness than the White British group, whereas people from these ethnic groups living in London had higher illness rates. Arab men and women had considerably more limiting long-term illness than the White British group in London, but better health than the White British outside London.

Pakistani men were the only group to have better health than the White British group in London than outside London, although the differences are small (see Figure 9.8).

The pattern of health inequalities for the Indian ethnic group, which differs across genders (Indian men have lower rates of poor health than White British men, whereas Indian women have higher rates of poor health than White British women), also shows geographical differences. Indian men reported lower rates of limiting long-term illness as compared to White British men both outside and in the London region (see Figure 9.8). Indian women, however, reported slightly higher rates of limiting long-term illness than White British women in London, but slightly lower rates of limiting long-term illness than White British women outside of London (see Figure 9.9).

London and other regions in the South (South East, South West and East of England) have a better health profile than the Northern regions (Sloggett and Joshi, 1994). This North-South divide in health can be mostly explained by socioeconomic differences across regions, although there are also important socioeconomic differences *within* regions – London has high levels of socioeconomic inequalities, with some of the richest and poorest people in the country living in close proximity. London is also the most ethnically diverse region of England and Wales, which, together with its socioeconomic profile, creates a different pattern of ethnic health inequalities from the other regions. Although the health of minority ethnic people is better when they live in diverse areas, as compared to when they live in areas where a greater proportion of the residents is White (Bécares et al, 2009), the increased levels of socioeconomic inequality that exist in London place some minority ethnic groups in the lowest and most disadvantaged level of the inequality spectrum, patterning the health disadvantage observed in the regional analyses of census data.

Figure 9.8: Regional analysis of ethnic inequalities in limiting long-term illness for men, 2011

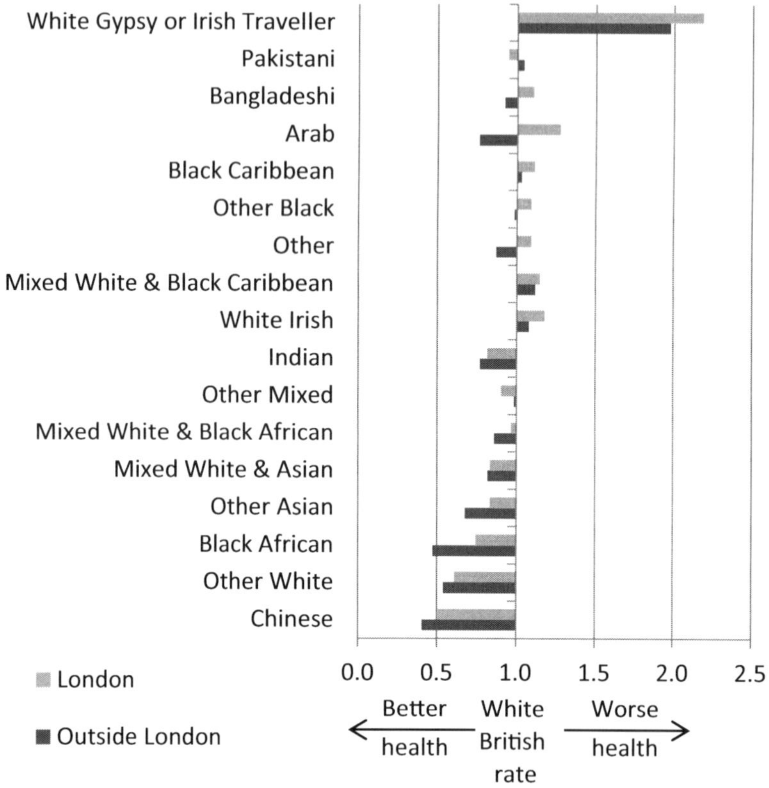

Note: Age-standardised illness ratio, each group relative to the White British group. A value of 0.5 indicates half the White British illness, and 2 indicates twice the White British illness. See information on age standardisation on page 125. Groups have been sorted in the chart from highest to lowest illness for women.

Conclusions and implications

This chapter shows that the health of the Pakistani, Bangladeshi, Black Caribbean and White Irish groups is much worse than the health of the White British group. These health inequalities can be observed from census data since 1991 (excluding the White Irish group, which was not measured in that census year). The 2011 Census results show marked inequalities between the health of the disadvantaged White Gypsy or Irish Traveller minority ethnic group, as compared to the health of the White British group. Although some minority ethnic groups, like the Chinese group, have better health than the White British group, persistent and pernicious inequalities in health have been consistently documented for the majority of minority ethnic groups.

Figure 9.9: Regional analysis of ethnic inequalities in limiting long-term illness for women, 2011

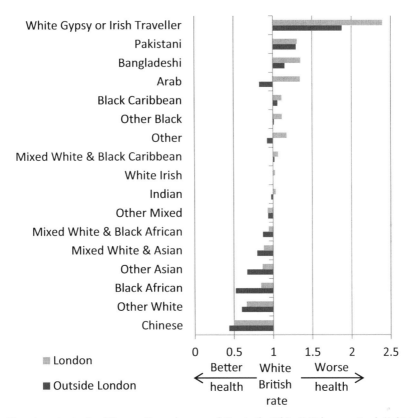

Note: Age-standardised illness ratio, each group relative to the White British group. A value of 0.5 indicates half the White British illness, and 2 indicates twice the White British illness. See information on age standardisation on page 125. Groups have been sorted in the chart from highest to lowest illness for women.

Marked gender inequalities within ethnic groups, when compared to the White group, are also observed in census data. For most minority groups, women report greater illness than men, relative to the White British group. Usually these gender differences are small. However, in 2011, Pakistani and Bangladeshi women had illness rates 20-25 per cent higher than White British women, while those groups' men have very similar illness to White British men. Furthermore, Indian women do not enjoy Indian men's 25 per cent advantage over White British health. Although women live longer than men, they experience higher rates of illness (Wingard et al, 1989). This inequality is not due to differences in health reporting (Macintyre et al, 1999), but to differential exposure to the determinants of health (Denton et al, 2004).

Health inequalities are preventable and unjust, and a reflection of underlying social inequalities. The ethnic and gender groups that suffer disproportionately from poorer health are also disadvantaged in terms of insecure housing tenure (Chapter Ten), reduced labour participation (Chapter Eleven), poorer educational outcomes (Chapter Twelve), and residence in the most deprived neighbourhoods (Chapter Thirteen). Findings in other sections of this book, which relate to the economic resources in our households, the safety of our neighbourhoods, the conditions of the houses we live in, and the quality of our education and subsequent employment opportunities, have severe implications for health, as they determine our levels of stress, availability of social and economic resources, exposure to health-promoting or health-deterring environments, and experiences of other harmful insults to health such as racism and discrimination. The unequal distribution of these socioeconomic factors across ethnic groups, and the influence that the underlying social inequalities have on health, pattern the inequalities in health experienced by some minority ethnic groups when compared to health of White British and of the England and Wales average.

Ethnic health inequalities can be reduced by improvements in the social status and living conditions of disadvantaged groups resulting from policies that explicitly target social inequalities. A recent publication suggested that to reduce ethnic inequalities in health in the short term, policies should focus on changing welfare, tax and benefit systems to decrease economic inequalities. However, much needed long-term policies must promote equitable life chances and address racism, discrimination and the marginalisation of people from different ethnic backgrounds (Nazroo, 2014).

Note

Further information about data and sources are available from http://www.ethnicity.ac.uk/dynamicsofdiversity/

References

Acheson, D. (1988) *Independent inquiry into inequalities in health (the Acheson Report)*, London: HMSO.

Bécares, L., Nazroo, J. and Stafford, M. (2009) 'The buffering effects of ethnic density on experienced racism and health', *Health & Place*, vol 15, pp 670-8.

Cohen, G., Forbes, J. and Garraway, M. (1995) 'Interpreting self reported limiting long term illness', *British Medical Journal*, vol 311, pp 722-24.

Commission on Social Determinants of Health (2008) *Closing the gap in a generation: Health equity through action on the social determinants of health*, Geneva: World Health Organization.

Davey Smith, G., Chaturvedi, N., Harding, S., Nazroo, J. and Williams, R. (2000) 'Ethnic inequalities in health: a review of UK epidemiological evidence', *Critical Public Health*, vol 10, no 4, pp 375-408.

Dahlgren, G. and Whitehead, M. (1991) *Policies and strategies to promote equity in health*, Copenhagen: Institute for Future Studies.

Denton, M., Prus, S. and Walters, V. (2004) 'Gender differences in health: a Canadian study of the psychosocial, structural and behavioural determinants of health', *Social Science & Medicine*, vol 58, no 12, pp 2585-600.

Idler, E. and Benyamini, Y. (1997) 'Self-rated health and mortality: a review of twenty-seven community studies', *Journal of Health and Social Behavior*, vol 38, no 1, pp 21-37.

Macintyre, S., Ford, G. and Hunt, K. (1999) 'Do women "over-report" morbidity? Men's and women's responses to structured prompting on a standard question on long-standing illness', *Social Science and Medicine*, vol 48, no 1, pp 89-98.

Nazroo, J.Y. (1997) *The health of Britain's ethnic minorities: Findings from a national survey*, London: Policy Studies Institute.

Nazroo, J.Y. (2003) 'The structuring of ethnic inequalities in health: economic position, racial discrimination and racism', *American Journal of Public Health*, vol 93, no 2, pp 277-84.

Nazroo, J.Y. (2014) *'Ethnic inequalities in health: Addressing a significant gap in current evidence and policy', in "If you could do one thing..." Nine local actions to reduce health inequalities*, London: The British Academy, pp 91-101.

Sloggett, A. and Joshi, H. (1994) 'Higher mortality in deprived areas: community or personal disadvantage?', *British Medical Journal*, vol 309, no 6967, pp 1470-4.

Sproston, K. and Mindell, J. (2006) *Health Survey for England 2004: The health of minority ethnic groups*, London: The NHS Information Centre.

Wingard, D.L., Cohn, B.A., Kaplan, G.A., Cirillo, P.M. and Cohen, R.D. (1989) 'Sex differentials in morbidity and mortality risks examined by age and cause in the same cohort', *American Journal of Epidemiology*, vol 130, no 3, pp 601-10.

TEN

Which ethnic groups are hardest hit by the 'housing crisis'?

Nissa Finney and Bethan Harries

Key findings

- Analyses of census data from 1991, 2001 and 2011 highlight stark and persistent ethnic inequalities in housing tenure and occupancy (overcrowding).
- The private rental sector is increasingly being relied on to make up for the shortfall in affordable homes to buy and the availability of social housing. The speed of increase in private renting between 1991 and 2011 was greatest for the Indian, Pakistani and Black Caribbean ethnic groups whose proportion in private renting more than doubled.
- Chinese, Black African, Bangladeshi and Pakistani ethnic groups have had persistently high levels of private renting over the last two decades.
- Concerns about a 'generation rent' are particularly relevant for the more than half of young adults in Indian, White Irish, Chinese and Arab groups and three-quarters of Other White young adults who live in privately rented accommodation.
- Ethnic inequalities in overcrowding persist: a third of households with a household reference person (HRP) who identifies as Bangladeshi are overcrowded, while over two-thirds of White British households have spare rooms.
- The 'housing crisis' has manifestations throughout the country that affect ethnic groups in different ways in different parts of England and Wales; it is not solely a London issue.
- To effectively remedy the 'housing crisis', policy needs to take account of the particular disadvantages facing some minority ethnic groups, and to distinguish

policy responses to address the needs of recent immigrants and persistent ethnic inequalities in housing.

Introduction: the 'housing crisis' and the significance of ethnicity

A 'housing crisis' has been identified in Britain by the housing charity Shelter and others (Smith et al, 2014), and housing issues have surfaced as key social and public policy issues. The main problem is disparity between housing need, provision and access, which is a consequence of economic, political and demographic factors including the globalisation of banking systems, shifts in the role of the welfare state as regards housing, neglected investment in housing infrastructure and changing demographics and living arrangements (Lowe, 2011; Pawson and Wilcox 2012). What this means in practice is that it has become more difficult for people to find adequate, affordable and secure accommodation in the place they want to live. This does not, however, affect people equally: some people are at greater housing disadvantage than others (Dorling, 2014). In this chapter we focus on how different ethnic groups are affected by housing disadvantage, and point to key areas of concern that require attention in attempts to redress housing inequalities.

At the core of the housing problem is the relationship between supply and demand. Although regeneration was a feature of urban change in the late 20th century, this focused on specific places rather than being part of a broader scheme to assess the long-term needs and sustainability of housing provision in Britain (Jones and Watkins, 1996). Overall there persists a deficiency in the number of homes and especially affordable homes, and the number of homes being built annually is failing to redress this balance. The Barker Review conducted in 2003 (Barker, 2004) identified the need for 260,000 private sector homes to be built annually in order to meet demand and to reduce house price inflation to 1.1 per cent. However, in England in the period 2003-14 the average number of new private houses built each year was just 114,000, and in the same period house prices rose annually on average by 9.1 per cent (ONS, 2014). The Barker Review also recommended that 17,000 homes be built per annum in England to meet the needs of social housing, yet, since 2003, the average number of new social houses each year (including local authority and housing association) has been 11,000 (ONS, 2014). In addition, the Homes and Communities Agency (2014) reported that during the period 2011-12 only 15,698 affordable homes were built (including affordable and intermediate rent, social rent and affordable home ownership).

The lack of housing and of affordable housing means that the size and role of the private rental market is changing. Private renting is providing the only viable option for many people who cannot afford to buy and cannot access social housing. This is worrying because, while in other parts of Europe private renting is a norm for secure, long-term housing, it remains the most precarious and insecure form of tenure in the UK. This is because the private rented sector in the UK is largely unregulated, which contrasts with the situation in other European counties. Private renting can offer flexibility which can suit people at particular life stages and in particular labour markets, but the insecurity of tenure and the associated concerns about lack of regulation of landlords, unpredictability of rental prices and maintenance of private rental housing can have adverse effects on people's lives, especially on families with young children (Ball, 2010; Albanese, 2013). Furthermore, there is concern over the cost and condition of housing stock on offer (Jones, 2010), and over the prospects for young people who are at a particular disadvantage in the context of rising house prices and a constricting social housing sector. The housing charity, Shelter, has described this as the creation of a 'generation rent' (Lindsay and Earley, 2013) in which young people increasingly have to rely on the private rented sector.

Due to the lack of available and affordable housing and reduced mortgage lending, there is also an emerging trend for young people to live longer at their parents' homes. The percentage of young adults living with their parents in the UK in 2013 was 26 per cent (ONS, 2013), and it is predicted that more than half of those aged 20-34 will be living with their parents by 2040 (Smith et al, 2014). This raises concerns about the possibilities of overcrowded housing conditions.

In this chapter we investigate how two key markers of the 'housing crisis' – the rise in private renting and overcrowding – have affected ethnic groups differently. It is important to consider how ethnic groups experience housing in order to develop policies and interventions that take heed of any differences. There is already evidence that some ethnic groups are discriminated against in the housing market (Harrison and Phillips, 2003) and reside disproportionately in poorer parts of cities (Phillips, 1998). We also know (and other chapters in this book demonstrate) that ethnic inequalities persist in a number of other spheres including in employment, education and health, and these have direct social and economic consequences for people's housing trajectories.

This chapter highlights how ethnic inequalities in housing manifest and are experienced. It lays out the key areas in which inequalities are evident across the different ethnic groups identified in the census categories for 1991, 2001 and 2011 in the following areas of housing concern: differences in tenure, the rise in private renting and levels of overcrowding and under-occupancy.

How do we know about people's housing situation? Data and measures from England and Wales censuses

This chapter uses two indicators of housing situation: tenure and occupancy rating. Tenure is used to indicate the security of housing; occupancy rating measures the degree to which housing size is appropriate for the number, age and sexes of the residents.

Measuring household or individual characteristics?

2011 Census data on tenure and occupancy are published for people and households. However, for 1991 and 2001, the equivalent tables are available for households but not people. It is therefore only in the analyses presented for 2011 that the units of analysis are people. In the analyses that make comparisons over time we use data for households. In these data, the ethnic group of the HRP is used to characterise the ethnic group of the household. In effect, the assumption is that all people within a household identify with the same ethnic group, although the 2011 Census shows that 12 per cent of households with two or more people in England and Wales have more than one ethnic group within them (see Chapter Two). Slightly different results are obtained if data on ethnic group of people are used, but this does not change the substantive findings of this chapter.

How does the census find out about tenure?
The 2011 Census data on tenure originate from these census questions:

Does your household own or rent this accommodation?
    Owns outright
    Owns with a mortgage or loan
    Part owns and part rents (shared ownership)
    Rents (with or without Housing Benefit)
    Lives here rent-free

Who is your landlord? (Asked of individuals who do not own their accommodation)
    Housing association, housing cooperative, charitable trust, registered social landlord
    Council (local authority)
    Private landlord or letting agency
    Employer of a household member
    Relative or friend of a household member
    Other

Tenure data based on similar questions are available from the 1991 and 2001 Censuses, and are used in this chapter.

To reflect different experiences of housing security, we have condensed the responses to these questions into three categories: home ownership (with or without a mortgage), social renting (renting from a housing association or similar or from a local authority), and private renting (renting from another individual or organisation). Home ownership can be considered the most secure form of tenure affording ownership rights. Private renting can be considered the least secure form of tenure because it does not offer assurance for stay in the property or an assured standard of maintenance, because private landlords are less regulated than social landlords.

How does the census find out about overcrowding?
The 2011 Census data measures overcrowding using an 'occupancy rating'. It is calculated from information from the census household questions which identify who usually lives at the address, the number of people who usually live there and the relationship between residents, together with the age and sex of each resident, all of which are combined with responses to the following questions:

How many rooms are available for use only by this household?

Do not count bathrooms, toilets, halls or landings, rooms that can only be used for storage such as cupboards

Count all other rooms, for example: kitchens, living rooms, utility rooms, bedrooms, studies, conservatories

If two rooms have been converted into one, count them as one room

How many of these rooms are bedrooms?

Include all rooms built or converted for use as bedrooms, even if they are not currently used as bedrooms

An occupancy rating of 0 indicates that the accommodation meets the requirements of the residents, a value of 1 or greater indicates the number of rooms in the accommodation that are in addition to the required number, and a value of −1 or less indicates by how many rooms the accommodation does not meet the needs of the residents. Thus, an occupancy rating of 0 shows required size accommodation, a positive value shows under-occupancy, and a negative value shows overcrowding. In 2001 Census tables, occupancy was calculated on the basis of number of rooms. In the 2011 Census tables, occupancy was calculated on the basis of number of rooms and number of bedrooms.

These definitions are used to inform government policy, for example, on entitlement to social housing (as outlined in the Welfare Reform Act 2012 which includes the measure commonly known as the 'Bedroom Tax' or 'size criteria' for social housing allocation). In government and policy, occupancy measures based on rooms have been superseded by occupancy based on bedrooms. It is also noteworthy that these measures of occupancy are a shift from overcrowding defined as people per room that has been provided since the 1971 Census.

Census definitions of room requirements and bedroom requirements used to calculate occupancy ratings

The Office for National Statistics (ONS) measures occupancy using the ages of the household members and their relationships to each other to derive the number of rooms and bedrooms required, as below (ONS, 2011):

- The 2001 Census calculation of room standard is based on the definition described in the Housing Act 1985. The 2011 Census calculation of bedroom standard is based on the Housing Overcrowding Bill 2003.
- A bedroom is defined as any room that was intended to be used as a bedroom when the property was built, or any room that has been permanently converted for use as a bedroom. It also includes all rooms intended for use as a bedroom even if not being used as a bedroom at the time of the census.
- Bedsits and studio flats are counted as having one bedroom.
- A one-person household requires three rooms including one bedroom.

The *room* requirements for a multi-person household used in the 2001 and 2011 Censuses are:

1   One room per couple or lone parent
2   One room per person aged 16 and above who is not a lone parent or in a couple
3   One room for every two males aged 10-15, rounded down
4   One room for every pair of males of whom one is aged 10-15 and one is aged 0-9, if there are an odd number of males aged 10-15
5   One room for a remaining unpaired male aged 10-15
6   Repeat steps 3-5 for females
7   One room for every two remaining children aged 0-9 (regardless of gender), rounded up
8   Add two rooms to this total.

The *bedroom* requirements for a multi-person household used in the 2011 Census are:

1   One bedroom per couple
2   One bedroom per person aged 21 or over not in a couple
3   One bedroom for every two males aged 10-20, rounded down
4   One bedroom for every pair of males of whom one is aged 10-20 and one is aged 0-9, if there are an odd number of males aged 10-20
5   One bedroom for a remaining unpaired male aged 10-20
6   Repeat steps 3-5 for females
7   One bedroom for every two remaining children aged 0-9 (regardless of gender), rounded up.

Who is most affected by the rise of private renting?

In 2011, 9.8 million people in England and Wales (or 18 per cent of the population) were living in privately rented accommodation. This equates to almost one in five households (18 per cent), an increase from one in eight a decade earlier (12 per cent), as shown in Figure 10.1. The increase equates to an additional 1.6 million households renting privately in 2011 compared with 2001, representing a 63 per cent increase over that decade. In comparison, the number of households in owned and social rented accommodation has remained stable, meaning that over the decade 2001-11 the proportion of households who owned their accommodation and who rented from a social landlord decreased (from 69 to 64 per cent and 19 to 18 per cent respectively). This shift in the tenure patterns of England and Wales represents an important social change over the 2000s.

Has this rise in private renting affected ethnic groups equally? Certainly not – census data tell us that some ethnic groups have experienced particularly large increases in private renting since 1991, and that there were large ethnic differences in private renting in 2011. The highest levels of private renting have consistently been recorded for the Chinese and Black African groups, in 1991, 2001 and

Figure 10.1: Number of households in owned, social rented and private rented accommodation, 2001 and 2011, England and Wales

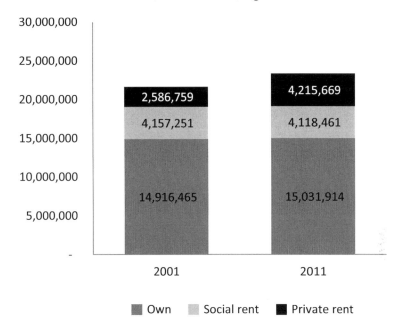

Figure 10.2: Percentage of ethnic groups in private rented accommodation, 1991, 2001, 2011 (England and Wales)

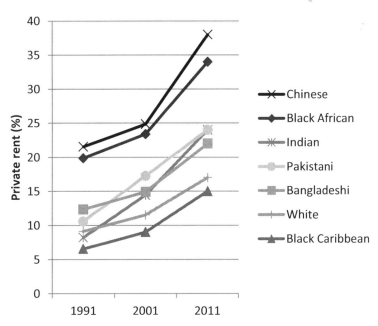

2011; proportions in private renting have been consistently lowest over the two decades for White and Black Caribbean ethnic groups.

All ethnic groups have seen an increase in the proportion of their population living in private rented housing since 1991 and the rate of increase has escalated since 2001 for all groups. Figure 10.2 gives the changes in the proportion of people living in private rented accommodation between 1991, 2001 and 2011, with a line for each ethnic group. The speed of increase in private renting between 1991 and 2011 was greatest for the Indian, Pakistani and Black Caribbean populations whose proportion in private renting more than doubled. The case of the Indian ethnic group is particularly notable: over the 20 years from 1991 to 2001 the proportion of this ethnic group in private rented accommodation grew from 8 to 24 per cent.

If we consider 2011 Census data only, it is possible to look at more detailed ethnic group categories. Figure 10.3 gives the percentage of each ethnic group in private rented, social rented and owned accommodation in 2011, for households (ethnic group determined by HRP). When we compare data based on people and data based on households, there is little difference in the proportions of

Figure 10.3: Percentage of 18 ethnic groups in owned, private rented and social rented accommodation, 2011, England and Wales

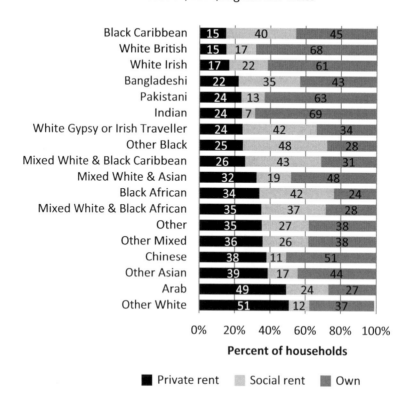

ethnic groups across the three main tenures and in the ranking of ethnic groups according to the proportion in private renting. When we focus on the results based on households, the chart shows that there is a more than three-fold variation between ethnic groups in the proportion in private renting. This ranges from 15 per cent for Black Caribbean and White British groups to 50 per cent for Arab and Other White groups. The Arab and Other White groups are notable for their high levels of private renting in 2011 (49 and 51 per cent respectively). This can partly be explained by these groups comprising recent immigrants from origins such as Europe, the US and Australia (see Chapter Three).

Is there a 'generation rent' for all ethnic groups?

Young adults are particularly disadvantaged in terms of purchasing a home in the current economic climate of increased competition for employment, stagnant incomes, rising housing prices and more restrictive access to mortgage products. The concerns of a 'generation rent' may, however, be particularly pertinent for some ethnic groups. Figure 10.4 shows that levels of private renting are higher for young adults than for the population as a whole: at least a third of young

Figure 10.4: Percentage aged 25-34 in owned, private rented and social rented accommodation, by ethnic group, 2011, England and Wales

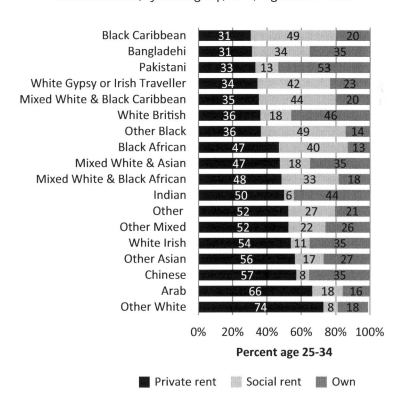

adults in all ethnic groups lived in private rented housing in 2011, more than half of young adults in Indian, White Irish, Chinese and Arab groups, and as many as three-quarters of Other White young adults. For other groups, however, there is quite a different housing story. The tenure profile of Black Caribbean young adults is noteworthy: a relatively low proportion live in private rented accommodation (15 per cent) while a high proportion live in social rented and owned accommodation (40 and 45 per cent respectively). For young adults of other ethnic groups one form of tenure tends to dominate. Social housing was the most common tenure for Mixed White & Black Caribbean, Other Black and White Gypsy or Irish Traveller young adults. In comparison, high levels of home ownership for White British (46 per cent), Indian (44 per cent) and in particular, Pakistani young adults (53 per cent), suggest security of tenure for these young adults. One factor here may be the tendency for Pakistani and Bangladeshi ethnic groups to live in more deprived neighbourhoods where there are familial and cultural connections, and where house prices are more affordable. Owning a home in a deprived neighbourhood can, however, bring its own housing market restrictions. Owner-occupiers in deprived neighbourhoods can find it difficult to afford a move to a better quality neighbourhood because of the house price difference between these places.

How do levels of private renting vary across England and Wales?

The proportion of people living in private rented housing varies between local authority districts in England and Wales: each ethnic group has a distinct geography of private renting. This is illustrated in Figure 10.5 (a, b and c) for three ethnic groups: the White British group, the Black Caribbean group, who had the lowest level of private renting in 2011, and the Other White group, who had the highest level of private renting in 2011. For the White British group, districts with the highest levels of private renting are clustered in London plus other large cities such as Manchester and Birmingham. In contrast, the Black Caribbean group, whose average national level of private renting is only a little less than the White British, has its lowest levels of private renting in London. This reflects the importance of social housing for this ethnic group in the capital.

Figure 10.5c depicts geographical variation in private renting for the Other White ethnic group, and illustrates its significance for this group throughout the country. High levels of private renting are found not only in large cities but also in more rural areas such as in North Yorkshire, Lincolnshire and Mid Wales. This is likely to reflect the high levels of mobility of the Other White group, associated with its young age structure and high proportion of recent economic migrants, as well as the locations of temporary and seasonal work. The private rental market can meet a preference for being able to move quickly to employment opportunities for some people in this population group in traditional and non-traditional immigrant settlement areas. It can also leave people particularly at risk of insecure tenure and rental price rises in a precarious housing sector.

Figure 10.5: Private renting across England and Wales, percentage of ethnic group (people), local authority districts, 2011

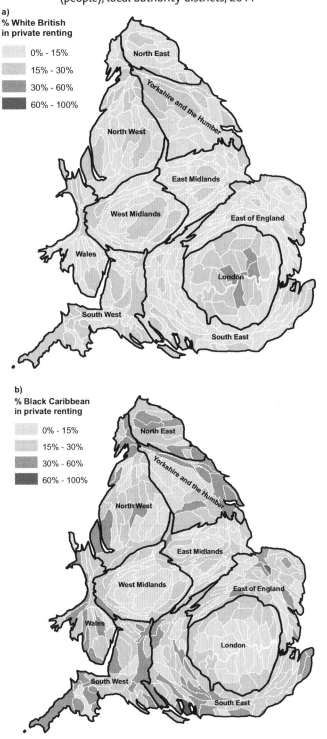

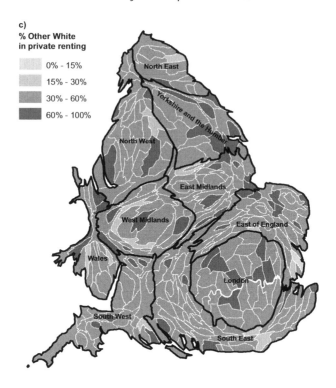

c)
% Other White
in private renting

- 0% - 15%
- 15% - 30%
- 30% - 60%
- 60% - 100%

North East

Yorkshire and the Humber

North West

East Midlands

West Midlands

East of England

Wales

London

South West

South East

What is happening to home ownership?

Although the preference for home ownership is common across ethnic groups (Harries et al, 2008), there are stark differences between groups in levels of home ownership. Between 1991 and 2011 levels of home ownership decreased for all ethnic groups, but particularly so for Pakistani, Chinese and Indian households.

Despite this decline, home ownership levels are high, and remain the dominant experience for households of Indian (69 per cent of households), White British (68 per cent), Pakistani (63 per cent), White Irish (61 per cent) and Chinese (51 per cent) ethnic groups. Home ownership in 2011 is notably low for Black African (24 per cent) and Arab (27 per cent) households. This may reflect the disadvantaged position of these groups in the labour market (see Chapter Eleven) and resulting difficulties obtaining mortgages to buy a home.

What is happening to social housing?

The trend in social renting has been one of decline: in 2011 a smaller proportion of most ethnic groups lived in social rented housing than in 1991. The proportional decrease in social rented housing between 1991 and 2011 was greatest for the Chinese and Indian ethnic groups. There remain, however, persistent differences between ethnic groups in levels of social housing.

In 2011 the Black African, and also the Other Black, White Gypsy or Irish Traveller and Mixed White & Black Caribbean groups, had the highest proportions of their population in social rented housing – over 40 per cent for each of these groups. Social renting is lowest for the Indian (7 per cent), Chinese (11 per cent), Other White (12 per cent) and Pakistani (13 per cent) groups.

The Bangladeshi and Pakistani ethnic groups were the only ones to see a rise in social renting between 1991 and 2001, which may reflect the success of housing strategies in the 1990s to improve access of minority ethnic groups to social housing. Between 2001 and 2011 these groups, consistent with all others, saw a decrease in social housing.

Who lives in overcrowded housing?

Figure 10.6 indicates the proportion of each ethnic group in 2011 that was in under-occupied housing, overcrowded housing and housing that meets the standard and statutory requirements based on number of bedrooms. Bangladeshi, Pakistani and Black African households have the highest levels of overcrowding (30, 22 and 22 per cent of households respectively); White British and White

Figure 10.6: Percentage of ethnic groups in under-occupied, required size and overcrowded accommodation, based on number of bedrooms, 2011, England and Wales

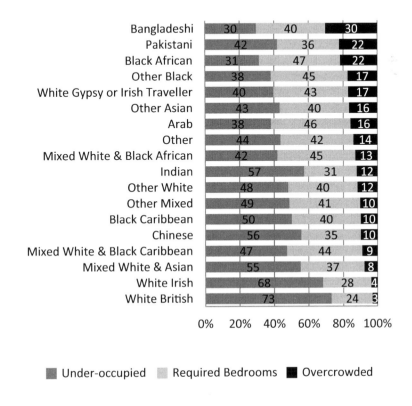

153

Irish groups have lowest levels of overcrowding (3 and 4 per cent of households respectively).

For censuses prior to 2011, the statutory measure of overcrowding was based on rooms, rather than bedrooms (see 'How does the census find out about overcrowding?' earlier). The room-based measure gives a similar range and ranking of overcrowding across ethnic groups as the bedroom-based measure: from 6 per cent of White British to 35 per cent of Black African and Bangladeshi ethnic groups in overcrowded accommodation (see Figure 10.7). However, levels of overcrowding are higher for each ethnic group when calculated on the basis of rooms compared with bedrooms: the newer bedroom-based measure implies lower levels of overcrowding. This is particularly marked for the Arab, Black African and Chinese ethnic groups, and suggests that the switch to a bedroom-based measure of overcrowding hides the experience of these ethnic groups having fewer than the required number of rooms for daily life activities other than sleeping.

The data relating to under-occupancy in 2011 highlight how there are considerable ethnic differences in whether a household has spare rooms. The proportion of households in each ethnic group that has at least one 'spare' bedroom varies from under a third of the Bangladeshi and Black African ethnic groups to more than two-thirds of the White British and White Irish ethnic

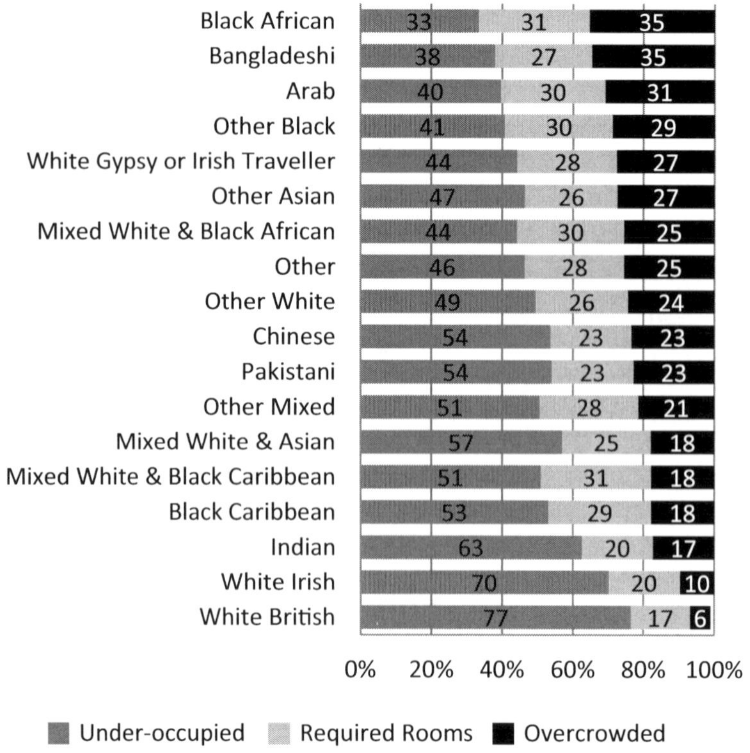

Figure 10.7: Percentage of ethnic groups in under-occupied, required size and overcrowded accommodation, based on number of rooms, 2011, England and Wales

groups (Figure 10.6). Four times as many White British as Black African and Bangladeshi groups live in houses with two or more spare bedrooms. For White British and White Irish ethnic groups, 36 per cent live in households with two or more spare bedrooms, whereas for the Black African ethnic group, the figure is 9 per cent, and for the Bangladeshi ethnic group, 10 per cent. It has been argued that chronic under-occupancy represents reproduction of inequalities as the wealthy effectively store their assets in surplus rooms (Dorling, 2014). These data show that this inequality is not only manifest along lines of wealth or class, but also ethnicity.

It is possible to compare change over time in overcrowding and under-occupancy using the room-based measure available in both 2001 and 2011 Census data. Figure 10.8 shows that during this decade levels of overcrowding decreased, particularly for Black African and Bangladeshi groups, and ethnic inequalities were reduced. Nevertheless, levels of overcrowding (based on rooms) remain high, at over a third of Bangladeshi and Black African households in 2011.

Figure 10.8: Percentage of ethnic group in overcrowded accommodation, 2001 and 2011 (rooms)

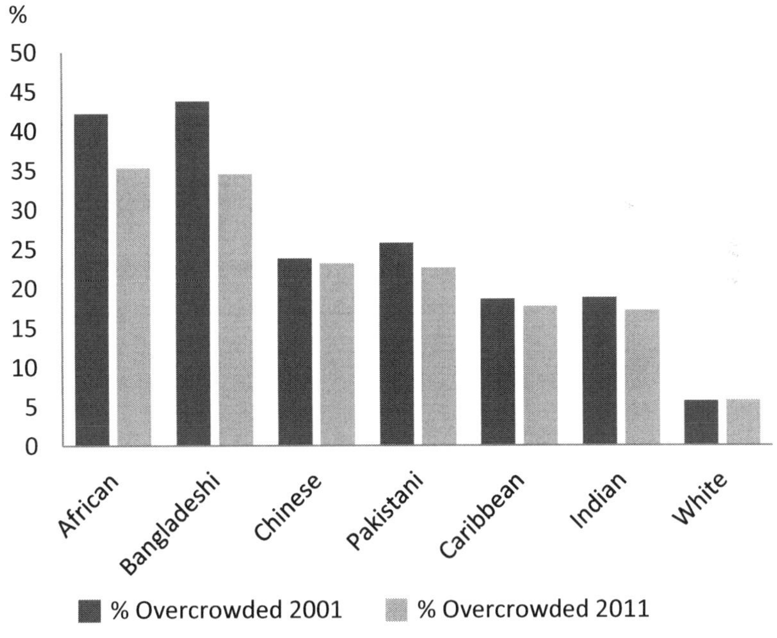

Is overcrowding worse in some parts of England and Wales?

The places where different ethnic groups experience overcrowding most are not the same. Figure 10.9 (a, b and c) illustrates the geographical variation in overcrowding by presenting maps for three ethnic groups, White British, Pakistani and Black African, with distinct and contrasting patterns. High levels of

Figure 10.9: Percentage of households in districts of England that are overcrowded, 2011

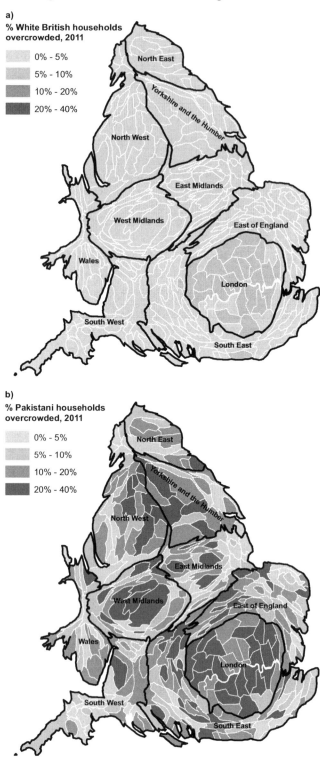

Which ethnic groups are hardest hit by the 'housing crisis'?

c)
% Black African households overcrowded, 2011

- 0% - 5%
- 5% - 10%
- 10% - 20%
- 20% - 40%

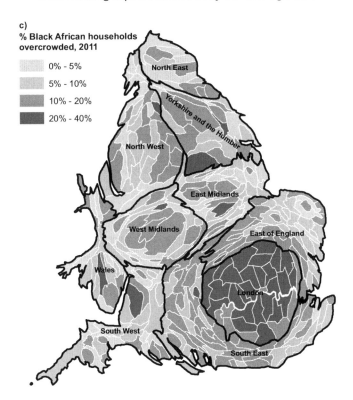

North East

Yorkshire and the Humber

North West

East Midlands

West Midlands

East of England

Wales

London

South West

South East

overcrowding are concentrated in London: one in five Black African households in inner and North London is overcrowded and White British overcrowding is highest in inner London. However, for some ethnic groups, London should not be the focus as far as overcrowding is concerned. For the Pakistani ethnic group, for example, the cartogram shows that there are high levels of overcrowding in districts in the Midlands and north of England, with one in four Pakistani households being overcrowded in some of these areas.

Conclusions and implications

The 'housing crisis' raises questions of the role of the state in housing provision, both in terms of planning and building, and welfare policies. Housing status in Britain is a clear marker and producer of wealth inequalities, and our analysis of census data has demonstrated that there are stark ethnic differences in who is advantaged in terms of housing. It seems pertinent that those attempting to understand and address contemporary housing problems pay attention to who is being hardest hit.

The 63 per cent proportional increase in private renting between 2001 and 2011 represents a major social shift in Britain, where this tenure can be considered to be insecure. On average a fifth of households rent privately, but this is higher for minority ethnic groups – a third of Chinese and Black African households, and half of Arab and Other White households. It is these households who are in the most precarious housing situations. Concerns about a 'generation rent' can also be directed to certain ethnic groups: Other White, Indian, White Irish, Chinese and Arab.

The shift to private renting over the last two decades has been particularly marked for Pakistani, Black Caribbean and Indian ethnic groups. The case of the Indian group, a relatively advantaged ethnic group in other respects (see Chapters Nine, Eleven and Twelve), is noteworthy as it has seen a tripling of its proportion renting privately since 1991, together with one of the largest decreases in home ownership and persistently the lowest levels of social renting. Unpicking the housing story of the Indian ethnic group, and others, will require further investigation.

However, the Indian case does draw attention to the need to distinguish between recent immigrants and more established residents for understanding ethnic differences in housing experience. This has not been possible with the census data available for this chapter, but will be an important feature of future work. For example, the Indian ethnic group is comprised of established first, second and third generation migrants, and a relatively large number of young adults who have migrated to Britain in the 2000s (see Chapter Three). The housing experience of these sub-populations of the Indian ethnic group may be very different, with the established residents accounting for the high levels of home ownership and the recent immigration accounting for the high levels and large increase in private renting. Policy will need to respond to both the housing needs of recent immigrants, and the persistent housing disadvantage of some established minority ethnic groups.

This chapter has evidenced how the growth in the private rental sector in England and Wales means that a majority of some ethnic groups, particularly where young adults are concerned, now live in this tenure. It is therefore imperative that action is taken to address the insecurity of private renting, for example, in terms of rent control, length of tenancy agreements and quality of housing, if deepening of the 'housing crisis' is to be avoided.

There is a positive story on overcrowding: levels of overcrowding and ethnic inequalities have reduced slightly over the 2000s. However, it remains the case that one in three Bangladeshi households are overcrowded while over two-thirds of White British households have spare rooms. Furthermore, overcrowding affects ethnic groups differently in different parts of the country: in some districts of England and Wales one in four Pakistani households live in overcrowded accommodation.

The reasons for ethnic differences in overcrowding (and, indeed, other aspects of housing) are not well understood. It is likely that the socioeconomic disadvantages for some minority ethnic groups demonstrated in other chapters of this book are a large part of the explanation. There may also be demographic drivers, to do with ethnic variations in household size and living arrangements. Although there is convergence over time between ethnic groups in the number of children in a household, some minority ethnic groups, notably Indian, Pakistani and Bangladeshi groups, continue to have larger than average households due to multigenerational living (Catney and Simpson, 2013). This raises a challenge for policymakers about how housing provision and regulation can respond to variation in household composition and the ongoing need for larger accommodation.

The findings of this chapter about ethnic inequalities in housing would have remained hidden without the rich and high-quality UK census data. A particular and unique quality of these census data is not only that they allow detailed analysis for relatively small (minority ethnic) sub-groups of the population, but also that they allow policy analysts to look at the experience for neighbourhoods across the country. In terms of tenure and overcrowding, it is clear that the 'housing crisis' is widespread and not confined to London and the South East of England.

After a period of relatively little interest in housing in political spheres, and among those concerned with social inequalities, the results from this chapter are a call for housing inequalities to feature more prominently, and for the ethnic dimension of these inequalities to be given due attention. After all, the housing conditions in which we live have very real implications for our everyday lives, and a society concerned with social justice should be troubled that some minority groups are so starkly disadvantaged.

Note
Further information about data and sources are available from
http://www.ethnicity.ac.uk/dynamicsofdiversity/

References

Albanese, F. (2013) *Growing up renting: A childhood spent in private rented homes*, London: Shelter.

Ball, M. (2010) *The UK private rented sector as a source of affordable accommodation*, York: Joseph Rowntree Foundation.

Barker, K. (2004) *Review of housing supply*, Norwich: HMSO.

Catney, G. and Simpson, L. (2013) 'How persistent is demographic variation between ethnic groups? The case of household size in England and Wales', *Population, Space and Place*, vol 20, pp 201-21.

Dorling, D. (2014) *All that is solid: How the great housing disaster defines our times, and what we can do about it*, London: Penguin.

Harries, B., Richardson, L. and Soteri-Proctor, A. (2008) *Housing aspirations for a new generation: Perspectives from white and South Asian British women*, York and London: Joseph Rowntree Foundation and Chartered Institute for Housing.

Harrison, M. and Phillips, D. (2003) *Housing and black and minority ethnic communities: Review of the evidence base*, London: Office of the Deputy Prime Minister.

Homes and Communities Agency (2014) *Housing statistics* (www.homesandcommunities.co.uk/housing-statistics).

Jones, A. (2010) *Black and minority ethnic communities' experience of overcrowding*, Better Housing Briefing 16, London: Race Equality Foundation.

Jones, C. and Watkins, C. (1996) 'Urban regeneration and sustainable markets', *Urban Studies*, vol 33, no 7, pp 1129-40.

Lindsay, D. and Earley, F. (2013) *A home of their own*, London: Shelter.

Lowe, S. (2011) *The housing debate*, Bristol: Policy Press.

ONS (Office for National Statistics) (2011) *Census quality notes and classifications*, Newport: ONS (www.ons.gov.uk/ons/guide-method/census/2011/census-data/2011-census-user-guide/quality-and-methods/quality/quality-notes-and-clarifications/index.html).

ONS (2013) *Young adults living with parents in the UK, 2013*, Newport: ONS (www.ons.gov.uk/ons/rel/family-demography/young-adults-living-with-parents/2013/info-young-adults.html).

ONS (2014) *Live tables on house building*, Newport: ONS (www.gov.uk/government/statistical-data-sets/live-tables-on-house-building).

Pawson, H. and Wilcox, S. (2012) *UK housing review, 2012 briefing paper*, Coventry: Chartered Institute of Housing.

Phillips, D. (1998) 'Black minority ethnic concentration, segregation and dispersal in Britain', *Urban Studies*, vol 35, no 10, pp 1681-702.

Smith, M., Albanese, F. and Truder, J. (2014) *A roof over my head: The final report of the Sustain project, a longitudinal study of housing outcomes and wellbeing in private rented accommodation*, London: Shelter and Crisis.

ELEVEN

Have ethnic inequalities in the labour market persisted?

Dharmi Kapadia, James Nazroo and Ken Clark

Key findings

- Younger (aged 25-49) White men had a consistent advantage in the labour market between 1991 and 2011 compared with those in other ethnic groups, who were more likely to be not working or working in less secure employment.
- White women aged 25-49 also had a consistent employment advantage over the last 20 years compared with women in other ethnic groups.
- Exceptions to the pattern of White advantage were Indian and Chinese men, whose initial high unemployment and self-employment rates converged with those of the White group over the 20-year period. Black Caribbean women had similar labour market participation rates to White women from 1991 to 2011.
- At older ages (50-74), Black African men and women had the highest rates of labour market participation over the past 20 years. This is likely due to the age structure of the Black African group, where there are relatively few people aged over 65.
- Younger Pakistani and Bangladeshi men saw large falls in unemployment rates over the period 1991-2011 (respectively, from 25 to 10 per cent and from 26 to 11 per cent), but unemployment rates for these groups remain much higher than for White men.
- Black Caribbean and Black African younger men had rates of unemployment consistently more than double those of White men throughout the period 1991-2011.
- For Bangladeshi men, the fall in unemployment was balanced by a rise in part-time work; the 11-fold increase in part-time work for this group between 1991

and 2011 was larger than for any other ethnic group. In 2011, over one-third of Bangladeshi working men were employed part time.

- Pakistani and Bangladeshi women were the least likely, in the 25- to 49-year-old age group, to be in the labour market, but also experienced the highest rises in rates of economic activity between 1991 and 2011 (from 24 to 43 per cent for Pakistani women and from 17 to 40 per cent for Bangladeshi women).
- In the 50- to 74-year-old age group Pakistani and Bangladeshi women were the least likely to be in the labour market. From 1991 to 2011, these were the only groups that had increases in the proportion of women out of the labour market due to sickness.
- The advantage of younger White women in relation to unemployment reduced over the period, but was still present in 2011. Unemployment rates were particularly high for Bangladeshi (19 per cent), Black African (17 per cent), Pakistani (15 per cent), and Black Caribbean (11 per cent) women.

Introduction

Minority ethnic groups in England and Wales have a history of lower rates of employment and higher rates of unemployment than the White majority population (Clark and Drinkwater, 2007). Previous research indicates that this can be partly explained by between group differences in demographic and other characteristics, but substantial disadvantage remains even after these are taken into account. This unexplained ethnic penalty is thought to be due to racial and religious discrimination inherent in job application processes and the workplace (Modood, 1997; Heath and Cheung, 2006), as well as the geographical concentration of some groups in deprived areas with less access to thriving labour markets (Simpson et al, 2006). Some minority ethnic groups are further disadvantaged due to their increased likelihood to be employed in insecure, low-paid jobs (Brynin and Guveli, 2012).

The Department for Work and Pensions (DWP) has put in place policies to address these inequalities, with initiatives such as Ethnic Minority Outreach, specialist employment advisers and Partners Outreach for Ethnic Minorities, and with the establishment of the Ethnic Minority Employment Stakeholder Group. The success of these policies and initiatives to increase minority ethnic employment has been limited, and ethnic inequalities in employment are still apparent (Bourn, 2008).

Using census data from 1991, 2001 and 2011, we document changes over time to understand the degree to which inequalities have persisted over the last 20 years. We first present the changes in labour market activity for both younger and older workers from 1991 to 2011, using seven ethnic groups that are comparable over time (see Chapter One). Next we present a more detailed picture of the labour market experiences of the 18 ethnic group categories used in the 2011 Census. Finally we consider the policy implications of the ethnic differences in labour market participation.

Definitions

Economic activity: people are classed as economically active if they are in employment or actively looking for work. This category consists of people who are employed, self-employed or unemployed. The terms 'economic activity' and 'labour market participation' are used interchangeably throughout this chapter. People who are retired, students, looking after the home or family, or long-term sick or have a disability are classed as economically *inactive*. Among the economically active, we distinguish four categories:

- *Unemployed:* people who are not in employment and are either actively looking for work, or waiting to start jobs that they have already obtained.
- *Self-employed:* people who operate their own businesses or enterprises or work freelance, with or without employees. This category contains those who are self-employed, either full time or part time.
- *Full-time employment:* working 31 or more hours per week in a main job, including paid and unpaid overtime, but not self-employed. For 1991 data, those who were 'on a government scheme' have been put in the same category as those in full-time employment.
- *Part-time employment:* working 30 or less hours per week in a main job, including paid and unpaid overtime, but not self-employed.

In Figures 11.7 and 11.8 we show the percentage of the economically active population and the percentage of the total population in full-time work (full- and part-time work for women). It is important to look at both measures, as the unemployment rate (based on only those who are economically active) is subject to fluctuations in different periods due to the economic climate (that is, number of vacancies) and contemporary welfare benefit rules.

For most of the data presented here, economically active full-time students are excluded from numerators and denominators in calculations. The exception is the 1991 data, where economically active students are subsumed into the full-time, part-time and self-employed totals, and therefore cannot be removed from the counts.

The census data reflect levels of economic activity, unemployment, hours of employment and self-employment. They do not allow us to examine whether some ethnic groups are more concentrated in employment associated with poorer working conditions (for example, less secure jobs, or jobs with poorer promotion prospects), or whether the wage level may be on average less for some ethnic groups, including being paid less for equivalent work.

Younger and older working age groups

We have defined younger workers as those aged 25-49. This is the group where economic activity is highest, at over 85 per cent, compared with the national average of 63 per cent. This age category also contains few retired people and students.

We have classed those who are aged 50-74 as older workers. The upper age limit is above the current state pension age, so those at the younger end of this age group are more likely to be in the labour market compared to those that are older. However, this age breakdown was the only one available in the 2011 Census at the time of writing. Other research, from the Labour Force Survey, suggests that the economic activity rates of 50- to 74-year-old men is 10 to 15 percentage points lower than for men below the state pension age (50- to 64-year-olds); for women, it is up to 30 percentage points lower compared with those below the state pension age (50- to 59-year-olds). The state pension age for women increased in 2010, but in 2011, women aged 60 were eligible for a state pension.

For Figures 11.3 and 11.4, we have used the categories 'economically active', 'retired', 'permanently sick' and 'other inactive'. The 'other inactive' category consists of economically inactive students, those looking after the home and family and other inactive. Students made up a very small (although increasing) percentage of this older age group (0.05 per cent of all people in 1991, 0.15 per cent in 2001 and 0.24 per cent in 2011). Those looking after the home and family were not separately identified in the 1991 data. Therefore, in Figures 11.3 and 11.4, we include economically inactive students, those looking after the home and family and other inactive as one group.

Change in labour market participation, 1991-2001-2011

White men aged 25–49 had a consistently higher rate of labour market participation compared with men in other ethnic groups, with the exception of Indian men, over the period 1991–2011 (see Table 11.1). The difference between White men and all minority ethnic groups, except for Indian and Chinese groups, widened during the 1990s, and then narrowed by 2011 to 1991 levels for all groups, except Black Caribbean and Black African men. Men in most ethnic groups saw a small decline in labour market participation over the 20 years, but for men in the Black African group, participation rates increased from 75 per cent in 1991 to 84 per cent in 2011. This closed the gap between White men and Black African men; however, there remained an 8-percentage point deficit relative to the White men's rate of 92 per cent in 2011.

There were also large differences between ethnic groups in terms of economic activity for older male workers (aged 50–74). For this age group, Black African men had consistently the highest rate of economic activity of any ethnic group between 1991 (71 per cent) and 2011 (75 per cent). Older working men in all ethnic groups saw a large drop in economic activity between 1991 and 2001, except for White men, who had only a 1 percentage point decrease. This sharp fall was greatest for Bangladeshi (from 61 per cent in 1991 to 26 per cent), Pakistani (61 to 39 per cent) and Black Caribbean (69 to 43 per cent) men. During the 2000s, the economic activity rate in this age group rose for all ethnic groups and by the greatest amount for those that had the sharpest fall in the 1990s, including Bangladeshi (26 to 51 per cent), Black Caribbean (43 to 62 per cent) and Pakistani (39 to 58 per cent) groups. These substantial fluctuations are partly explained by the changing age structure of these populations. Census data indicate that for these three ethnic groups, but not others, the 50-74 age group shifted very strongly towards the younger 50- to 59-year-olds from 2001 to 2011, and shifted the other way between 1991 and 2001. Comparing economic activity rates in 1991 with those in 2011 showed that over this total period they only increased for Black African, White and Indian men in this age group; for all other groups there was a fall.

In contrast to men, economic activity rates for 25- to 49-year-old women increased for all ethnic groups between 1991 and 2011 (see Table 11.2), reflecting a general pattern of increasing female participation rates during this period (ONS, 2013). The rate of increase was smallest for Black Caribbean and Black African women (a 6-percentage point increase for both groups). Black Caribbean women had the highest rate of labour market participation in 1991 (77 per cent), followed by White women (71 per cent), but by 2011, the rate of economic activity for these

Table 11.1: Economic activity, younger and older male workers, 1991-2001-2011

	Men 25-49 years % economically active			Men 50-74 years % economically active		
	1991	2001	2011	1991	2001	2011
White	95.4	91.0	91.8	54.0	53.3	59.4
Black Caribbean	92.9	85.2	86.3	68.6	42.5	61.8
Black African	75.4	78.6	83.8	70.6	62.4	75.2
Indian	94.8	90.5	92.3	64.7	54.2	66.6
Pakistani	89.5	82.0	87.1	61.5	39.0	57.5
Bangladeshi	90.3	80.7	86.4	61.4	25.5	51.1
Chinese	86.4	83.8	82.9	69.1	54.7	66.0

two ethnic groups had converged. Increases in economic activity were greatest for women in the Pakistani and Bangladeshi groups, who had, respectively, a 19- and 23-percentage point increase between 1991 and 2011, and were the only groups to narrow the gap from the White women's rate during the same period. This increased participation in the labour market among women in these groups has been associated with smaller families and increased levels of education (Dale et al, 2002). However, Pakistani and Bangladeshi women continued to have the lowest rates throughout this period, with fewer than half of women aged 25-49 in these groups working or looking for work.

As for Black African older men, Black African women had the highest rate of economic activity between 1991 and 2011 (55 per cent in 1991 rising to 62 per cent in 2011). This could be due to the young age structure of the Black African group; in 2011, only 2 per cent of Black African women were over 65 years of age (compared with the national average of 16 per cent). The low rates of economic activity that were present for younger Bangladeshi and Pakistani women were also seen for older women. In 2011, fewer than one in five older

Table 11.2: Economic activity, younger and older female workers, 1991-2001-2011

	Women 25-49 years % economically active				Women 50-74 years % economically active		
	1991	2001	2011		1991	2001	2011
White	71.4	76.2	82.2		31.4	38.0	47.1
Black Caribbean	76.6	77.0	82.7		53.3	37.7	57.3
Black African	65.8	63.2	71.9		54.8	47.6	62.1
Indian	67.4	70.9	78.3		30.6	32.4	46.2
Pakistani	23.5	28.5	42.6		13.5	11.0	18.8
Bangladeshi	16.8	20.8	39.3		12.6	7.6	12.5
Chinese	64.9	67.1	73.7		36.9	40.5	51.4

Bangladeshi and Pakistani women aged 50-74 were in the labour market compared with around half in all other ethnic groups.

Younger workers, 1991-2011

Unemployment

Unemployment rates for those aged 25-49 decreased between 1991 and 2001, with little change between 2001 and 2011, for all ethnic groups and both men and women. Pakistani and Bangladeshi men had the greatest reduction in unemployment rates over the whole period: in 2011 their unemployment rate was one-third of the rate in 1991 (see Figure 11.1). Black African men had consistently the highest rates of unemployment, although in 2011 the rate for Black Caribbean men was similar.

In contrast to Black African and Black Caribbean men, the reduction in unemployment rates narrowed the disadvantage of Pakistani and Bangladeshi men relative to White men. For Pakistani men the unemployment rate fell from 2.8 times as high in 1991 to 1.7 times as high in 2011, while for Bangladeshi men the fall was from 2.9 times as high to 1.9 times as high.

Among women aged 25-49, unemployment rates decreased from 1991 to 2011 by one-quarter in the Black African group, around one-third in the Indian and Pakistani groups, and almost two-fifths in the Bangladeshi group (see Figure 11.2). These large falls in unemployment, compared with a very small fall for White women, led to a narrowing in the ethnic differences for some ethnic groups. For Black African and Pakistani women, rates fell from 4.5 times the rate for White women to just over three times as high, while for Black Caribbean women they remained more than twice as high.

Figure 11.1: Type of employment and levels of unemployment for men aged 25-49, percentage of economically active, 1991-2001-2011

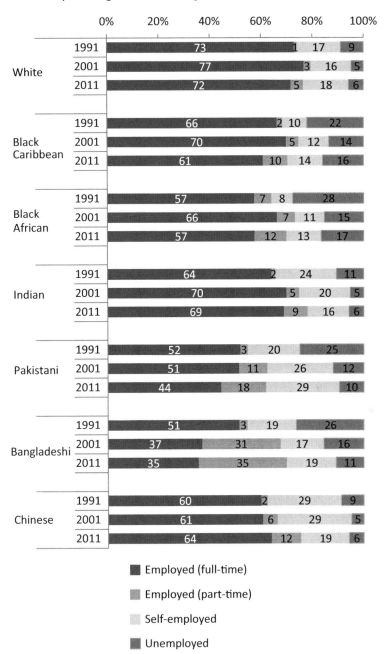

- ■ Employed (full-time)
- ▨ Employed (part-time)
- ░ Self-employed
- ▓ Unemployed

Figure 11.2: Type of employment and levels of unemployment for women aged 25-49, percentage of economically active, 1991-2001-2011

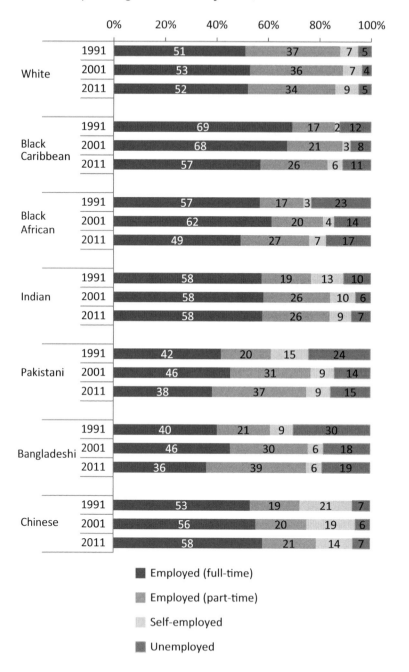

Types of employment, 1991-2011

Rates of full-time employment were reasonably stable for 25- to 49-year-old men in the White and Black African groups, and there was a substantial rise in full-time employment rates for Indian and Chinese men. The lower rates of full-time employment for 25- to 49-year-old Black Caribbean, Pakistani and Bangladeshi men compared with the White group in 1991 persisted to 2011. For younger women, full-time employment was stable for the White and Indian ethnic groups, but decreased in the Black Caribbean group (from 69 per cent in 1991 to 57 per cent in 2011) and in the Black African group (57 per cent decreasing to 49 per cent). The full-time employment rates for Pakistani and Bangladeshi women decreased slightly (by 4 percentage points between 1991 and 2011), and remained at the lowest level of all ethnic groups. Black Caribbean women's rate of full-time employment dropped by 11 percentage points in the 2000s.

Part-time employment rates increased from 1991 to 2011 for men in each ethnic group. High levels of part-time work for men indicate barriers to secure work, and those in part-time work are more likely to receive lower wage rates than those in full-time work (Whittaker and Hurrell, 2013). The largest rise was for Bangladeshi men – an increase from just over 3 to 35 per cent (most of this rise occurred between 1991 and 2001). The high rate for Bangladeshi men may reflect the sectors of employment in which they often work (for example, the catering industry, where part-time work is common), as well as difficulties in finding jobs with more hours (Tackey et al, 2006). Economically active men in other ethnic groups had a steady increase in part-time employment over the period, with rates in 2011 around four times as high as those in 1991. Overall this meant that, with two exceptions, the rate of part-time employment for men in minority ethnic groups did not change much relative to White men. The two exceptions were a fall in the relative rate for Black African men (from six to two-and-a-half times as high) and a rise in the relative rate for Bangladeshi men (from three to seven times as high). For women, between 1991 and 2011 all minority ethnic groups saw an increase in part-time employment, in contrast to White women whose rate reduced by 3 percentage points. By 2011, Bangladeshi and Pakistani women had the highest rates of part-time employment (39 and 37 per cent respectively).

The pattern of change in self-employment between 1991 and 2011 for 25- to 49-year-old men was more mixed than for part-time employment. For White men, self-employment rates remained stable (between 16 and 18 per cent). The higher rates of self-employment among Indian, Bangladeshi and Chinese men in 1991 had disappeared by 2011. However, the rate of self-employment for Pakistani men remained higher than that for White men throughout this period. Analysis from the Labour Force Survey shows that a large proportion (53 per cent) of self-employed Pakistani men work in the transport sector, mainly as taxi drivers (Clark, 2014). Although there have been suggestions that self-employment is a positive choice that enables more flexible working and potentially higher earnings, for Pakistani men this form of activity may be due more to the inability to find work as paid employees (Kalra, 2000). Self-employment in trades such as taxi driving entails long working hours and benefits such as pensions and sick pay are rare, and hence men in these positions could be in more vulnerable positions than employees.

Older workers

The decrease in older men's labour market participation between 1991 and 2001 coincided with a drop in the unemployment rate which decreased by half for the Pakistani, Bangladeshi, Chinese, Indian and White groups over this period. However, it was the rise in the number of retired older men in the period 1991 to 2001 that was the main factor in the decrease in economic activity. This may reflect the demographic structure of different ethnic groups. Many migrants from India, Pakistan, Bangladesh and the Caribbean arrived in the UK in their twenties in the 1950s and 1960s, and thus will have reached retirement age around the turn of the millennium.

The decrease in economic activity over this period was not due to increased levels of sickness in the older male workforce, as rates decreased for men in most ethnic groups from 1991 to 2001, and there was a small (1 to 2 percentage points) increase for the White, Black Caribbean and Black African groups. Throughout the period, Pakistani and Bangladeshi men had the highest rates of not working due to sickness, and in 2011 their rates remained twice as high as White men. The percentage of men in each ethnic group that classed themselves as economically inactive due to other reasons increased between 1991 and 2001. Among those at the younger end of the older age group, this may reflect a rise in the number of discouraged workers – those who, after an extended period of unemployment, have given up searching for work and thus do not fall into the standard definition of the unemployed.

The overall increase in economic activity rates for older women was due to the decrease in the number of women who were looking after home and family, which dropped considerably from 1991 to 2011 (see Figure 11.4). The drop in economic activity rates that were seen for older men in minority ethnic groups between 1991 and 2001 were also seen for Black Caribbean, Black African, Pakistani and Bangladeshi women. This is partly explained by an increase in the proportion in retirement, which increased by about half from 1991 to 2001 for Black Caribbean and Black African women and doubled for Pakistani and Bangladeshi women. Pakistani, Bangladeshi and Black African women also saw an increase in the percentage not working due to sickness in the period 1991 to 2001, which was another reason for their decreased levels of economic activity in 2001. By 2011, Bangladeshi and Pakistani women had the highest rates of not working due to sickness (18 per cent) (see Chapter Nine for a detailed description of the change in poor health between 1991 and 2011). Older Pakistani and Bangladeshi women were persistently the least likely to be in the labour market between 1991 and 2011. This is largely due to the high propensity of these groups to be responsible for looking after the home and family.

Figure 11.3: Economic activity, and inactivity (permanently sick, other inactive and retired), men aged 50-74, 1991-2001-2011

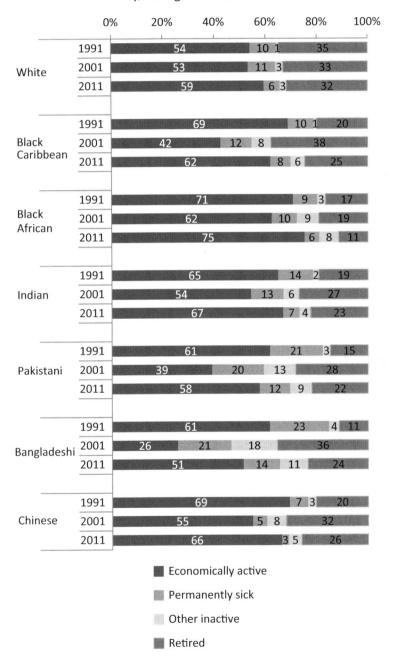

Economically active

Permanently sick

Other inactive

Retired

Figure 11.4: Economic activity, and inactivity (permanently sick, other inactive and retired), women aged 50-74, 1991-2001-2011

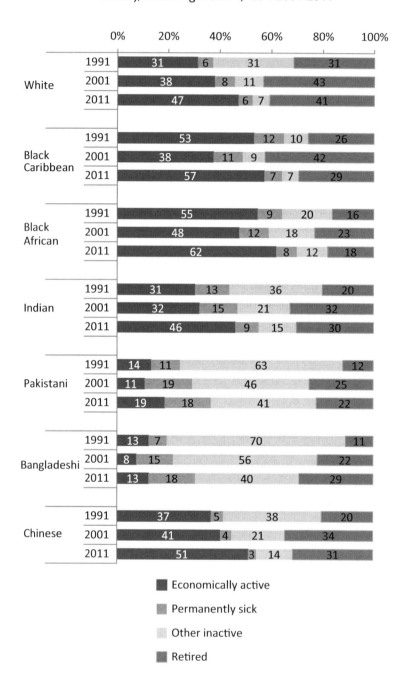

Economic activity and employment in 2011: a more detailed picture of inequalities

For this section, we present data for all 18 ethnic groups that were available in the 2011 Census. In 2011, over 90 per cent of 25- to 49-year-old men were economically active in the Indian, White British, White Irish and Other White ethnic groups (see Figure 11.5). For the other groups, rates of economic activity were between 80 and 88 per cent for all but the Arab and White Gypsy or Irish Traveller groups, that had considerably lower rates (69 and 67 per cent respectively). For older male workers in 2011, the ethnic patterning of economic activity was different to that for younger male workers. Black African (75 per cent), Other White (71 per cent) and Other Asian (68 per cent) men had the highest rates of economic activity, which may be as a result of these groups' younger age structures. Economic activity was lowest for White Gypsy or Irish Traveller (41 per cent), Bangladeshi (51 per cent) and White Irish (53 per cent) men.

Figure 11.5: Percentage of economically active, 25- to 49- and 50- to 74-year-old men, 2011

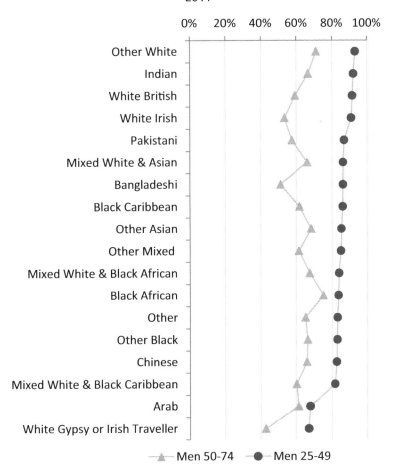

Among women aged 25–49, rates of economic activity varied more than they did for men (see Figure 11.6). Only women in the White British, Other White and Black Caribbean groups had rates that were above 80 per cent. The rates of economic activity were lowest (at around 40 per cent) for women in the White Gypsy or Irish Traveller, Pakistani, Bangladeshi and Arab groups. For older women, economic activity was highest for the Black African (62 per cent), Mixed White & Black African (60 per cent) and Other Black (59 per cent) groups. It was lowest in the same four groups as for younger women: Bangladeshi (13 per cent), Pakistani (19 per cent), White Gypsy or Irish Traveller (28 per cent) and Arab (32 per cent).

Figure 11.6: Percentage of economically active 25- to 49- and 50- to 74-year-old women, 2011

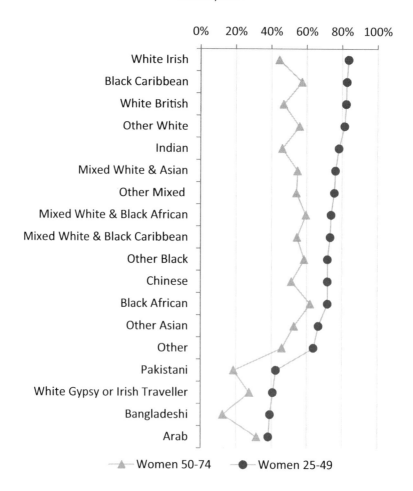

Full-time employment for men, 2011

For men in the 25–49 year age group, we consider the most positive labour market outcome to be full-time employment (as an employee, rather than self-employed). Although some men prefer to be self-employed or employed part-time, full-time paid employment typically offers greater economic returns and job security (Whittaker and Hurrell, 2013). Employment rates are usually expressed as a proportion of the whole population, but can be depressed simply because of a high number of older people, students, people not working due to illness or disability, or people looking after the home and family, which makes it useful to show the rate also as a proportion of the economically active. In 2011, there were large ethnic inequalities in the rates of full-time employment (see Figure 11.7). For White British men, the rate of full-time employment was 66 per cent

Figure 11.7: Full-time rates of employment for men aged 25-49, compared with the White British rate, 2011

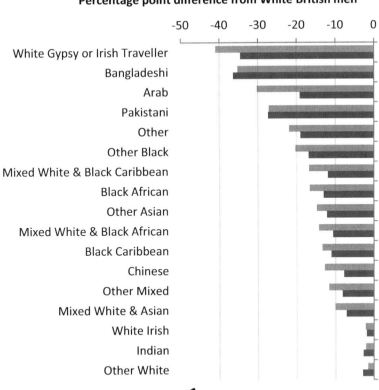

Percentage point difference from White British men

Further away from the White British rate of full time employment

▨ Full time employment rate, of all people

▪ Full time employment rate, of economically active

out of all White British men aged 25–49, and 72 per cent of those who were economically active, the highest of any ethnic group. Other White, Indian and White Irish men had very similar rates, only 1 to 2 percentage points less than White British men. However, the disparity was much larger for White Gypsy or Irish Traveller, Bangladeshi, Arab and Pakistani men, who had rates that were between 27 (Pakistani) and 41 (White Gypsy or Irish Traveller) percentage points lower than the White British rate. For the Arab group, the low rate in part reflects high rates of participation in full-time education for this age group, at 18 per cent, almost 13 times as high as the national average. However, this was not the case for the White Gypsy or Irish Traveller men, for whom only 2 per cent were in full-time education, but as many as 15 per cent in this age group were not working due to sickness or disability – more than three times the national average.

Full and part-time employment for women, 2011

For women, we define the most positive employment outcome as being in either full-time or part-time work (as an employee rather than self-employed). In 2011, 71 per cent of all White British women were in full- or part-time employment, while 87 per cent of economically active White women were in full- or part-time employment (see Figure 11.8). Only White Irish women had a rate that was similar. The rates were over 40 percentage points lower for White Gypsy or Irish Traveller, Arab and Bangladeshi women, and very close to this level for Pakistani women. As for men, the low levels of employment for women in the Arab group in part relate to high rates of participation in full-time education (at 14 per cent, eight times as high as the national average) and, as for men, in the White Gypsy or Irish Traveller groups they reflect high rates of sickness and disability (at 14 per cent, also over three times the national average). There were high proportions of Pakistani and Bangladeshi women (43 and 40 per cent respectively) who were out of the labour market because they were looking after the home or family; this was four times the rate of White British women.

Figure 11.8: Rates of employment for women aged 25-49, compared with the White British rate, 2011

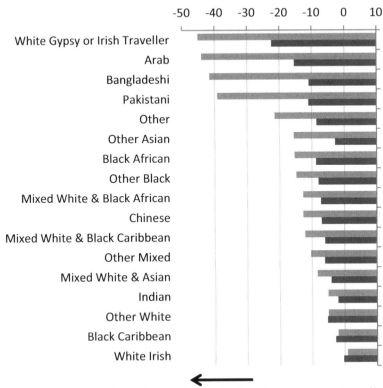

Percentage point difference from White British women

Further away from the White British rate of full- and part-time employment

■ Full- and part-time employment rate, of all people

■ Full- and part-time employment rate, of economically active

Conclusions and implications

Between 1991 and 2011, there were many changes in the ethnic patterning of economic activity, unemployment and employment. While some minority ethnic groups saw their disadvantage relative to the majority White group fall over this period, the overall picture is one of persistent inequality for many minority ethnic groups in England and Wales.

With the exception of Indian and Chinese men, all minority ethnic younger (aged 25-49) males had lower rates of economic activity compared with their White counterparts in 2011. Younger Pakistani and Bangladeshi men saw large falls in unemployment over the period 1991-2011 (respectively, from 25 to 10 per cent and from 26 to 11 per cent), and the differential unemployment rate relative to the White group also fell. This may reflect the increase in higher educational qualifications experienced by members of these groups (see Chapter Twelve). Despite this fall, however, the unemployment differential with the White group remained substantial, and for both groups the fall in unemployment was balanced by a rise in part-time work. For Bangladeshi men the 11-fold increase in part-time work between 1991 and 2011 was much larger than for any other ethnic group. Black Caribbean and Black African men also experienced falling unemployment rates but, given that the labour market was generally more favourable in 2011 compared to 1991, their relative position compared to White men hardly improved.

Younger White women also had a consistent advantage from 1991 to 2011, although Black Caribbean women had similar rates of economic activity. Younger Pakistani and Bangladeshi women were the least likely to be in the labour market, but also experienced the highest rises in rates of economic activity between 1991 and 2011, which again may reflect improvements in human capital and decreases in family size (Dale et al, 2002).

These persistent ethnic inequalities in the labour market are alarming, especially for the younger age groups where most minority ethnic groups have higher levels of educational qualifications compared to their White counterparts (see Chapter Twelve). Hence, a lack of human capital cannot be cited as the main reason for the higher levels of unemployment for these groups. It is more likely that there continues to be significant racial and religious discrimination in the labour market, both at the recruitment stage and in the workplace, that works more strongly against certain ethnic groups and that accounts for these differences (Runnymede Trust, 2012; Cheung, 2014).

Policymakers in Britain have acknowledged ethnic labour market disadvantage for some time, and a number of initiatives have been introduced. A criticism of these policies is that they are fragmented (Bourn, 2008), and although some measures have had a degree of success, in general, progress towards ethnic equality in the labour market is slow. Adjusting existing policies in the light of the patterns of inequality documented in this chapter, and learning from and building on the progress made by some groups may help; however, the persistence of inequalities over time and into new cohorts suggests the need for a more fundamental, national response to ethnic group disadvantage in the labour market.

Note

Further information about data and sources are available from http://www.ethnicity.ac.uk/dynamicsofdiversity/

References

Bourn, J. (2008) *Increasing employment rates for ethnic minorities. A report by the Controller and Auditor General*, London: The Stationery Office.

Brynin, M. and Guveli, A. (2012) 'Understanding the ethnic pay gap in Britain', *Work, Employment and Society*, vol 26, no 4, pp 574-87.

Cheung, S.Y. (2014) 'Ethno-religious minorities and labour market integration: generational advancement or decline?', *Ethnic and Racial Studies,* vol 37, no 1, pp 140-60.

Clark, K. (2014) 'Is the picture of Pakistani self-employment really so rosy?', 9 April, *Manchester Policy Blogs* (http://blog.policy.manchester.ac.uk/featured/2014/04/pakistani-self-employment-in-the-recession/).

Clark, K. and Drinkwater, S. (2007) *Ethnic minorities in the labour market: Dynamics and diversity*, Bristol: Policy Press.

Dale, A., Shaheen, N., Kalra, V., and Fieldhouse, E.A. (2002) 'Routes into education and employment for young Pakistani and Bangladeshi women in the UK', *Ethnic and Racial Studies*, vol 25, no 6, pp 942-68.

Heath, A. and Cheung, S.Y. (2006) *Ethnic penalties in the labour market: Employers and discrimination*, DWP Research Report 341, London: Department for Work and Pensions.

Kalra, V. (2000) *From textile mills to taxi ranks: Experiences of migration, labour and social change*, Aldershot: Ashgate Publishing.

Modood, T. (1997) 'Employment', in T. Modood, R. Berthoud, J. Lakey, J. Nazroo, P. Smith, S. Virdee and S. Beishon (eds) *Ethnic minorities in Britain*, London: Policy Studies Institute, pp 83-149.

ONS (Office for National Statistics) (2013) *Full report – Women in the labour market*, Newport: ONS (www.ons.gov.uk/ons/dcp171776_328352.pdf).

Runnymede Trust (2012) *First report of Session 2012–2013. All-Party Parliamentary Group on Race and Community. Ethnic minority female unemployment: Black, Pakistani and Bangladeshi heritage women*, London: Runnymede Trust.

Simpson, L., Purdam, K., Tajar, A., Fieldhouse, E., Gavalas, V., Tranmer, M., Pritchard, J. and Dorling, D. (2006) *Ethnic minority populations and the labour market: An analysis of the 1991 and 2001 Census*, DWP Research Report 333, London: Department for Work and Pensions.

Tackey, N.D., Casebourne, J., Aston, J., Ritchie, H., Sinclair, A., Tyers, C., Hurstfield, J., Willison, R. and Page, R. (2006) *Barriers to employment for Pakistanis and Bangladeshis in Britain*, DWP Research Report No 360, London: Department for Work and Pensions.

Whittaker, M. and Hurrell, A. (2013) *Low pay Britain 2013*, Resolution Foundation (www.scribd.com/doc/165161949/Low-Pay-Britain-2013).

TWELVE

Is there an ethnic group educational gap?

Kitty Lymperopoulou and Meenakshi Parameshwaran

Key findings

- Between 1991 and 2011 there was an overall improvement in educational attainment, but minority ethnic groups experienced greater improvements compared with the White British group. In 2011 people from minority ethnic groups were more likely to have academic qualifications than White British people (17 and 24 per cent respectively had no qualifications).
- The Indian, Pakistani and Bangladeshi groups experienced an increase in those with degree-level qualifications, by 27, 18 and 15 percentage points respectively, between 1991 and 2011.
- Members of the Indian, Chinese and Black African groups in 2011 had higher educational attainment than other minority ethnic groups and the White British group.
- In 2011, 60 per cent of the White Gypsy or Irish Traveller group had no qualifications. This was the highest proportion for any ethnic group, and was two-and-a-half times that of the White British group.
- The Bangladeshi and Pakistani groups saw a 19- and 16-percentage point decrease respectively in those without any qualifications between 2001 and 2011.
- Although the educational disadvantage of Pakistani and Bangladeshi groups compared to the White British group declined between 1991 and 2011, it was still present in 2011.
- Nearly one in three women in the Pakistani or Bangladeshi groups had no qualifications compared with one in four White British women. However, Pakistani and Bangladeshi young people aged 16-24, both females and males,

were considerably more qualified than their older counterparts, and more qualified than White British young people of the same age.
- Over a third of people born outside of the UK had degree-level qualifications compared with a quarter of people born in the UK.
- Migrants who arrived in the UK between 2001 and 2011 were better qualified than those who arrived in the UK in previous decades.

Introduction

Policymakers in Britain are concerned with education as it provides a pathway for the broader integration of immigrants and minority ethnic groups into economic, political and civil society. Education facilitates social mobility for all ethnic groups: higher educational attainment is associated with improved employment outcomes, such as avoiding unemployment and securing higher-level jobs and higher incomes (Heath and Cheung, 2006). Historically, minority ethnic groups in the UK have been disadvantaged in education compared with the White British group; however, over the last 20 years, the educational attainment of minority ethnic groups has increased. This is the result of better access to education overseas and increasing proportions of minority ethnic people receiving education in Britain. Nevertheless, ethnic gaps in educational attainment persist in Britain for a number of reasons.

According to Heath and Brinbaum (2007), there are structural and cultural explanations for ethnic gaps in educational attainment. These are based on the social class positions of different groups. Structural explanations focus on parental occupation, the role of material resources and the valuation of education across social classes. Individuals belonging to ethnic groups that are typically lower in the social class hierarchy would be expected to have lower educational attainment because the costs of education outweigh the benefits, they do not have sufficient resources to continue in school, and they perceive education to be of lower value. Cultural explanations focus on parental education and suggest that educational inequality can be explained by social class differences in parental knowledge of the education system, parental abilities in helping their children with schoolwork, and parental familiarity with high-status culture (including use of the English language). Individuals belonging to ethnic groups that on average have higher socioeconomic status are more likely to have high educational attainment because they have more of the relevant knowledge and cultural resources to gain an advantage in education.

Ethnic gaps in educational attainment can also be explained by *ethnic penalties*. These are the lower employment outcomes experienced by minority ethnic groups compared to similar White British people that may be attributed to discrimination by employers (Heath and Cheung, 2006). Ethnic penalties exist even after taking account of social background, educational qualifications, age and labour market experience. Minority ethnic individuals may choose to stay on in education to avoid exposure to potential employer discrimination in low-skilled labour markets, or because they believe that higher educational attainment will give them access to the potentially more meritocratic high-skilled labour markets.

The typically higher educational aspirations of minority ethnic students compared to White British students of the same social class may help compensate for ethnic educational disadvantages (Heath et al, 2008). High aspirations are evident despite the negative ethnic group stereotypes and low educational expectations of some teachers (Gillborn, 1997), and the concentration of some minority ethnic groups in socially and economically disadvantaged areas, where schools are more likely to be of poorer quality (Heath et al, 2008). Many minority ethnic groups do less well in school in terms of grades; however, when comparing students who do equally well at school, minority ethnic students are more likely to continue in further and higher education than White British students (Jackson, 2012), but often at lower-status institutions (Boliver, 2006).

Ethnic differences in educational attainment can also be explained by selective migration (Feliciano, 2005). The argument is that the immigrant generation does not represent a random sample from the population of the origin country. Rather, the immigrant generation is likely to be more highly educated (positively selected) than the population that remains in the origin country. The degree of positive educational selectivity varies by country of origin, period of migration and migration motivation, and depends on changes in government migration policies. The degree of positive selectivity is likely to have increased in recent years as a result of the tightening of immigration controls of successive governments in the UK. If the degree of positive selectivity of immigrants has increased, then we would expect some improvement in the educational attainment of minority ethnic groups in the UK over the past decade, as a result of greater proportions of new immigrants to the UK entering with higher-level qualifications on arrival than in earlier decades.

Ethnic group differences in education also have a gender dimension. Gender disparities in the propensity to continue in education reveal differences in cultural expectations across ethnic groups. The Pakistani group, in particular, is notable for the lower likelihood of girls remaining in post-compulsory education, despite Pakistani girls typically having higher qualifications than Pakistani boys (Dale et al, 2002). One explanation for this is the greater prevalence of the preference for traditional gender roles and early marriage among this group (Dale et al, 2002). There is also a geographical dimension, with school pupils in the UK's large cities (London, Manchester and Birmingham) outperforming their economic peers elsewhere (Social Mobility and Child Poverty Commission, 2014).

This chapter explores the ethnic group educational gap using data from the last three censuses (1991, 2001 and 2011). The methodology used in the chapter is described on p 184. The next sections examine the educational attainment of ethnic groups in 2011 – by sex and age, countries of birth and years of arrival – and how it changed over time. The chapter concludes with a discussion of the implications of the results.

Measuring educational attainment in the census

This chapter uses data from the 1991, 2001 and 2011 Censuses to provide an overview of the educational attainment of ethnic groups in England and Wales, and to examine how educational attainment has changed over time. In order to examine which ethnic groups are more or less advantaged in terms of educational attainment, this chapter focuses on the distribution of high educational outcomes (degree level or equivalent qualifications) and low educational outcomes (no qualifications). The analysis also examines age, sex, country of birth and year of arrival, wherever possible, to explore potential explanations for differences in educational attainment among ethnic groups.

In 2011, people aged 16 and over were asked by the census to indicate all the types of educational qualifications they held from 13 options, ranging from no formal qualifications through to degree-level qualifications. People with qualifications gained outside the UK were asked to tick the 'foreign qualifications' box and the nearest UK equivalents. Responses were combined into five categories for the highest level of qualification held, plus one category for no qualifications, and one for other qualifications. Other qualifications included foreign qualifications where an equivalent qualification was not indicated. The 2011 qualifications question is broadly comparable with the 2001 Census question, although in 2001 this question was only asked of people aged 16-74.

In 1991 people aged 18 or over were asked to write the name of any degrees or vocational qualifications attained, excluding school-level qualifications. The 1991 Census qualifications question was only processed for a 10 per cent sample of households and people in communal establishments. It is possible to compare degree-level or equivalent qualifications across 1991-2001-2011, but comparisons of no qualifications can only be done for 2001 and 2011, since information on these was not recorded in the 1991 Census. Degree-level or equivalent qualifications denote completed education at Level 4 or above, which correspond to degree (for example, BA, BSc), higher degree (for example, MA, PhD, PGCE), NVQ Level 4-5, HNC, HND, RSA Higher Diploma, BTEC higher level, and Foundation degree (NI) qualifications (see QAAHE, 2008, for details of the framework for higher education qualifications).

Despite the census being the most complete source of information on the population of England and Wales, it is likely that it undercounts certain migrant populations, such as irregular migrants, casual migrant workers and migrants who have remained in the country after their visas have expired (over-stayers). Under-reporting of lower-level qualifications has been highlighted as an issue in both the 2001 and 2011 Censuses (ONS, 2012). The 2011 Census recorded foreign qualifications as a separate category, but for respondents reporting multiple qualifications it is not possible to identify which qualifications were obtained outside the UK. While determining UK equivalent qualifications may be easier for higher qualifications, such as university degrees, for those without knowledge of the UK education system, identifying lower-level qualifications may be more difficult. The census outputs available for this chapter combine qualifications acquired abroad and in the UK, which may conceal differences in the quality of education received.

Educational attainment of ethnic groups in 2011

People from minority ethnic groups other than White British were generally more likely than White British people to have degree-level qualifications or equivalent (34 and 26 per cent respectively). In 2011, only people from the White Gypsy or Irish Traveller, Pakistani, Bangladeshi, and White & Black Caribbean groups were less likely than White British people to have degree-level qualifications or equivalent (see Figure 12.1). The groups with the highest proportion of people with degree-level qualifications were the Chinese (43 per cent), Indian (42 per cent) and Black African (40 per cent) groups.

People from minority ethnic groups were also less likely to have no qualifications compared with White British people (17 and 24 per cent respectively). People from the Black African group, which has grown mainly through migration (see Chapter Three), and includes a substantial number of international students, were the least likely to have no qualifications (11 per cent). The Other White group and the Mixed groups also had a lower proportion of people with no

Figure 12.1: Percentage of people aged 16 and over with no qualifications and degree-level qualifications, by ethnic group, 2011

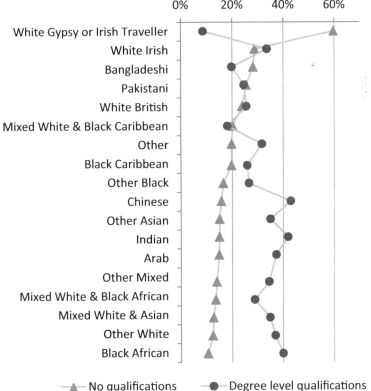

185

qualifications (between 12 and 20 per cent) than the average for England and Wales (23 per cent).

In 2011, 60 per cent of White Gypsy or Irish Traveller people had no qualifications. This was the highest proportion for any ethnic group, and was two-and-a-half times higher than for White British people. Only around one in ten (9 per cent) White Gypsy or Irish Traveller people had degree-level qualifications or equivalent. Taken together, these figures indicate the serious educational disadvantage experienced by the White Gypsy or Irish Traveller group. There were also higher proportions of people with no qualifications in the White Irish (29 per cent), Bangladeshi (28 per cent) and Pakistani (26 per cent) groups than in the White British group (24 per cent).

Educational attainment: ethnic group, sex and age in 2011

Figures 12.2-12.4 show large differences in educational attainment by gender and age. Women were noticeably more likely to have no qualifications than men in the Bangladeshi, Pakistani and White Gypsy or Irish Traveller groups. These differences were more pronounced for the older groups. In contrast, women were noticeably more likely to have a degree than men in the Black Caribbean, Mixed and Other White groups.

Members of minority ethnic groups in the younger age groups have particularly high levels of attainment. Among men aged 16-24, the Indian and Chinese groups had the highest attainment, with 28 per cent of each group having degree-level qualifications and only 5 and 6 per cent (respectively) having no qualifications. Among men aged 16-24, the White Gypsy or Irish Traveller and White British groups were among the most educationally disadvantaged, being more likely to have no qualifications (44 and 12 per cent), and less likely to have degree-level qualifications (6 and 11 per cent) than any other ethnic group. The proportion of Pakistani and Bangladeshi men with degree-level qualifications in the same age group was one-and-a-half times higher that of White British men. The proportion of women aged 16-24 without qualifications was higher among the White Gypsy or Irish Traveller and White & Black Caribbean group (49 and 13 per cent) compared with that of women from other minority ethnic groups (ranging between 5 and 12 per cent) and White British women (10 per cent).

In the oldest age group, lower levels of attainment for all ethnic groups are evident, with much greater proportions of males and females in each ethnic group having no qualifications. Among men aged 50 or above, 72 per cent of White Gypsy or Irish Traveller, 53 per cent of Bangladeshi, 44 per cent of White Irish and 43 per cent of Pakistani men had no qualifications compared with 33 per cent of White British, 20 per cent of Arab and 12 per cent of Black African men. Among women aged 50 or above, 78 per cent of White Gypsy or Irish Traveller, 75 per cent of Bangladeshi and 64 per cent of Pakistani women were without qualifications, as were 45 per cent of White Irish, 43 per cent of Indian and 33 per cent of Black Caribbean women. The proportion of women from other minority ethnic groups with no qualifications within this age group was lower (ranging between 21 and 43 per cent) than that of White British women (44 per cent). The different age composition of minority ethnic groups and the lower rates of participation in education among some minority ethnic women can explain some of the differences in attainment across minority ethnic groups. For example, the White Irish group have an older age structure than other groups, while Pakistani and Bangladeshi women participate less in education due to earlier marriage, family formation and cultural practices (Dale, 2002), although this is less evident in younger cohorts.

The proportion of Pakistani men aged 25-49 with no qualifications was nearly double that of the 16-24 age group (18 per cent compared with 10 per cent respectively). Differences were even larger for women. For example, the proportion of Bangladeshi women aged 25-49 without qualifications was three times higher than that of Bangladeshi women in the 16-24 age group (31 and 10 per cent respectively). Across all ages, one in three Pakistani women (30 per cent) and Bangladeshi women (33 per cent) had no qualifications in 2011 compared with one on four (26 per cent) White British women. The lower proportions of men and women with no qualifications in the younger age group compared to the middle age group suggest improvements in educational attainment for all ethnic groups. White British males are the exception to this, with the proportion of White British males with no qualifications in the 16-24 and 25-49 age groups being identical (12 per cent). Although progress has been made for all ethnic groups, the White Gypsy or Irish Traveller group lags well behind. While similar proportions of females aged 50 and above in the Bangladeshi group and White Gypsy or Irish Traveller group have no qualifications (75 and 78 per cent respectively), in the 16-24 age group only 10 per cent of Bangladeshi females have no qualifications compared to 49 per cent of the White Gypsy or Irish Traveller group. Bangladeshi females show clear signs of improving educational attainment in the younger generations, but the White Gypsy or Irish Traveller group has not experienced the same success.

Educational attainment in 2011: country of origin and year of arrival

The foreign-born population in 2011 was less likely to be without any qualifications than the UK-born population (19 and 23 per cent respectively). Over a third (35 per cent) of people born outside the UK had degree-level qualifications compared with a quarter (26 per cent) of people born in the UK. Recently arrived migrants were more likely to be better qualified than those who arrived in the previous decades. This is evident from differences in the proportion of people without any qualifications (Figure 12.5) and with degree-level qualifications (Figure 12.6) that arrived in the UK over the last decade compared with previous decades.

Figure 12.2: Percentage of people aged 16-24 with and without qualifications, by ethnic group, 2011

Figure 12.3: Percentage of people aged 25-49 with and without qualifications, by ethnic group, 2011

Figure 12.4: Percentage of people aged 50 or above with and without qualifications, by ethnic group, 2011

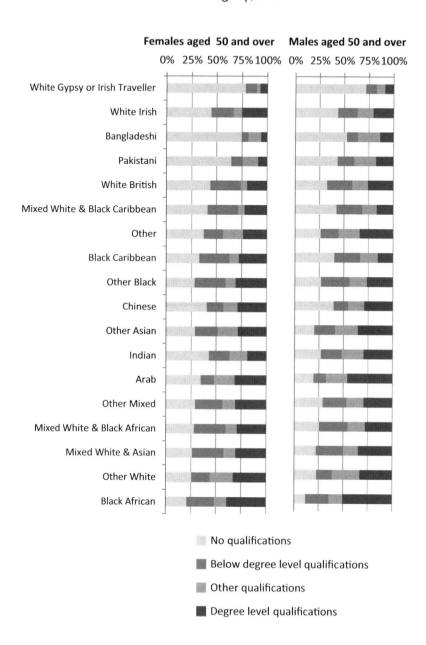

Figure 12.5: Percentage of people with no qualifications, by year of arrival and country of birth, 2011

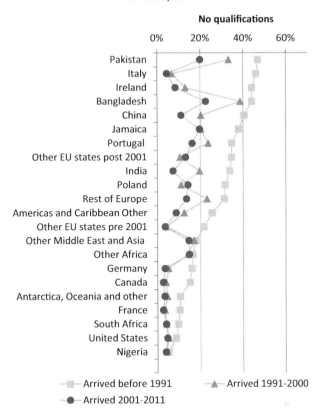

Notes for Figures 12.5 and 12.6: The figures show the country or broad region in which people were born. The Office for National Statistics (ONS) has grouped countries into five broad regions: Europe (European Union [EU], Rest of Europe), Africa (Nigeria, South Africa, Other Africa), Middle East and Asia (China, Bangladesh, Pakistan, India, other Middle East and Asia), the Americas and the Caribbean (Canada, US, Jamaica, other Americas and the Caribbean), and Antarctica and Oceania. Countries in the EU are grouped into those that were EU members in 2001 (France, Germany, Italy, Spain, Other EU) and those that joined the EU subsequently as part of the EU enlargement (Poland and Other EU Accession states). Rest of Europe includes all other (non-EU) countries in Europe.

There were large differences in the qualifications of Pakistani migrants by year of arrival, with nearly half (47 per cent) of those who arrived prior to 1991 having no qualifications compared with a third (33 per cent) and a fifth (20 per cent) of those who arrived in the UK between 1991 and 2001, and between 2001 and 2011 respectively. These differences were more pronounced for people born in Italy and Ireland, with 46 and 44 per cent of those who arrived in the UK prior to 1991 having no qualifications compared with 5 and 8 per cent respectively of those who arrived in the UK between 2001 and 2011. In contrast, there was less variation in the qualifications of people by year of arrival for the groups that were better qualified in 2011, including those born in France, Canada, South Africa and the US.

Figure 12.6: Percentage of people with degree-level qualifications, by year of arrival and country of birth, 2011

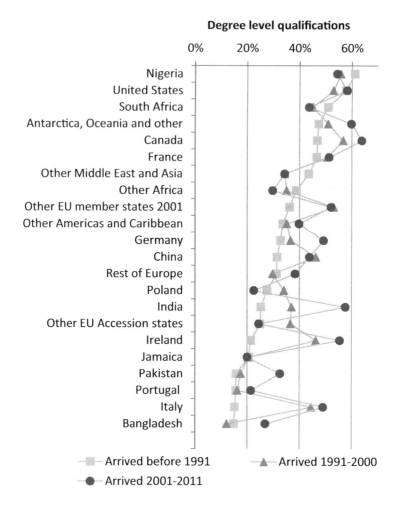

The proportion of Nigerian migrants with degree-level qualifications was higher (61 per cent) among those who arrived in the UK prior to 1991 compared with those who arrived between 1991 and 2001, and between 2001 and 2011 (56 and 54 per cent respectively). This is because earlier immigration waves from Nigeria and the rest of Africa to the UK comprised African elites (including East African Indians of high socioeconomic status), students and professionals, while subsequent waves were more diversified and included economic migrants, refugees and undocumented migrants (Koser, 2003). The proportion of Nigerian migrants without any qualifications who arrived in the UK over the last decade compared with those who arrived at earlier decades was similar, at around 5 per cent, suggesting that the vast majority of Nigerian migrants had at least some education before arriving in the UK, irrespective of when they came.

There were higher proportions of people with degrees from Poland and the rest of the EU Accession countries among those who arrived in the UK between 1991 and 2001 (34 and 37 per cent respectively) than among those who arrived in the UK after 2001 (23 and 25 per cent respectively). This reflects the large numbers of labour migrants from the EU Accession states, who arrived in the UK following the 2004 EU enlargement to work predominantly in low-skilled sectors (UKBA et al, 2009). In 2011, EU Accession migrants had a lower proportion of people with degree-level qualifications and a higher proportion of people with other qualifications (including unknown foreign qualifications) than other migrant groups. Overall, those who arrived in the UK after 2001 were more likely to have degrees than earlier migrants; for example, 25, 21 and 15 per cent of pre-1991 migrants born in India, Ireland and Italy respectively were educated at degree level compared with 58, 56 and 49 per cent of post-2001 migrants. The growth in the number of international students and skilled migrant workers over the last decades assisted by selective immigration policies accounts for some of the differences in the composition of migrants across different years. China, India and Nigeria are the top three countries of domicile of international students at UK higher education institutions (HESA, 2013), suggesting that ethnic educational gaps are also narrowing through more places for international students at UK universities. However, international student numbers (especially those from the Asian sub-continent) declined for the first time in 29 years in 2012-13, most likely because of changes to student visa policies (HEFCE, 2014).

Educational attainment, 1991 to 2011

A comparison of the 1991, 2001 and 2011 Censuses suggests that all ethnic groups experienced improvements in educational attainment over the last 20 years. These improvements reflect, to a large extent, the expansion of the higher education sector in the UK and abroad, and the higher number of places for international students in the UK. Women have benefited the most from this expansion. There have also been improvements at the primary and secondary stages of education, both in the UK and abroad.

According to the census, between 2001 and 2011, there was a reduction in the proportion of people without any qualifications (see Figure 12.8). The Bangladeshi and Pakistani groups saw the greatest improvement in educational attainment, with a 19- and 16-percentage point decrease respectively in those without any qualifications. In contrast, the proportion of people with no qualifications in the Black African group was low and roughly equivalent in 2001 and 2011 (14 and 11 per cent).

Overall, more of the increase in the proportion of people with degrees occurred between 1991 and 2001 than between 2001 and 2011. The smallest improvement between 1991 and 2011 in the proportion of people with degree-level qualifications was in the White group. There were large increases in degree-level qualifications for people from the Chinese and Black Caribbean groups (17 percentage points in each). The largest improvements between 1991 and 2011 were for the Indian and Pakistani groups, which experienced an increase in those with degree-level qualifications by 27 and 18 percentage points respectively (see Figure 12.7). These groups, with the exception of the Pakistani and Black Caribbean group, grew mainly through immigration rather than through natural change between 2001 and 2011 (see Chapter Three). In particular, these groups comprise a large number of international students. Family reunification is also likely to have played a part. For example, European Court-mandated changes to UK immigration rules in 1989, allowing husbands as well as wives to immigrate to the UK, contributed to significant increases in male adult immigrants to the UK in the 1990s (Simpson, 1997).

Figure 12.7: Percentage of people with degree-level education, by ethnic group, 1991, 2001 and 2011

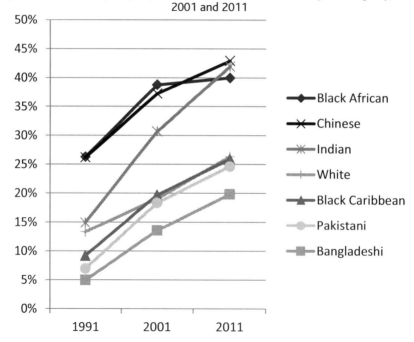

Note: The 1991 figures are based on a 10% sample (see Measuring educational attainment in the census methodology box, p 184).

Figure 12.8: Percentage of people with no qualifications, by ethnic group, 2001 and 2011

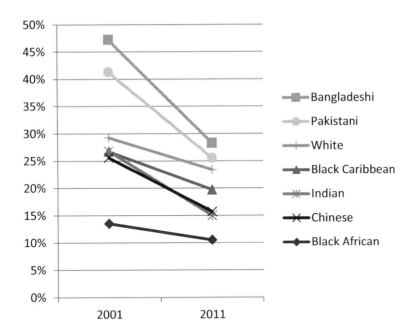

Conclusions and implications

The analysis presented in this chapter indicates that in 2011 members of minority ethnic groups in England and Wales, on average, had higher educational attainment than members of the White British group, with one in three people from minority ethnic groups having degree-level qualifications compared with one in four White British people. All minority ethnic groups experienced an increase in educational attainment (between 14 and 27 percentage points), and were more likely to hold degrees in 2011 than in 1991. However, while some groups have experienced educational success, others continue to face disadvantage in terms of education.

Looking first at educational advantage, the Indian, Chinese and Black African groups had higher educational attainment than other minority ethnic groups, and were more than one-and-a-half times more likely to be educated to degree level than the White British group. These minority ethnic groups grew mostly through immigration rather than through natural change (see Chapter Three), and include a large number of international students, typically from higher social class backgrounds. The educational success of these groups is partly due to positive selection at migration. The positive selection of migrants to the UK has meant that foreign-born members of these groups are significantly more likely to be highly qualified than UK-born people, and that recent arrivals are typically more highly qualified than earlier immigrants. These highly qualified more recent arrivals also typically belong to the two younger age groups, which partly explains the lower qualifications of older generations compared to younger generations. The characteristics of educated immigrants will continue to help narrow the gap as the children of these positively selected migrants benefit through their parents' cultural resources (high aspirations and improved parental knowledge of British systems and language) and structural position (improved socioeconomic situation and anticipation of discrimination) to improve their own educational attainment.

The ethnic education gap has also narrowed because of changes in educational policy. The UK higher education sector went through a significant expansion in the early 1990s, with the Further and Higher Education Act 1992 permitting polytechnics to become universities. This increased university places, which opened up access to universities for minority ethnic students. The global shift towards a services-based economy, with corresponding wage differentials between graduates and non-graduates, has also significantly increased demand for degree-level qualifications (Blanden and Machin, 2004). Government policies at earlier stages of education, such as the Ethnic Minority Achievement Grant, were intended to help minority ethnic pupils do better in school, thereby allowing them to enter university. Taken together, both immigration and educational policies can explain much of the improvements in the educational attainment of minority ethnic groups over the last 20 years.

Gender gaps in educational attainment across ethnic groups seem to have narrowed over time, with women from the Pakistani and Bangladeshi groups experiencing dramatic improvements in their educational achievement over the past two decades. This is evident from the much lower gender gap in the younger age groups compared with the older age groups, where females are far more likely to have no qualifications than males. Although the gender gap has narrowed, the Pakistani and Bangladeshi groups in the 25-49 age group shows greater concentrations of males and females in the highest and lowest educational attainment categories (educational polarisation) than the 16-24 age group. This polarisation in educational attainment could indicate that while some members of these ethnic groups are succeeding in education, others are being left behind. In contrast, the White British, Other Black, and Mixed White & Black Caribbean groups feature greater proportions with qualifications below degree level, suggesting less educational polarisation for those aged 25-49 in these groups. However, differences in the proportions of people qualified to degree level in these three groups could indicate institutional barriers to accessing higher education for the Other Black group and the Mixed White & Black Caribbean group.

Alongside institutional barriers, economic deprivation and geographical location are also key drivers of educational disadvantage. For example, large proportions of the Pakistani group live in the North and the Midlands, where neighbourhood deprivation is higher and school quality lower (Social Mobility and Child Poverty Commission, 2014; and see also Chapter Thirteen). Large proportions of the Bangladeshi group live in deprived places in London, but benefit from better performing schools. Mobility, poor school attendance, low parental aspirations and low levels of parental literacy can help explain the educational disadvantage of the White Gypsy or Irish Traveller group (DCLG, 2012), but prejudice, discrimination and bullying also play a role (Carlson and Casavant, 1995). Policymakers should make renewed efforts to ensure all ethnic groups are able to attain in education so as to avoid a stalling in the closure of the ethnic gap in education in the future.

Despite school achievement gaps between minority ethnic groups and the White British group narrowing or even disappearing, some minority ethnic groups continue to experience inequalities in higher education and the labour market. Most minority ethnic groups, even those with the highest educational attainment such as the Indian, Chinese and Black African groups, are not performing as well as their White British counterparts in the labour market, given their educational attainment (see Chapter Eleven). Although evidence from the 2011 Census paints an optimistic educational picture, there is clearly more to be done to close the ethnic group educational gap for all groups and enable those with qualifications to better utilise them.

Notes

Further information about data and sources are available from
http://www.ethnicity.ac.uk/dynamicsofdiversity/

References

Blanden, J. and Machin, S. (2004) 'Educational inequality and the expansion of UK higher education', *Scottish Journal of Political Economy*, vol 51, no 2, pp 230-49.

Boliver, V. (2006) *Social inequalities of access to higher status universities in the UK: The role of university admissions decisions*, Sociology Department Working Paper 2006-07, Oxford: University of Oxford.

Carlson, H.M. and Casavant, C.M. (1995) 'Education of Irish Traveller children: some social issues', *The Irish Journal of Psychology*, vol 16, no 2, pp 100-16.

Dale, A. (2002) 'Social exclusion of Pakistani and Bangladeshi women', *Sociological Research Online,* vol 7, no 3.

Dale, A., Shaheen, N., Kalra, V. and Fieldhouse, E. (2002) 'Routes into education and employment for young Pakistani and Bangladeshi women in the UK', *Ethnic and Racial Studies*, vol 25, no 6, pp 942-68.

DCLG (Department for Communities and Local Government) (2012) *Reducing inequalities for Gypsies and Travellers: Progress report* (www.gov.uk/government/publications/reducing-inequalities-for-gypsies-and-travellers-progress-report).

Feliciano, C. (2005) 'Does selective migration matter? Explaining ethnic disparities in educational attainment among immigrants' children', *International Migration Review*, vol 39, no 4, pp 841-71.

Gillborn, S. (1997) 'Ethnicity and educational performance in the United Kingdom: racism, ethnicity, and variability in achievement', *Anthropology & Education Quarterly*, vol 28, no 3, pp 375-93.

Heath, A. and Brinbaum, Y. (2007) 'Explaining ethnic inequalities in educational attainment', *Ethnicities*, vol 7, no 3, pp 291-305.

Heath, A. and Cheung, S.Y. (2006) *Ethnic penalties in the labour market: Employers and discrimination*, DWP Research Report 341, London: Department for Work and Pensions.

Heath, A., Rothon, C. and Kilpi, E. (2008) 'The second generation in western Europe: education, unemployment, and occupational attainment', *Annual Review of Sociology*, vol 34, pp 211-35.

HEFCE (Higher Education Funding Council for England) (2014) *Global demand for English higher education: An analysis of international student entry to English higher education courses* (http://dera.ioe.ac.uk/19838/1/HEFCE2014_08a.pdf).

HESA (Higher Education Statistics Agency) (2013) *Higher education statistics for the UK 2012/13*, Cheltenham: HESA.

Jackson, M. (2012) 'Bold choices: how ethnic inequalities in educational attainment are suppressed', *Oxford Review of Education*, vol 38, no 2, pp 189-208.

Koser, K. (ed) (2003) *New African diasporas*, London: Routledge.

ONS (Office for National Statistics) (2012) *2011 Census: User guide 2011-2001 Census in England and Wales questionnaire comparability* (http://www.ons.gov.uk/ons/guide-method/census/2011/census-data/2011-census-user-guide/comparability-over-time/2011-2001-census-questionnaire-comparability.pdf).

QAAHE (Quality Assurance Agency for Higher Education) (2008) The framework for higher education qualifications in England, Wales and Northern Ireland (http://www.qaa.ac.uk/en/Publications/Documents/Framework-Higher-Education-Qualifications-08.pdf).

Simpson, S. (1997) 'Demography and ethnicity: case studies from Bradford', *New Community*, vol 23, no 1, pp 89-107.

Social Mobility and Child Poverty Commission (2014) *Lessons from London schools for attainment gaps and social mobility* (www.gov.uk/government/uploads/system/uploads/attachment_data/file/321969/London_Schools_-_FINAL.pdf).

UKBA (UK Border Agency), DWP (Department for Work and Pensions), HMRC (HM Revenue & Customs) and DCLG (Department for Communities and Local Government) (2009) *Accession monitoring report May 2004-March 2009* (http://webarchive.nationalarchives.gov.uk/20100422120657/http:/www.ukba.homeoffice.gov.uk/sitecontent/documents/aboutus/reports/accession_monitoring_report/report-19/may04-mar09?view=Binary).

THIRTEEN

How likely are people from minority ethnic groups to live in deprived neighbourhoods?

Stephen Jivraj and Omar Khan

Key findings

- All minority ethnic groups living in England are more likely to live in a deprived neighbourhood than the White British group.
- More than 30 per cent of Bangladeshi and Pakistani people live in deprived neighbourhoods – three times the England average.
- The proportion living in deprived neighbourhoods fell for most ethnic groups between 2001 and 2011 as a result of each group growing faster outside deprived neighbourhoods.
- Minority ethnic groups are most concentrated in neighbourhoods that are deprived because of low income, barriers to housing, crime or poor living environment, and less concentrated in neighbourhoods that are deprived because of low employment, poor health or poor educational results.
- The inequality between ethnic groups in the proportion living in deprived neighbourhoods is greatest in the northern regions of England.
- Inequalities between the White British group and minority ethnic groups in unemployment and labour market participation are not greater in deprived neighbourhoods than in other neighbourhoods, suggesting that minority groups are disadvantaged wherever they live.

Introduction

The 2011 Census tells us that unemployment among minority ethnic groups is almost twice that of the White British population in England and Wales (see

Chapter Eleven). This disadvantage can only be partially accounted for by the individual characteristics of minority ethnic groups which mean they are more likely to be unemployed, including being younger, having fewer educational qualifications, being born abroad, and not speaking English well (Berthoud, 2000; Carmichael and Woods, 2000). The remainder not accounted for by these characteristics is often regarded as an 'ethnic penalty', which refers to unmeasured effects including direct and indirect discrimination by employers (Heath and Cheung, 2006; Simpson et al, 2009). Although discriminatory practices are difficult to measure, there is evidence to suggest that discrimination continues to impede the progress of certain minority ethnic groups in housing markets in 21st-century Britain (Lynn and Davey, 2013).

An additional explanation for the presence of ethnic penalties is that minorities are unevenly distributed in poor parts of urban areas in Britain where unemployment and competition for jobs are high (Fieldhouse, 1999; Clark and Drinkwater, 2009). Their concentration in these neighbourhoods is a legacy of the availability of employment and housing opportunities when most immigrant groups settled in the country. The speed at which minority ethnic groups have dispersed to surrounding areas varies and is often tied to socioeconomic differences (Catney and Simpson, 2010). The persistent inequalities in housing options (see Chapter Ten), as a result of financial limitations and discriminatory practices, has meant some minority ethnic groups, Bangladeshi and Pakistani people in particular, have remain clustered in deprived parts of towns and cities.

The effect of neighbourhoods on individual outcomes is thought to operate through a number of processes, including stigma attached to deprived neighbourhoods, negative socialisations with others out of work, institutional under-investment, over-demand for public services and a lack of networks to better opportunities (Buck, 2001). Although many studies find a statistical association of deprived neighbourhoods with unemployment and low economic activity among minority ethnic groups (Clark and Drinkwater, 2009; Feng et al, 2013), the causal pathways through which these effects occur are disputed (Fieldhouse and Tranmer, 2001; Simpson et al, 2009).

Critics of the theory that a deprived neighbourhood affects all those living in it suggest that apparent 'neighbourhood effects' reflect a sorting of individuals into neighbourhoods. For example, only those who cannot afford to move away from a deprived neighbourhood choose to remain there. This is often referred to as a selection effect. Fieldhouse and Tranmer (2001) find support for selection effects by taking account of individual household tenure when predicting unemployment, and assuming that private renting is a mechanism by which unemployed people become spatially clustered. They find that variation in unemployment between areas can largely be attributed to housing. Fieldhouse and Tranmer do not rule out the potential of accumulated neighbourhood effects, which refers to a situation where those living in rented housing experience greater disadvantage the longer they live in the neighbourhood.

Whether some minority ethnic groups are more likely to be unemployed because of discrimination, or through a disadvantaged neighbourhood, the ethnic composition of deprived neighbourhoods differs strikingly from the average. This chapter uses aggregate data from the 2011 Census to show how minority ethnic groups are more clustered in deprived neighbourhoods than the White British ethnic group in England, and to consider whether they face similar disadvantages in the labour market in deprived neighbourhoods and all other neighbourhoods. We go on to show how the clustering has changed since 2001, and how it varies according to the type of neighbourhood deprivation and region of England. We end by exploring whether particular ethnic groups are more disadvantaged relative to the White British group in deprived neighbourhoods or not.

We do not present analysis using individual data, and are therefore cautious about the inferences we can draw on as to whether neighbourhoods affect individuals. We are also not able to show how many people in each ethnic group live in a deprived household, but rather how many live in deprived neighbourhoods by highlighting the spatial distribution of minority ethnic groups according to neighbourhood deprivation and the disadvantages they are likely to face dependent on where they live. We focus on England because the government measure used to define a deprived neighbourhood is calculated differently in each country of Britain.

Measuring neighbourhood deprivation

We use the English Index of Multiple Deprivation 2010 (IMD 2010) to identify neighbourhood concentrations of multiple deprivation. It uses broadly the same methodology to earlier releases in 2004 and 2007 (DCLG, 2011). The IMD has been widely used in the formulation of government policies in England, most notably as a tool to deliver the 1997-2010 Labour government's National Strategy for Neighbourhood Renewal, which aimed to ensure that, within 20 years, no one will be disadvantaged by where they live (Social Exclusion Unit, 2001). It has been used by subsequent governments and usefully summarises neighbourhood multiple deprivation.

The IMD's multiple deprivation refers to seven dimensions or 'domains': income, employment, health, education, barriers to housing and services, crime, and living environment. The domains are brought together using a weighting scheme to create an overall deprivation score, where income and employment carry the most importance. The overall score and domain scores are calculated for each lower layer super output area (LSOA) in England using 2001 Census boundaries, which have relatively even population size containing, on average, 1,500 people. LSOAs are referred to as 'neighbourhoods' throughout this chapter.

The standardised scores for the overall IMD measure do not give an indication of how deprived a neighbourhood is, but whether it is more deprived than other areas determined by its ranking among all neighbourhoods. We generally use a cut-off of the 10 per cent most deprived on the overall IMD and on each domain, and refer to these as deprived neighbourhoods. In this chapter, 10 per cent is therefore the standard: values above 10 per cent show that a group is more concentrated in deprived areas than all people. Thresholds of 3 and 10 per cent most deprived on the IMD have been used to allocate neighbourhood-based funding.

Neighbourhood deprivation of each ethnic group

Table 13.1 shows the cumulative distribution of the population in each ethnic group living in neighbourhoods at selected percentiles of the IMD 2010 overall score, where 0-3 per cent indicates the most deprived neighbourhoods and 80-100 per cent indicates the least deprived neighbourhoods. The only ethnic group that has the majority of its population who live in the least deprived 50 per cent of neighbourhoods is the White British group (54 per cent). The inverse is the case for all minority ethnic groups who are more likely to live in the 50 per cent most deprived neighbourhoods. Nonetheless, the concentration across the 50 per cent most deprived neighbourhoods varies by ethnic group.

At least half of people in the Bangladeshi and Pakistani groups, and almost half in the Other Black and Black African groups, live in the most deprived fifth of neighbourhoods compared with only a tenth of the White British group. The Pakistani and Bangladeshi groups are particularly concentrated in neighbourhoods at the very top of the distribution, with 10 and 9 per cent respectively living in neighbourhoods in the most deprived 3 per cent. The Indian ethnic group had the smallest proportion of people living in the most deprived 3 per cent of neighbourhoods than any other ethnic group (2 per cent). These findings are in line with the under-performance of Pakistani and Bangladeshi groups in the labour market relative to the White British group, but with the almost equal performance of the Indian group (see also Chapter Eleven).

At the other end of the distribution, the ethnic group with most people living in the relatively better-off fifth of neighbourhoods (or least deprived) was the White British group (22 per cent). The Bangladeshi group had the lowest proportion, with only 4 per cent of its population living in these neighbourhoods. The Indian ethnic group was the most over-represented in the middle of the deprivation distribution, especially in the 20-50 per cent most deprived neighbourhoods, where 39 per cent of the group lived. This suggests that although people in the Indian ethnic group are performing similarly to the White British population in the labour market, they have not been able to relocate to the least deprived neighbourhoods in England.

Comparing deprivation over time
The IMD was updated in 2004, 2007 and 2010, each time referring to the same LSOA boundaries. Here we use the IMD 2004 and 2010 matched to 2001 Census estimates and 2011 Census data respectively. We allocate the 2011 Census ethnic group output area (OA) data to 2001 LSOA boundaries used in both the IMD 2004 and 2010. We then use a look-up table for 2011 to 2001 OAs, and then a look-up table for 2001 OAs to LSOAs.

Table 13.1: Cumulative percentage of population living in neighbourhoods at selected percentiles on the IMD 2010 distribution, by ethnic group, 2011 (%)

	Most deprived				Least deprived	
	0-3%	3-10%	10-20%	20-50%	50-80%	80-100%
Pakistani	10	32	52	84	95	100
Bangladeshi	9	35	60	87	96	100
Arab	7	20	37	73	92	100
Other Black	6	24	49	86	96	100
Black African	6	23	48	84	95	100
Mixed White & Black Caribbean	6	19	37	72	91	100
Mixed White & Black African	5	18	36	71	90	100
Black Caribbean	5	21	44	83	95	100
Other	4	17	35	71	91	100
White Gypsy or Irish Traveller	4	12	25	57	86	100
Chinese	4	11	25	58	84	100
Other Mixed	4	13	29	64	87	100
Other Asian	4	13	27	66	89	100
Mixed White and Asian	3	11	23	55	81	100
Other White	3	11	25	61	87	100
White British	3	8	17	46	78	100
White Irish	3	10	21	55	83	100
Indian	2	10	24	63	87	100
England average	3	10	20	50	80	100

Note: Ethnic groups sorted by proportion living in 3% most deprived neighbourhoods.

Change over time in the most deprived neighbourhoods

Figure 13.1 shows the proportion of each ethnic group living in the 10 per cent most deprived neighbourhoods in 2001 and 2011. For most ethnic groups the proportion living in the most deprived neighbourhoods has decreased. The Bangladeshi and Pakistani groups have seen the largest absolute reduction in the proportion of people living in the most deprived neighbourhoods, by 9 and 6 percentage points respectively, between 2001 and 2011. The relative change in the proportion living in deprived neighbourhood was greatest for the White Irish group, with a 25 per cent decrease. The Other White ethnic groups were the only comparable group, 2001–11, to experience an increase in the proportion of people living in deprived neighbourhoods. This is likely to reflect recent immigration to relatively more deprived neighbourhoods in England that have affordable rented housing, especially by those arriving from Eastern Europe.

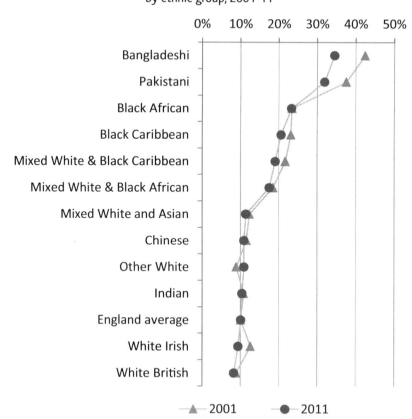

Figure 13.1: Percentage of population living in the 10% most deprived neighbourhoods, by ethnic group, 2001-11

Type of neighbourhood deprivation

The seven domains of the IMD 2010 measure separate dimensions of neighbourhood deprivation. Figure 13.2 shows the proportion of each ethnic group that live in the 10 per cent most deprived neighbourhoods on each domain. The differences across ethnic groups are greatest for income deprivation and smallest for employment deprivation. A higher proportion of an ethnic group living in, for example, a health-deprived neighbourhood does not necessarily mean that most people in that group have health problems, but that more people have health problems in the neighbourhoods where the group is concentrated.

The income domain of the IMD 2010 measures the proportion of people in receipt of at least one of the following: Income Support, income-based Jobseeker's Allowance, Pension Credit, Child Tax Credit or asylum-seeker subsistence support. The Bangladeshi group have by far the highest proportion of people living in income-deprived neighbourhoods, at 47 per cent compared with as low as 8 per cent for the White British group. The Pakistani (37 per cent), Other Black (32 per cent), Black African (31 per cent) and Black Caribbean (27 per cent) groups each have more than a quarter of their population living in the 10 per cent most deprived neighbourhoods on the income domain.

The employment domain measures the proportion of the working-age population who are involuntarily excluded from the labour market, and not those who choose not to work to look after a family, for example. The indicators comprise claimants of Jobseeker's Allowance, Incapacity Benefit, Severe Disablement Allowance, Employment and Support Allowance and participants in New Deal. The proportion of people in each minority ethnic group living in an employment-deprived neighbourhood is lower than the proportion living in income-deprived neighbourhoods.

Employment-deprived neighbourhoods are considerably less concentrated in London, where labour markets are more buoyant. They are more concentrated in the North of England, which contrasts with income-deprived neighbourhoods heavily concentrated in the capital. The Pakistani group, 18 per cent, have the highest percentage of people living in an employment-deprived neighbourhood, reflecting the spatial concentration of this group in depressed parts of the Midlands and North of England. The Indian group have the lowest proportion living in employment-deprived neighbourhoods, at 7 per cent. We explore the regional differences by ethnic group in the next section.

Health deprivation measures premature death and poor health using the following indicators: years of potential life lost; illness and disability ratio; acute morbidity rate; and adult mood and anxiety disorder rates. The Pakistani group have the highest percentage of its population living in health-deprived neighbourhoods, at 23 per cent, followed by the Bangladeshi, 20 per cent, and Arab, 17 per cent, groups. The Indian group have the lowest proportion living in health-deprived neighbourhoods, at 9 per cent.

The Pakistani group have by far the highest proportion of its population, 24 per cent, living in education-deprived neighbourhoods. The education domain is measured using average point scores of pupils at Key Stages 2-4; secondary school absence rates; the proportion of 16-year-olds not staying on in education; the proportion of people aged under 21 not entering higher education; and the proportion of adults aged 25-54 with no or low qualifications. The White Irish group have the lowest proportion, 6 per cent, living in education-deprived neighbourhoods, which is surprising given that this group has the second highest proportion of its population without any qualifications (see also Chapter Twelve).

The 'barriers to housing and services' domain measures household overcrowding; homelessness; housing affordability; and road distance to a GP, food shop, primary school and Post Office. The Pakistani group have a low proportion (10 per cent) living in neighbourhoods deprived on this domain. This may be a result of affordable house prices in the places where this group is most concentrated, which is reflected by their relatively high rate of home ownership (see Chapter Ten). The Bangladeshi group (33 per cent) have the highest proportion living in neighbourhoods with barriers to housing and that are services-deprived, which is unsurprising given this group's concentration in London. Other groups clustered in London, including Other Black, Black African, Black Caribbean and Arab, have a quarter of their population living in neighbourhoods deprived on this domain. The White British group had the lowest proportion of its population living in such neighbourhoods, at 9 per cent.

Crime deprivation is measured using rates of violence; burglary; theft; and criminal damage. The Black African group have the highest proportion living in neighbourhoods with high crime rates, at 26 per cent. This reflects the concentration of this group in South and East London and other large cities. The Other Black, Pakistani, Black Caribbean and Bangladeshi groups all had more than a fifth of their population located in the neighbourhoods most deprived on the crime domain. The White British group (9 per cent) had the lowest proportion living in high crime neighbourhoods.

The living environment deprivation domain combines indicators of housing in poor condition; houses without central heating; poor air quality; and road traffic accidents. The Pakistani group have by far the highest proportion of its population living in living environment-deprived neighbourhoods, at 39 per cent. The Bangladeshi, Other Black, Arab and Black Caribbean groups all have more than a quarter of their population living in environment-deprived neighbourhoods. The White British group have the lowest proportion, at 8 per cent.

Regional variation

Figure 13.3 shows for each ethnic group the proportion of people living in a neighbourhood in the 10 per cent most deprived nationally on the overall IMD 2010, separately for each region. There are few deprived neighbourhoods in the South East and the East of England, and so, for all groups, the proportions are low in these two regions. The Bangladeshi group is the most concentrated in five out of the nine English regions: London, South East, East of England, West Midlands, and Yorkshire and the Humber. The Other Black group is the most concentrated in deprived neighbourhoods in the South West and East Midlands, and the Black African group is the most concentrated in the North West and the North East.

The inequality between ethnic groups in the proportion living in deprived neighbourhoods varies substantially across regions. In the West Midlands and Yorkshire and the Humber, the proportion is as high as 60 and 61 per cent for the Bangladeshi group, and as low as 11 and 14 per cent for the White British group, a 49- and 47-percentage point difference respectively. In contrast, the proportion in the South East is only as high as 7 per cent for the Bangladeshi group and as low as 1 per cent for the Pakistani group, a 6-percentage point difference. This is, in part, a result of different characteristics of ethnic groups in parts of the North compared with the South East, which could be explored in more detail using individual census data from the Sample of Anonymised Records (SARs).

Figure 13.2: Percentage of population living in the 10% most deprived neighbourhoods, by type of deprivation and ethnic group, 2011

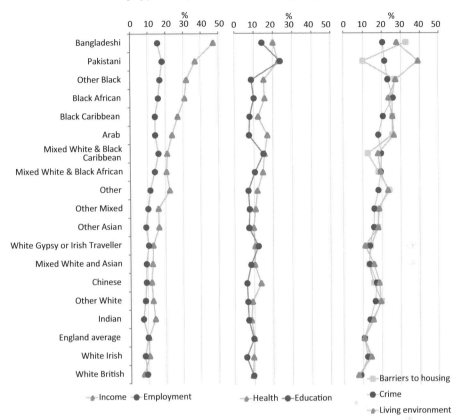

Figure 13.3: Percentage of population living in the 10% most deprived neighbourhoods, by region and ethnic group, 2011

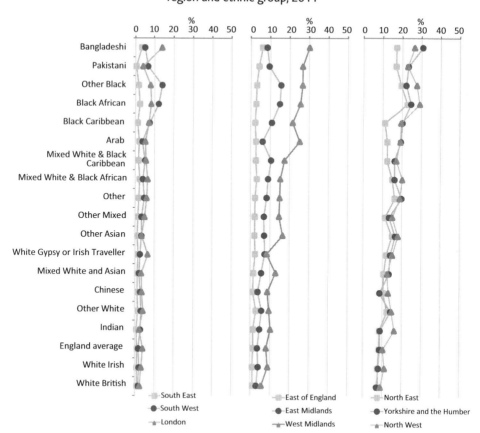

Unemployment, economic inactivity and neighbourhood deprivation

Figures 13.4 and 13.5 combine the neighbourhood characteristics of where minority ethnic groups live with their chances of being unemployed or economically inactive relative to the White British group. This section asks: are ethnic inequalities greater or less in deprived neighbourhoods among people aged 25-49? The figures show that all minority ethnic groups have a greater rate of unemployment and economic inactivity than the White British group in less deprived neighbourhoods (that is, not 10 per cent most deprived), except Other White and White Irish, which have rates less than 1 percentage point lower.

The advantage of the White British group is considerably less in the 10 per cent most deprived neighbourhoods. Moreover, the Other White, Indian and Chinese groups have unemployment rates more than 3 percentage points lower than the White British group, and the Other White, Black Caribbean, White Irish and

Figure 13.4: Unemployment rate for people aged 25-49, relative to the White British group, 2011

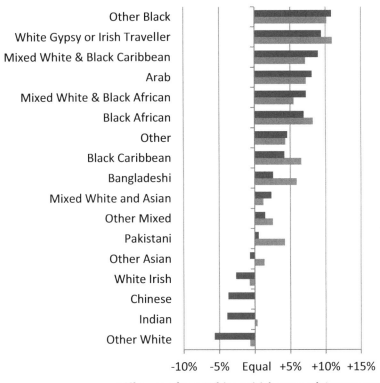

Difference from White British unemployment rate

■ Deprived neighbourhoods (White British rate: 12.5%)

▨ All other neighbourhoods (White British rate: 4.6%)

Note: The chart shows the difference between the unemployment rate for each minority ethnic group and the White British group; ethnic groups are ordered by decreasing difference in the unemployment rate for those living in deprived neighbourhoods.

Chinese groups have economic inactivity rates 3 percentage points lower than the White British group in the most deprived neighbourhoods.

For most other groups, there is a relative disadvantage in unemployment and inactivity compared with the White British group, whether they lived in a deprived neighbourhood or not. For example, the Other Black group have an unemployment rate more than 10 percentage points higher in deprived neighbourhoods and all other neighbourhoods, and the White Gypsy or Irish Traveller group have an economic inactivity rate more than 25 percentage points higher than the White British group. However, for all groups other than Mixed, the disadvantage relative to the White British group was lower in the 10 per cent most deprived neighbourhoods than in all other neighbourhoods. This suggests that ethnic inequalities in the labour market are greater in less deprived neighbourhoods.

Figure 13.5. Economic inactivity for people aged 25-49, relative to the White British group, 2011

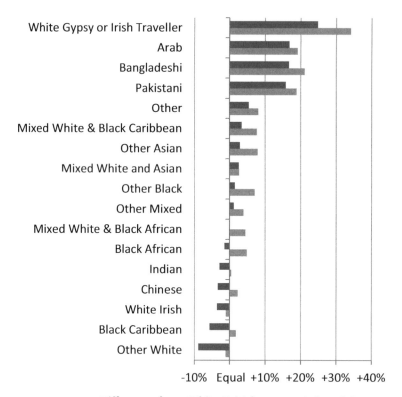

Difference from White British economic inactivity rate

■ Deprived neighbourhoods (White British rate: 23.3%)

▨ All other neighbourhoods (White British rate: 12.0%)

Note: The chart shows the difference between the economic inactivity rate for each minority ethnic group and the White British group; ethnic groups are ordered by decreasing difference in the economic inactivity rate for those living in deprived neighbourhoods.

Conclusions and implications

Minority ethnic groups are more likely to live in deprived neighbourhoods in England than the White British majority. There is considerable variation between groups, with the Bangladeshi and Pakistani groups considerably more likely to live in the most deprived neighbourhoods, and especially the very most deprived, than any other ethnic group. The Indian ethnic group is less likely to live in deprived neighbourhoods than other minority groups, and is particularly under-represented in the 3 per cent most deprived neighbourhoods in England. However, the Indian group, and other groups less concentrated in the 10 per cent most deprived neighbourhoods, including White Irish, Other White, Chinese, Other Asian and Mixed White & Asian, are not more likely than the White British group to live in the 50 per cent least deprived neighbourhoods.

This will concern policymakers who are worried about the negative effects of neighbourhood disadvantage, if they believe that living in more deprived places is likely to have an impact on labour market prospects. There is much debate about the existence of what are commonly referred to as 'neighbourhood effects' in the academic literature. Most research suggests there is some residual influence of the area where a person lives on individual outcomes over and above their own circumstances and their history that led them to live there. Minority ethnic groups have often faced limited choices about where to live because of the limited availability of housing when they or their families arrived as immigrants, which forced many to find a home in deprived neighbourhoods (Phillips, 1998).

The neighbourhood disadvantage faced by minority ethnic groups has been compounded by the different house values between neighbourhoods, which makes it difficult for people who have settled in deprived neighbourhoods to afford to move away (Kearns and Parkes, 2003). This provides part of the explanation as to why some ethnic groups, for example, Pakistani and Bangladeshi groups, have remained concentrated in some of the most deprived parts of England. There are indicators, however, that these groups, and most other minority ethnic groups, are becoming less concentrated in deprived neighbourhoods (see Figure 13.1 and Chapter Two). Evidence suggests that there is a social gradient in outward movement from these places, where those with the fewest socioeconomic resources are least likely to move (Catney and Simpson, 2010). This provides support for targeted interventions at those who remain in the most deprived neighbourhoods.

All minorities without exception are more likely than the White British ethnic group to live in neighbourhoods deprived because of low income, barriers to housing and services, crime and a poor living environment. Low-income characterises neighbourhoods where minorities live much more so than unemployment. Income-deprived neighbourhoods have the greatest concentration of minority ethnic groups, particularly the Bangladeshi group, of which almost half live in these 10 per cent of neighbourhoods. There is a lower proportion of most minority ethnic groups living in employment-deprived neighbourhoods and less variation between ethnic groups, which reflects the fact that low income does not coincide in all the same places as unemployment. The other deprivation domain that particularly bucks the trend is educational qualifications. Sufficient minorities manage to live in areas where more people are employed and where educational tests are passed. The nature of the employment may be part-time and low-paid, and the qualifications may not turn into better-paid jobs. For example, Black African, Black Caribbean and Other Black groups are not concentrated in areas with education-deprived neighbourhoods, but are in neighbourhoods deprived due to health, housing and crime. Chinese people are not concentrated in neighbourhoods deprived by employment or health, but are concentrated in neighbourhoods deprived on other factors.

The concentration of minority ethnic groups in deprived neighbourhoods is greatest in the North West, Yorkshire and the Humber and West Midlands regions in England, where inequalities between ethnic groups are also greatest. In the West Midlands, 60 per cent of the Bangladeshi group live in deprived neighbourhoods compared with 11 per cent of the White British group. These findings on the type of deprived places and regions where minority ethnic groups are most concentrated will provide evidence for policymakers to steer efforts to alleviate neighbourhood disadvantages specific to each ethnic group.

Nonetheless, it also appears that neighbourhood only explains a small part of ethnic disadvantage, and therefore policies need to target the particular needs of each ethnic group. For example, the disadvantage that minority ethnic groups face relative to the White British group are not more but less when living in a deprived neighbourhood compared with others places, at least in respect to unemployment and economic inactivity. This suggests that most minority ethnic groups are not disadvantaged by where they live, but wherever they live. The Mixed groups are an exception and appear to experience a neighbourhood effect (for example, higher unemployment) when living in deprived neighbourhoods more than any other group. However, this may reflect the different individual characteristics of people in the Mixed groups living in deprived neighbourhoods compared with those living in other all neighbourhoods. For example, people in the Mixed ethnic groups living in the most deprived neighbourhoods may have less human capital than those living in all other neighbourhoods. The individual census data available in the SARs would enable a more thorough test of this hypothesis.

Note

Further information about data and sources are available from
http://www.ethnicity.ac.uk/dynamicsofdiversity/

References

Berthoud, R. (2000) 'Ethnic employment penalties in Britain', *Journal of Ethnic and Migration Studies*, vol 26, no 3, pp 389–416.

Buck, N. (2001) 'Identifying neighbourhood effects on social exclusion', *Urban Studies*, vol 38, no 12, pp 2251-75.

Carmichael, F. and Woods, R. (2000) 'Ethnic penalties in unemployment and occupational attainment: evidence for Britain', *International Review of Applied Economics*, vol 14, no 1, pp 37-41.

Catney, G. and Simpson, L. (2010) 'Settlement area migration in England and Wales: assessing evidence for a social gradient', *Transactions of the Institute of British Geographers*, vol 35, no 4, pp 571-84.

Clark, K. and Drinkwater, S. (2009) 'Dynamics and diversity: ethnic employment differences in England and Wales, 1991-2001', *Research in Labor Economics*, vol 29, pp 299-333.

DCLG (Department for Communities and Local Government) (2011) *English indices of deprivation 2010*, London: DCLG (www.gov.uk/government/publications/english-indices-of-deprivation-2010).

Feng, X., Flowerdew, R. and Feng, Z. (2013) 'Does neighbourhood influence ethnic inequalities in economic activity? Findings from the ONS Longitudinal Study', *Journal of Economic Geography*, pp 1-26.

Fieldhouse, E. (1999) 'Ethnic minority unemployment and spatial mismatch: the case of London', *Urban Studies*, vol 36, no 9, pp 1569-96.

Fieldhouse, E. and Tranmer, M. (2001) 'Concentration effects, spatial mismatch or neighbourhood selections? Exploring labour market and neighbourhood variations in make unemployment risk using census microdata from Great Britain', *Geographical Analysis*, vol 33, no 4, pp 353-69.

Heath, A. and Cheung, S. (2006). *Ethnic penalties in the labour market: Employers*, London: DWP Research Report 341, London: Department for Work and Pensions.

Kearns, A. and Parkes, A. (2003) 'Living in and leaving poor neighbourhood conditions in England', *Housing Studies*, vol 18, no 6, pp 827-51.

Lynn, G. and Davey, E. (2013) 'London letting agents "refuse black tenants"', BBC News, 14 October (www.bbc.co.uk/news/uk-england-london-24372509).

Phillips, D. (1998) 'Black minority ethnic concentration, segregation and dispersal in Britain', *Urban Studies*, vol 35, no 10, pp 1681-702.

Simpson, L., Purdam, K., Tajar, A., Pritchard, J. and Dorling, D. (2009) 'Jobs deficits, neighbourhood effects, and ethnic penalties: the geography of ethnic-labour-market inequality', *Environment and Planning A*, vol 41, no 4, pp 946-63.

Social Exclusion Unit (2001) *A new commitment to neighbourhood renewal*, London: Cabinet Office.

Conclusions

FOURTEEN

Policy implications

Ludi Simpson and Stephen Jivraj

Introduction

The chapters of this book have highlighted the ethnic dimension of Britain's diverse population. When averaged across an ethnic group, the characteristics of individuals have striking differences compared to other groups' education, health, housing, employment and location within Britain. The analysts who have presented and interpreted these chapters have explained many of these differences by referring to the historical development of Britain's ethnic diversity, through immigration, adjustment, integration and contribution to the life of this country.

In this chapter we discuss the implications of these findings for three main policy areas that have motivated the government to measure ethnicity. The first is the *set of policies that address inequality* brought about by discrimination on the grounds of race, ethnic or national background that has been illegal since the first Race Relations Act of 1965. The second area of policy addresses the *diversity of preferences and needs* that are associated with ethnicity, and the respect for these differences that goes hand-in-hand with equal access to services. The third area is concerned with *community relations in a diverse society*, which more recently has been associated with community cohesion and national security issues.

The last but no less substantial part of this chapter attempts to clarify some of the concepts and measurements that such policies require of social statistics, and asks how far we can rely on ethnic group differences to direct public policy.

Discrimination

Despite improvements in the health, employment, education, housing and neighbourhood deprivation of minority ethnic groups over the last 20 years, clear disadvantage persists in comparisons with the average experience of the White

British group. The Pakistani and Bangladeshi groups continue to have poorer health and higher unemployment than the White British majority. Household overcrowding disproportionately affects people in the Bangladeshi and Black African groups. Black African men and women continue to face disadvantage in the labour market with lower levels of labour market participation and, along with Black Caribbean men and women, higher rates of unemployment if they are available for work. In 2011, Black Caribbean and Black African men's unemployment among 25- to 49-year-olds was 1 in 6, 10 percentage points higher than the 6 per cent of White British men of the same age.

Minority disadvantage in the labour market has persisted despite successful educational attainment. Minorities taken as a whole now have higher educational attainment than the White British group as a whole, whether measured by having at least one qualification or by gaining a degree. These qualifications gained, especially by younger adults, are not matched by success in employment and the resources that it brings, or by living in better quality neighbourhoods.

It is clear from the evidence presented in this book that minority ethnic groups in Britain have suffered disproportionately during the past 20 years' restructuring of the labour and housing markets. For example, the rise of part-time work has affected all groups, with White men aged 25-49 increasing their proportion working part time from 1 per cent in 1991 to 3 per cent in 2001 and to 5 per cent in 2011. But each minority ethnic group has much higher proportions working part time in 2011, from 9 per cent of Indian men, to 18 per cent of Pakistani men and 35 per cent of Bangladeshi men. In the housing market, the rise in private renting, which is associated with the most precarious tenancies and poorest home maintenance, has also affected all groups. But again, minorities have been hit hardest: Chinese and Black African households have more than twice the proportion renting privately than the White British group's 17 per cent, and more than 22 per cent rent privately in each of the Indian, Pakistani and Bangladeshi groups, the Indian group's proportion having increased most rapidly in the past two decades.

This pattern for some ethnic groups of relatively poor quality living conditions in spite of improvements in many indicators is confirmed by the analysis of residence in deprived neighbourhoods. Minority groups are without exception found more often in areas of low income than White British groups, and are more concentrated there than in areas of low employment or education.

The principal finding is that minority disadvantage in Britain suggests structural and widespread discrimination. Data from the census cannot directly identify discrimination, and surveys are limited to the measurement of experiences of discrimination. Experiments with dual applications using different photographs or names do directly identify discrimination by housing and labour agencies and employers (Riach and Rich, 2002). Attitudinal surveys show that despite steady and modest declines in self-reported racial prejudice since the early 1980s in Britain (Ford, 2014), minority ethnic groups continue to report experience of racism at work (Heath and Cheung, 2006). Discrimination may be applied by an individual or an institution. It is associated with those who have power to make decisions about others, and can be used to divide those with similar legitimate claims. These things are combated legislatively and through education, but require determined remedial action until it becomes customary to deal fairly, considerately and without prejudice with all people regardless of race and ethnicity, as with religion, gender, age and other characteristics unrelated to the ability to work or the need for services.

Around this principal finding there are specific stories for each ethnic group, and many differences within each group. For the first time the census in 2011 identified 'White Gypsy or Irish Traveller' as an ethnic group, which has revealed extremely poor conditions. For both men and women in the White Gypsy or Irish Traveller group, on average, illness is twice the rate of the White British group, nearly 50 per cent of young people aged 16-24 have no qualifications compared to the national average of under 10 per cent, and full-time employment is more than 40 percentage points below the White British rate. These new data will give impetus to understand and improve the conditions of this very marginalised group.

There are success stories to be learned too. The Chinese and Black African groups consistently report better health and less long-term limiting illness by a wide margin from other groups. Other research suggests that these differences reflect real health rather than cultural biases in reporting. The educational progress of the Indian, Black African and Chinese groups is remarkable, and more than can be accounted for from the number of overseas students in Britain.

Within groups, there are clear gender differentials that beg investigation and policy responses. For example, Indian women do not enjoy Indian men's 25 per cent advantage over White British men's health, and similarly Pakistani and Bangladeshi women's health is worse than that of White British women, although those groups' men's health is reported as very similar to White British men.

Some chapters have been able to point to geographical differences in inequality, but the result that stands out here is one of greater disadvantage in the labour market, compared to the White British group, outside deprived areas than inside them. This reflects a growing inequality within the White British group between those living in deprived areas and elsewhere, more than a relatively better labour market performance of minority ethnic groups living in deprived places. Therefore, minority ethnic disadvantage and discrimination are not associated with poverty and diversity but require policies that apply to all areas, perhaps especially in areas where there are more opportunities but less ethnic diversity, and thus where there is greater room for discriminatory access to the opportunities.

The recognition of differences within groups applies no less forcefully to the White British group, which makes up 80 per cent of the population of England and Wales. More people in this group face poor health, unemployment and precarious housing, and more lack any educational qualification than in all the minority groups taken together. A greater proportion of the minority populations face disadvantage, but they remain a minority among the disadvantaged in Britain. Policies to tackle discrimination and disadvantage often raise issues of equal opportunities for all people, whatever their background. These must be taken seriously when the aim is to give all people access to their potential and to acceptable living standards.

In summary, social policy must embody cultural and institutional encouragement of non-discriminatory practices. The fact that disadvantage persists in spite of existing legislation and social policy begs the question of what is systemic about disadvantage, and how can systemic faults be remedied? It is beyond this book to provide answers to these questions, but its spotlight on the data that provoke the questions is intended to make them harder to avoid.

Diverse preferences

While persistent disadvantage points to the need to recognise and deal with discrimination, the inclusion of an ethnic group question in the census in 1991 also responded to the rise of policies recognising culturally distinct traditions, whether affecting funereal services, school meals and dress, cultural festivals or housing size and style. Roy Jenkins' formulation of racial integration in 1966 as 'equal opportunity accompanied by cultural diversity, in an atmosphere of mutual tolerance' (Jenkins, 1967, p 267) was acted on in the 1980s through many new policies in education, social services and other public arenas.

While preferences and aspirations are individual, they partly derive from traditions for which ethnicity may be a good or an approximate description. Sometimes preferences and aspirations are expressed through organisations as well as by individual demands; the census provides independent evidence useful to planning services. Thus the number of older people in different ethnic and religious groups is a useful indicator of the current and future demand for particular characteristics of adult social care, including cultural specific requirements of paid and unpaid carers, supported housing, care homes and hospital care.

Recognition of different claims or preferences works best in parallel with humanitarian equality of services, rights, and of opportunities. An authoritarian approach may assess different claims negatively and expect that they be ignored or reduced, whether the claims refer to educational practices, food preparation, the size of planned housing, or preferred residential location. On the other hand, recognising and respecting diversity of preferences requires understanding and more nuanced responses in the provision of services. It is a difficult path to tread, but aims at greater social cohesion in a diverse Britain. Too often a negative attitude to differences has had an intimidating aspect, leading to discrimination rather than a sense of belonging.

An example in employment is the still relatively low economic activity of Pakistani and Bangladeshi women, and more generally of Muslim women. Although increasing in recent decades, as shown in this book, employment makes caring roles in the home more difficult, and threatens to contravene some traditional beliefs about contact between women and the commercial world, which are more common among Muslim groups (Dale et al, 2002). A policy expectation that all Pakistani and Bangladeshi women should consider working is unlikely to reap its intended goal of higher economic activity, and is more likely to instil a sense that policy is insensitive to personal preferences, or worse, that it is discriminatory in its demands. Increasing the availability of work in a variety of environments, along with support for learning English, is more likely to result in the integration of more women in work, as has indeed been the case over the past two decades. Increasing the economic activity of women of any background in Britain is a relatively new and slowly emerging development during the late 20th century that began with a rise in part-time work only (Hakim, 1993; ONS, 2011, p 9). Effective policies can be demanding in an encouraging way, rather than demanding conformity or undermining legitimate practices.

The relevance of this book is that it showcases the kinds of analyses that quantify the age, gender, ethnicity and social characteristics of people that may have preferences that are different from the mainstream expectation. This information is highly useful in planning services, even while keeping in mind that ethnicity is an approximation to individual differences, not a measurement of a fixed characteristic from which different claims or entitlements can be inferred.

Community relations and the management of diversity

The demand for conformity is especially strident when accompanied by claims of polarised residential patterns that, it is often said, maintain parallel cultures reinforced by twin responses of 'white flight' and 'minority self-segregation' (see, for example, Groves, 2013). Several of the early chapters in this book have addressed these claims and found a very different picture, one of slow but steady residential mixing and increasing diversity within families and communities.

These results are a good news story for policies relating to community relations and the future of Britain's diverse cities. The book's analysis of Scotland found evidence of this growth in diversity at all levels: regionally, in the movement of minorities beyond those areas in which they were most established in 2001; locally, in the rise of the number of households which include residents of more than one ethnicity; and personally, in the growth of those who describe themselves as being, in some sense, of 'mixed ethnicity'. These results were also found in England and Wales. Each minority ethnic group has spread more evenly across Britain, at the same time as their population has grown through immigration and through the natural growth of young populations having more births than deaths.

These demographic trends are the norm after migration from overseas in other European countries no less than in Britain, albeit with important local variations (Finney and Catney, 2012). There is 'brown' and 'black flight' from cities as much as 'white' flight, and both are better understood as counter-urbanisation, whereby people have moved from central urban areas to suburban and rural areas. Counter-urbanisation began before post-war immigration, and filled gaps left in British cities where migrants were attracted by employment opportunities in sectors that have since deindustrialised. This combination of trends results in cities with noticeably larger minority populations, which have nonetheless seen many more residents of all backgrounds leave them than have joined them from other parts of Britain. There is therefore a greater residential ethnic mix in all parts of Britain at the same time as a smaller White British population in the most diverse areas.

The study of neighbourhood segregation supports this general pattern of reduced segregation for minorities, and highlights how different trends can be found within different parts of England and Wales. We go to press as data from the 2011 Census on migration of each ethnic group within the UK are being released, which provide further direct evidence of the patterns described here. The evidence is summarised at http://www.ethnicity.ac.uk/research/outputs/briefings/dynamics-of-diversity/

In Chapter Four on plural cities, the development of diversity has been projected forward to 2031 for each of England and Wales' 348 local authority districts. If trends continue as in the past 10 years, the future is not one of islands of one ethnicity, but of a growing number of diverse areas.

Each city has and will continue to have its own character, a diversity of diverse forms rather than a single shape or form. This growth of new forms of inter-mixture and new patterns of living together, as again noted for Scotland and applying equally to England and Wales, has taken time and has come about organically. The geographical spreading of ethnic diversity has also occurred without direct intervention by government, and there is little that policy can do to change it.

However, the fastest future change in diversity will be in areas outside the neighbourhoods that are currently most diverse: in suburbs, outer estates and smaller towns. That is also where relative disadvantage and experiences of racism are greater for minority ethnic groups, and social policy could most usefully remove obstacles to mobility, ensure conditions for realising housing needs and neighbourhood preferences, firmly curb racism, and encourage community development that is supportive of new residents of different origins and backgrounds. Social policy on diversity should focus on the currently less diverse areas as much as it does on the most diverse areas.

'Management' of and planning for ethnic diversity has many aspects more positive than concern over residential patterns. The 2011 Census contains indicators of relevance that have not been the focus of this book, including the linguistic, transnational and other resources of diverse cities.

What should be measured?

Major social policies relate to the changing ethnic composition of Britain, its constituent countries and areas within them. To develop and implement these policies, what is it important to measure now, and in the future? As described earlier, the policies relate in part to appearance, to assess and act against discrimination, and in part to different cultural traditions and preferences. The questions asked in censuses of the UK since 1991, reproduced in Chapter One, have encompassed these two aspects. They use broad labels of White, Asian and Black, and within each heading they offer options for specific regional origins such as Caribbean or Pakistani.

However, the fact that more than 4 million people in England and Wales are not able to identify with any of the main response categories on the census form gives some pause for thought. They chose the 'residual' categories of 'Other White', 'Other Mixed', Other Black', 'Other Asian' or simply 'Other', and wrote in what they felt was their ethnic group. Our projection of ethnic diversity suggests that the population in these categories will grow, to the point where in some cities they will together be a larger population than any of the other ethnic groups including White British. Further, the growth of those that are known to be more internally diverse, for example, the Black African and the Mixed groups, also shows that it is becoming increasingly difficult to measure ethnicity. The proportion of people who swapped from one ethnic group to another between censuses doubled from 2 per cent between 1991 and 2001 to 4 per cent between 2001 and 2011 despite fewer changes to the question. Reliance on the ethnic group question to ensure equality of opportunity and allocation of resources is being stretched to a limit.

The addition of more response categories to the census form is likely, just as the number of categories has grown in each past census and developed differently in Scotland. More categories might ensure that the question is more meaningful to those being asked, but it runs the risk of the answers becoming so difficult to analyse and make sense of, that policymakers will find it of diminishing use as a guide to action. If this book's projection is correct, future UK social policy will be less concerned with the fate of the White British group in relation to other groups, less concerned about groups at all, and more concerned with diversity itself. How conceptualisation and measurement of ethnicity will develop in that future is rather unclear, especially given the drive to make use of large administrative datasets that do not routinely collect subjective markers such as ethnicity.

In the present and near future, clarity is required in concepts that can lead to effective policy. Immigration and race relations, described as a single entity, has become the biggest issue facing Britain according to political opinion monitoring (Ipsos MORI, 2014). The combination of these two separate issues, both by surveys and in the public consciousness, is a source of confusion. Immigration involves crossing a border with the intention to stay; controlling it through tighter restrictions does nothing to tackle the fears that many people have about demands for services and community tensions arising when an immigrant group (or a collection of groups) are already visible in a local area. Moreover, when does an immigrant become a resident who is as entitled to public services as their neighbour?

Immigration, then, is a concept measured by a date of entering the UK, for those not born in the UK or returning to it. Country of birth is a simple measure of different origins of immigrants. On the other hand, as described at the start of this section, ethnic group measures concepts of appearance and regional origins that have been useful to policies addressing discrimination and to policies respecting distinct cultural traditions and preferences.

'Integration' of peoples has been a policy theme of British governments since the early 2000s (DCLG, 2012). It has rather displaced the term 'community relations' used earlier. Integration has been given priority by governments in response to terrorist events, on the tenuous premise that a lack of integration is a cause of sympathy to terrorist actions. However, integration is a process through which immigrants and their descendants become able to feel and be part of a cohesive British society. Linking it in policy rhetoric to one's distance from terrorism does not help to create integration. Policies for integration would better focus on real problems raised by communities that can be tackled through relocation of responsibility or resources. These include English language support, racially aggravated crime, and the quality of schools' educational provision.

As a direct measure of Britishness, the census has already included a question on national identity. As discussed earlier in this book, the question may be interpreted as referring to citizenship or to cultural identity, but it confirms the adoption of one or other of the possible UK identities by the majority of each ethnic group except White Irish and Other White. The adoption of a UK identity is tempered mainly by birthplace outside the UK, but those born in the European Union (EU) are least likely to adopt a UK national identity. Adoption of a UK identity (usually British or English in England) takes time and is not influenced by a particular ethnic or religious background. Of greater concern are the prejudices held by some and discussed at the start of this chapter, who do not deem those who earn citizenship to have a right call themselves British.

Integration policy often also refers to the residential location of different ethnic groups with measures of segregation, as discussed earlier in this chapter. But an integrated and cohesive society is not well measured by simply sharing a neighbourhood with someone who may have a grandparent from a different part of the world. As argued earlier, the census has better measures of how people come to live in their neighbourhood, through immigration, birth and migration within the UK.

Within the limitations of the census, which addresses neither attitudes nor relationships of power, we have, nonetheless, a powerful description of Britain and its ethnic diversity that has done much to inform social policy over the past two decades. The characteristics of the census are its inclusiveness, both by asking its questions of all people and therefore providing the richness of local profiles, and by asking a multidimensional set of questions about housing, education, employment, demographic and other characteristics. The lack of any other sources for monitoring local policy issues related to diversity was one of the main reasons for the UK Statistics Authority's recommendation to continue the census to at least 2021 (ONS, 2014), which the government has accepted. In the meantime, there is much more to be gleaned from detailed analyses of the censuses' products, from national population surveys, and from administrative records.

References

Dale, A., Fieldhouse, E., Shadeen, N. and Kalra, V. (2002) 'The labour market prospects for Pakistani and Bangladeshi women', *Work, Employment & Society*, vol 16, no 1, pp 5-25.

DCLG (Department for Communities and Local Government) (2012) *Creating the conditions for integration*, London: DCLG.

Finney, N. and Catney, G. (eds) (2012) *Minority internal migration in Europe*, Farnham: Ashgate.

Ford, R. (2014) 'The decline of racial prejudice in Britain', *Manchester Policy Blogs: Ethnicity*, 21 August (http://blog.policy.manchester.ac.uk/featured/2014/08/the-decline-of-racial-prejudice-in-britain/).

Groves, J. (2013) 'How rise of "white flight" is creating a segregated UK: study reveals white Britons are "retreating" from areas dominated by ethnic minorities', *Mail Online*, 6 May (www.dailymail.co.uk/news/article-2320002/How-rise-white-flight-areas-dominated-ethnic-minorities-creating-segregated-UK.html).

Hakim, C. (1993) 'The myth of rising female employment', *Work, Employment & Society*, vol 7, no 1, pp 97-120.

Heath, A. and Cheung, S.Y. (2006) *Ethnic penalties in the labour market: Employers and discrimination*, DWP Research Report 341, London: Department for Work and Pensions.

Ipsos MORI (2014) Economist/Ipsos MORI April 2014 Issues Index, 29 April (www.ipsos-mori.com/researchpublications/researcharchive/3373/EconomistIpsos-MORI-April-2014-Issues-Index.aspx).

Jenkins, R. (1967) *Essays and speeches*, London: Collins.

ONS (Office for National Statistics) (2011) *Social Trends 41: Labour market*, Newport: ONS.

ONS (2014) *The census and future provision of population statistics in England and Wales: Recommendation from the National Statistician and Chief Executive of the UK Statistics Authority* (www.ons.gov.uk/ons/about-ons/who-ons-are/programmes-and-projects/beyond-2011/beyond-2011-report-on-autumn-2013-consultation--and-recommendations/index.html).

Riach, P.A. and Rich, J. (2002) 'Field experiments of discrimination in the market place', *The Economic Journal*, vol 112, F480-F518.

Index

References to figures and tables are in *italics*